Kai's Magic Toolbox

Daniel Giordan

Kai's Magic Toolbox

Library of Congress Catalog Number: 95-77729
ISBN: 1-56830-223-1

98 97 96 4 3 2 1

Interpretation of the printing code: the rightmost double-digit number is the year of the book's printing; the rightmost single-digit number is the number of the book's printing. For example, a printing code of 96-1 shows that the first printing of the book occurred in 1996.

This book was produced digitally by Macmillan Computer Publishing and manufactured using 100% computer-to-plate technology (filmless process), by Shepard Poorman Communications Corporation, Indianapolis, Indiana.

Trademark Acknowledgments

All products mentioned in this book are either trademarks of the companies referenced in this book, registered trademarks of the companies referenced in this book, or neither. We strongly advise that you investigate a particular product's name thoroughly before you use the name as your own.

Apple, Mac, and Macintosh are registered trademarks of Apple Computer, Inc.

The Hayden Books Team

Publisher	Lyn Blake
Editor-in-Chief	Michael Nolan
Acquisitions Editor	Robin Graham
Development Editor	Pat Soberanis
Production Editor	Rebecca Tapley
Interior Designer	Gary Adair
Cover Designer	Karen Ruggles
Production Team Supervisor	Laurie Casey
Production	Heather Butler, David Garrett, Erika Millen, Beth Rago, Gina Rexrode, Erich Richter, Laura Smith, Christine Tyner, Karen Walsh
Graphic Specialists	Sonja Hart, Clint Lahnen, Laura Robbins, Craig Small, Todd Wente
Indexer	Chris Cleveland

Colophon

This book was composed in *Apple Garamond* and *Syntax*.

To Our Readers

You can reach Hayden Books with your comments and book ideas at:

Hayden Books
201 W. 103rd St.
Indianapolis, IN 46290
800/428-5331 voice
800/448-3804 fax

America Online: Hayden Bks
Applelink: hayden.books
CompuServe: 76350.3014
Internet: hayden@hayden.com

Dedication

To Barbara, Donald, and Josephine.

About the Author

Daniel Giordan began his career as a conventional artist whose paintings and drawings have been shown extensively at nationally known museums, galleries, and universities. In addition to one-person and group shows, he has received fellowships and traveling scholarships from institutions such as Yale University in New Haven, Connecticut, and the Museum of Fine Arts in Boston.

He has gradually been seduced away from traditional artistic moorings by the possibilities held out by digital media. He currently works in both atom-based and pixel-based media, seeking to combine the strengths of each into a cohesive result. In addition to his own work, Daniel focuses on projects such as consulting, training, and product management of digital technology.

He received his undergraduate degree and fifth-year certificate from The Museum School in Boston, as well as a master's of Fine Arts from Bard College in Annandale, New York. He has traveled extensively, both domestically and internationally, and has been especially influenced by Renaissance art and architecture.

Daniel currently lives and works in Southbury, Connecticut, with his wife, Barbara. He welcomes any comments or inquiries, which may be sent via e-mail to: Giordan@aol.com.

Acknowledgments

Perhaps there is something to be said for naiveté. As a first-time author, I set very high standards during the planning stages of this book. I wanted to have in-depth background information on Kai Krause and MetaTools. Not just the facts, but the motivation behind the facts—background details and insider information. It also had to have concise, detailed information on four complex software products, not just one or two. All of the images had to be visually striking, and the book had to include step-by-step details on how to *design* with the tools, not just how to operate them. Naively, I wanted to create what amounted to four books in one, while demanding uncompromising quality in every area. If I had known then what I know now, I may not have demanded so much.

Fortunately, blind faith and raw aspiration won out, and all of these diverse components did come together. This is due to the assistance and support of many individuals whose efforts went above and beyond what could normally be expected. This project was not just important to me as the author; it was important to a lot of other people too, and I want to offer my thanks for all of their help.

Obvious thanks go to Kai Krause for the countless hours we spent in conversation, and for revealing much about his background, ideas, and motivations. He allowed us a unique, personal glimpse that went beyond the software creations themselves. Kai's willingness to address a wide range of questions, from future software products to the exact spelling of Gibert Jeune, gave this material a terrific clarity.

This project also owes a great debt to John Wilczak, founder, CEO, and president of MetaTools, and to the many individuals at MetaTools who went out of their way to answer questions and provide materials. Since I am not able to erect a statue of each of them, my thanks here will have to do. Special thanks go to Kristin Keyes, director of corporate communications, and Scott Hawthorne, business development manager, for all of their help. To Ben Weiss, Julie Sigwart, and all of the employees at MetaTools, thank you for all of your cooperation and support.

Special thanks go to Martin Schmitt for all of the effort he has put into this project. His involvement as a contributor, facilitator, and consultant played key roles throughout. Thanks again, Martin; you made a huge difference.

Robert Blumberg, cofounder and vice president of Live Picture, Inc., was immensely helpful in detailing information on Live Picture, specifically the workings of version 2.5. Thanks also go to Roger Dean for contributing his insights and images for the sidebar in Chapter 1 on his architectural designs, and to *Wired* magazine, Playboy, Inc., MACWORLD, and the other individuals and organizations that consented to the reprinting of materials for this book. Thanks also go to reviewer Stephen Noetzel for his observations and comments.

This project owes a debt to all of the artists who contributed images for the Gallery. Bill Ellsworth, Scott Tucker, Susan Kitchens, Justin Thyme, Dan Ecoff and Ron Shirley, and of course Kai, made significant contributions. Robert Bailey and Jackson Ting even went so far as to provide step-by-step techniques of how they arrived at some of the magical effects in their images. I thank you all for your collaboration.

My appreciation also goes to Pat Soberanis, development editor at Hayden Books, who went above and beyond the call of duty in bringing this project to fruition. She was able to take my broad strokes of ideas and concepts and focus them down to the specifics that make up this book. The result is exactly as I had envisioned...Thanks, Pat.

When all is said and done, a special thanks goes to Michael Nolan, Editor-in-Chief of Design Books at Hayden Books, who had the foresight to back this nonstandard, eclectic production. Thank you, Michael, for considering my input on design and format issues, and for consistently taking the ideas of a first-time author into consideration. In that same vein, thanks go to Robin Graham, Rebecca Tapley, Gary Adair, Sandra Stevenson, and the entire staff at Hayden Books.

I save the thanks for my wife for the very end. Her day-to-day support and encouragement have resonated through all of my efforts, and she has had a more positive impact on this project than perhaps even she is aware. Thank you, Barbara, for your unwavering encouragement, positive outlook, and patience. You are deserving of many treats . . . ;).

Table of Contents

Preface

At first glance, *Kai's Magic Toolbox* may appear to be a typical computer design book. There are step-by-step instructions on how to use software, with a lot of screen shots and callouts. It sits on a shelf surrounded by many other point-and-click computer books, and to some extent it blends in with its surroundings.

On closer look, you'll find that *Kai's Magic Toolbox* takes a different perspective on the digital imaging process. While others position themselves as elaborate manuals revealing the hidden secrets of technology, this book looks at technology as a means to an end. It is not about technology; it is about creativity.

Kai's Magic Toolbox places the emphasis on art—the art of creating, and the art of facilitating.

The art of creating focuses on digital art, loosely defined as images created on a computer using scans and specialized software. Digital art is one of the many new fields created by the digital revolution. In just a few years we have gone from crude, awkward attempts at graphic imaging to full-color photographic renderings, all generated on the computer with clicks of the mouse.

To this point, it has been mostly the tools that have gotten the attention: speedy computers, pressure-sensitive digital tablets, and color proofers. Given technology's fast-paced development, this comes as no surprise. In addition, the tools are integral to the digital art process—there would be no digital art without them. But the artist, who is the catalyst and animator of this new technology, has been ignored or forgotten in the rush to report on the latest Pentium chip or dye-sublimation printer. The rapid development of digital art is being reported and taught by technology experts, but with little or no aesthetic sense. As a result, there is a misconception that anyone who owns the tools can make the art, and that digital art is anything that the computer and printer spits out.

An artist who wants to develop digital artistic skills might be tempted to look for guidance to the art-school community, which in the past has upheld the aesthetic banner for the more conventional forms of art. With the exception of a few visionary and well-endowed institutions, however, this is also frustrating, for at least two reasons. The first is that, with the technology moving so fast, many colleges are unable to keep up with the trends and ideas associated with digital art. It requires an investment and commitment of time and money to stay on the upswing of the development curve. The second reason is the general reluctance in the art community to embrace digital media. Sadly, many aspiring digital artists are pushed toward painting and sculpture as more "valid" forms of expression.

One exception to this aesthetic void is the developments pioneered by Kai Krause and MetaTools. Kai is considered an artist first, and a technologist second. Since he is active in the creation of both visual art and music, he understands the creative process. One of the refreshing aspects about Kai's approach is in his realization that the field is in flux—he frequently says that we will have to throw away most of the tools we have now. He also understands that the digital art field is a fledgling one and that it still has a long way to go. When he speaks of digital art as an art form, he stresses that the tools and the path of creation should stay in the background—the work should exist on its own merits, without knowing how it was created.

That brings us to the second form of art discussed in this book: the art of facilitating. As an artist, Kai is extremely interested in facilitating the creative act, in empowering artists to push the envelope in using digital art as a mode of creative expression. Kai's software programs emphasize "creative exploration." They engage you on more than just a pragmatic, task-oriented level. They reach out and grab the artist in all of us, instilling a sense of wonder and curiosity about what the creative possibilities may be.

The role of facilitator is a double-edged sword: If your goal is to empower people, you must be careful not to discriminate with regard to whom you empower. Kai has encouraged and empowered a cross-section of our culture, many of whom have never considered themselves the least bit artistic. By Kai's own admission, this widespread, indiscriminate empowerment has resulted in a lot of very bad art. But it has also served as a catalyst in the rapid growth of digital art in general. And if widespread empowerment is your goal, then the tools that facilitate empowerment must be accessible. With almost all of MetaTools' software priced at around $100, accessibility is clearly a top priority.

The result of this empowerment is that a great many artists are stepping up to the plate and creating beautiful and expressive works. It is true that digital art has not quite "arrived," but it is developing at an accelerated rate, due in no small part to the efforts of Kai Krause and MetaTools.

My intention is also to play the role of facilitator. As you read this book, think about your own work, and how you can communicate your ideas more effectively. The artist Jeff Koons has said that art is about "the artist taking on the responsibility of power." This book will teach you how to use Kai's Power Tools, Live Picture, KPT Bryce, and KPT Convolver—but only as a means to an end. The technology and software are only valuable insofar as they facilitate the results. If these results were possible using two crayons and a blow drier, then this book just might have a different title and focus.

The fact remains, however, that many digital art works can only be created with digital software and hardware tools. It then becomes important to master these tools, in the same way that a sculptor masters the hammer and chisel. At some point, though, the sculptor forgets about the tools he is using and focuses all of his attention on what he is creating. And when people look at a great sculpture, such as Michelangelo's *David,* they don't scrutinize it and say, "Gee, it looks like he used a Craftsman number 12 chisel with a ball-peen hammer." All they see is the result, which speaks for itself.

I will leave you with this thought, then. Look at your digital creations as though they were being viewed 400 years in the future, when no one has ever heard of MetaTools or Kai Krause, and all they have to go on is the finished piece. In that future, digital technology is so common that it doesn't even have a name; it is simply part of daily life. Viewed in this light, how will your creation be received? Digital art, like all art, is about ideas, and it needs to communicate them clearly. This shifts the focus away from the tools, and puts the "responsibility of power" right back where it belongs, squarely on the shoulders of the artist.

Foreword

By Martin Schmitt

This is an unusual book.

It would have been easy enough for Dan to crank out yet another how-to guide. Instead he takes you behind the scenes of a software powerhouse and its creators. I think of the result as a "why-to" book. Some chapters will help you get the most out of MetaTools' software; in others, the history of the company and interviews with its founders, Kai Krause and John Wilczak, are an inspiration to take your own ideas and run with them.

I've known Kai since 1968, and in all those years of skipping classes, planning revolutions, and traveling the world, I have not met a more unique thinker than him. Nor can I think of anyone who couldn't learn a thing or two from his unique perspectives. And you'll find plenty of those in this book.

MetaTools is so far the most prominent instantiation of Kai's way of thinking. Not that there is "a way" of his thinking—some tip or trick one could learn and apply. Instead, Kai's personal evolution, and MetaTools' corporate evolution, are based on a profound ability to reject traditon, to deconstruct complex situations, and to reassemble them in an ingenious new way.

Kai used to tell me that what he values more than the possession of thinking tools is the ability to create them—to be, as he put it, at the source of the algorithms. Central to that is the ability to recognize patterns at all levels, from finding Waldo to visualizing the optimal path from pennyless immigrant to influential "metatoolmaker."

That ability became painfully aware to me when I taught Kai the game of Go many years ago (for more information on Go, click here . . . damn books!). That first game we played was also the last that I ever won. After my initial frustration, I realized how well the game reflected Kai's strengths: to predict, both analytically and intuitively, a sequence of moves in a highly decentralized and scalable environment of battles within battles that would eventually lead to success.

Kai plays the battles of life in the same style that he plays Go: forever questioning the status quo, leveraging moves, and managing chaos, all the while producing something that's not just powerful and efficient, but exciting and elegant as well.

Just as creating MetaTools was not about maximizing corporate earnings, to Kai winning at Go was not about clobbering the opponent. The real challenge was to combine the underlying rules to create an aesthetically pleasing pattern, as if growing a complex, domain-specific fractal.

As you read the book, you'll find that this quest for aesthetics was not limited to visuals (while we're at it, here are some more of Kai's favorite pseudo links: Monty Python, Woody Allen, and old Mel Brooks movies). In the '70s, Kai owned one of the first synthesizers on the market, basically a Lego kit of sound modules with inputs and outputs. With that machine, Kai produced sounds that years later, when we lived and worked in Hollywood, none of the studio musicians had ever heard. His secret: While everyone else was using inputs and outputs as intended, Kai connected outputs to other outputs, which caused unpredictable feedback loops.

This creative use of feedback is just one example of his pushing the envelope beyond the edge of linearity (in this case, with ADSR). I remember plenty of others, from the features in his first paint program in '82 that to this day haven't been implemented in commercial software, to his Roger Dean-esque oil paintings and "waxfalls" (ask him about those next time you're on AOL).

The harnessing of serendipity is a common thread in those examples. In Germany, Kai's home country, "this kind of behavior" consistently provoked *kopfschütteln* (serious head-shaking). It was that cultural attitude that eventually caused him to find pastures that nurtured, not tortured, pioneers, and that to this day confounds Uwe, MetaTools' German distributor.

In a country of great philosophers, ironically, art, surprise, and discovery seem to have no place in software. If it doesn't serve a purpose, solve a problem, or reduce valve-train noise in Mercedes engines, its existence can't be justified.

In this attempt to characterize the flying force behind MetaTools, there is still one unanswered question: "How does he come up with this stuff?" Although a common one, maybe it's not the right question. Maybe the creation of a masterpiece is really an iterative process of microvisions, with each step being equivalent to one click in the Texture Explorer, chipping away at the marble that encases the next KPT product.

On the other hand, software development is not a process of discovery. Every byte of code, every pixel of each screen is the product of lucid thinking—despite many, many sleepless nights. (Don't try this at home, kids!)

As much as I know about Kai, MetaTools, and all of their products, where Kai's visions—micro or macro—come from, I have no clue. Personally, I'm waiting for the Life Explorer module in KPT 27.0.

More Power Tools to you.

Martin Schmitt

Topanga, California

October 1995

Introduction

Kai Krause and MetaTools have released four of the most creative programs in the Macintosh world: Live Picture, Kai's Power Tools, KPT Convolver, and KPT Bryce.

Part I of *Kai's Magic Toolbox* introduces MetaTools' flagship products and captures the personalities and vision that went into their development. Chapters featuring Kai flesh out his adventurous background, his creative spirit, and the concepts behind his revolutionary interface designs. The next chapter describes how Kai met John Wilczak, and how the two of them started HSC Software (now MetaTools, Inc.). Part I closes with an insightful essay, written by Kai himself, describing the evolution of a MACWORLD event at which he single-handedly redefined the concept of the keynote speech.

In the four chapters of Part II, *Kai's Magic Toolbox* explores the design and technology of each of MetaTools' four flagship products, including the latest upgrade, KPT 3.0. These products are among the best-selling graphics software available today. The accompanying CD-ROM includes demo versions of each program, allowing you to explore the concepts of this book on your own. Each chapter in Part II provides a graphical introduction to key interface elements, and a solid description of the functionality of every icon, button, and menu. Next comes an overview for beginners, and topping off each chapter are strategies for creative exploration—a major theme of both Kai Krause and MetaTools—that digital artists will find invaluable.

Part III is a visual introduction to four of five creative exercises featured on the CD-ROM. These exercises show detailed, step-by-step instructions on how to use Live Picture, KPT Bryce, KPT Convolver, and Kai's Power Tools 3.0 to their best advantage. However, because Kai's Power Tools 3.0 was just released as this book was going to press, the figures in Part III reflect the KPT 2.1 interface; KPT 3.0 is covered in full detail in Part II. (Also included on the CD-ROM are deep Bryce techniques that further explore KPT Bryce's capabilities along with a Bryce materials reference chart.)

Part IV rounds out the book with a unique gallery of images created by the author, by Kai, and by contributing artists from around the country. *Kai's Magic Toolbox* is intended for all digital artists—graphic artists, production artists, fine artists, photographers, and digital imagers—as well as hobbyists and students, and, of course, Kai's many loyal fans.

The book covers the following versions of MetaTools' flagship software programs: Live Picture 2.0, Kai's Power Tools 3.0 (version 2.1 in Part II only), KPT Convolver 1.0, and KPT Bryce 1.0. It assumes a working knowledge of the Macintosh platform and Adobe Photoshop 3.0 (other applications supporting KPT plug-ins are not covered), and that the reader's equipment is powerful enough to run the respective applications.

Chapter 1

Renaissance Man

He has been described as a wizard, a recluse, and a charismatic visionary. His long hair, walrus mustache, and intense gaze do nothing to discourage those descriptions. On the surface, Kai Krause's intense expression suggests deep, profound thoughts, with his mind a thousand miles away. But those who know him realize that he might just as easily be thinking about what he's going to have for lunch, or about playing with his kids.

1.1 Courtesy of MetaTools

Although Kai seems distant at times, he is actually friendlier and more accessible than any other computer technology "guru" you could name, and he is easily found participating in the America Online graphics forums, answering questions and sharing ideas.

A thread that runs through many of Kai's experiences is his unique perspective and individualistic stance. Throughout his 38 years, he has always been compelled to put his own stamp on everything, questioning the status quo whenever he is asked to conform. This tendency was evident while he was in school; it was evident when he began to write software in the 1980s; and it is just as evident now that he is recognized as an innovator in graphics software.

1.1 Kai Krause

A Twist of Fate

When he was a young boy, Kai gave no signs of becoming a visionary or imaging guru. In his hometown of Essen, Germany, he would run around and play soccer just like any other nine-year-old boy. His father and mother allowed him to enjoy his childhood; although they exposed Kai to cultural things, there was no pressure for him to embrace them. In interviews for this book, Kai said, "My mom would draw, and we'd play piano and all those kinds of things. [But] it wasn't a fine-arts household, where the father is a free-flowing painter or the mom is a professor."

In 1967, when he was 10, Kai enrolled in a German Gymnasium school, which Kai has described as similar to a community college. Students enrolled for at least eight years; some continued on for ten. It featured an aggressive curriculum of Latin, Greek, calculus, and other classical studies, all taught by rote memorization. As Kai described it in a 1993 interview with writer James Watson, "We hated it, and even though in hindsight we have a decent general education, it is the missed potential and stupid rote memorization of tests that rubbed us the wrong way. We were passionate about philosophy and aesthetics, but nobody really wanted to engage in a discussion."

"We hated it, and even though in hindsight we have a decent general education, it is the missed potential and stupid rote memorization of tests that rubbed us the wrong way."

No one except another 10-year-old named Martin Schmitt. Kai met Martin during his first year at Gymnasium, and they have been close friends ever since. Kai said, "We began there, and [that] cemented us in a way that might not otherwise normally have happened."

Martin's friendship would prove especially invaluable just a few years later. When Kai was 13, tragedy struck: While on a business trip to Russia, his father was killed in a plane crash. In response, Kai shifted his focus from the casual things of boyhood to deeper, more philosophical pursuits. He said, "My father died when I was 13, which was a fairly pivotal change. I had a very, very happy childhood. And he died in a big plane crash, and somehow I remember distinctly that I thought, 'Gee, to be responsible and right about this I really shouldn't hop around and play soccer. I should be a bit more real and somber.' I turned inward a bit and stayed home. I started to write a lot....It triggered a rather pointed transition from a nonthinking childhood to trying to be the man in the family, the only son, trying to have a more responsible outlook."

Martin became the perfect counterpoint for Kai's newfound focus. Their mutual interest in philosophy and ideas served to propel each other forward. The two would go to Gibert Jeune, a store in Paris, and buy the unique, large notebooks available there (Figure 1.2). In these special notebooks, which Martin has called their "treasure chest of ideas," they tried to articulate their thoughts and feelings. Kai would write 40-page treatises on religion and aesthetics, attempting to know all things, prove all things. The two wrote, pondered, and challenged each other's notions, going further as a team than either of them would have separately. As Kai explained, "We had this sort of built-in rule; it's, "Look, either I'm right or you're right; we can't both be right. Let's see who's right." And so things that normally get tossed out in space—'Yeah, I believe in that, or maybe not ...Maybe. I don't know. Whatever ...'—that became, 'Let's figure it out: Is there a God or not? What's pro or con here?' We would go out; we'd research to the ends of it. It became almost like a game between us: Which had the better set of arguments to prove in this case?" As time went on, they recognized many other shared interests, such as traveling, exploring, and electronics.

Kai's interest in electronic music began in the early '70s, while still at the Gymnasium. At that time Kai bought his first instrument, an electronic keyboard called the ARP 2600, which cost him 12,000 Deutsche marks. He had been classically trained in piano, up to the conservatory level, and used that as a springboard in developing his own musical style. He bought a Farfisa electronic organ soon afterwards, and began composing his own music. His musical interests at that time ran along the lines of rock groups such as Pink Floyd and Yes.

Courtesy of Kai Krause

1.2

1.2 One of Kai's Gibert Jeune notebooks

Land of Opportunity

In 1973, at age 16, Kai visited an aunt who lived in Brockville, a small town in Ontario, Canada, between Montreal and Toronto. The landscape had a profound effect on him. “It was the antithesis of Germany—endless blue skies; open roads; very, very lovely,” he said. “It was just the right time to go when you’re 15 or 16; it completely twists your head around. And we met too many people, too, who took their own fate in their own hands, built their own houses.”

1.3

Kai Krause

The following summer, Kai brought Martin with him to Canada. “That’s where we spawned this whole notion of, We can’t end up 9-to-5 in some silly job; it isn’t for us,” Kai said. “And, not knowing where we belonged, we wanted to look around and sort of get a different view of the whole thing.” The two of them set about planning an ambitious trip around the world in a caravan of buses. The idea was to find the perfect place to live and, like the pioneering Canadians they had met, build a house there. The caravan would be needed because many of their friends wanted to come along. Kai said, “There was quite a gang. We meant to do this with about 15 people. I was a bit of the evangelizing leader.”

1.3 Kai at 12

During this time, Kai met his future wife, Barbara Freistuhler. “We met at some school party,” he recalled. “I took her to some restaurant and we sat there until three in the morning.” Kai shared his plan to travel and explore, which struck a chord with Barbara. Kai said, “I just related the idea, which...really hit a spot of, ‘My God, that really sounds like it’s the right thing to do; it really sounds true.’ We decided we wanted to be 81 together that night.” (They celebrated their 20th anniversary in 1995.)

The Perfect House

When Kai was 15 and visiting Canada, one of his dreams was to move to the most beautiful place on earth and build the best house he and his friends could imagine. A few years later, that same idea fueled his plans to travel and settle in a place other than Germany. Later still, that idea was in the forefront of his and Martin's minds when they left San Francisco searching for a spot of land in the Southwest.

Today, Kai has a terrific house in one of the most beautiful places on earth: Santa Barbara, California. It has spectacular views and an equally spectacular architectural design. And yet...there was once an opportunity to build the perfect house—an opportunity that could still come to pass.

In the mid-'80s, Kai and Martin heard about an incredible piece of land that was about to come on the market. It was an 11-acre site in the Santa Monica Mountains above Malibu, California, covering two hills, with a 180-degree view of the ocean. They seized the opportunity and, together with Kai's wife, Barbara, found themselves in a position they'd always dreamed of: owners of a perfect place on which to construct an amazing house.

For the house's design, Kai immediately thought of Roger Dean, whose *Views* book, published in the 1970s, described the principles of his unique brand of architecture. Roger is most renowned for his fantastical paintings and designs featured on the album covers of the rock band Yes, but his paintings and illustrations can be found in everything from corporate logos to computer-game scenes. At the time, Kai had a well-worn first edition of *Views,* so he was very familiar with and appreciative of Roger's vision. In 1985, Kai sent Roger a letter describing the land and its appropriateness for a Dean house. Both Kai and his ideas sounded intriguing to Roger, whose response consisted of one word: Yes.

One look at Roger's work and it's easy to see the similarities between Kai's and Roger's artistic visions. The incredible environments depicted on such Yes album covers as *Tales from Topographical Oceans* and *Relayer* come to life in Roger's 3D architectural designs. They maintain the emphasis on mushrooming, amorphous shapes; art-nouveau overtones; and a feeling of other-worldliness in the album art. Rarely in a Roger Dean painting will you find squares, corners, or symmetry, and the same goes for his architectural designs, which feature free-flowing and organic shapes. The underlying principles of Roger's dreamlike structures, he says, are based on his research on sleeping patterns and other aspects of the domestic environment.

In 1986, Roger presented Kai and Martin with detailed drawings for their newly acquired mountaintop site

(Figure 1.4). "Took about, oh, three seconds for us to look at it and each other and nod, 'Yep, that's it,'" Kai told interviewer James Watson in 1993. Although Roger had designed mostly public spaces such as a sports dome/atrium, luxury apartments, hotels, theme parks, and resorts, he was inspired by the site as well as by the enthusiasm Kai and Martin showed for his work.

1.4 Roger Dean

1.4 Roger Dean's design for Kai's and Martin's house

The challenge in building Roger's designs is formidable: How do you construct curved walls and ceilings in solid, secure structures while keeping costs in line? Roger, who had studied industrial design at the Royal College of Arts in London, found the answer. He designed the basic structures as a set of fiberglass molds. A key component in the construction process is a type of concrete known as gunite. This viscous material is sprayed under pressure into the pre-cast molds, as well as into intricate door and window molds. Molded gunite has an extremely smooth finish while providing exceptional insulation and strength, and once the gunite hardened, the fiberglass molds could be reused for other sections of the house. The outside of Roger's structures is often adorned with ceramic sculptural elements, which enhance the designs while serving utilitarian functions such as chimneys and vents.

But the process and budget for building a residence is much different than for building a hotel or theme park. The concrete molds would be created in England and shipped to California, where the ceramic and environmental facades would be fabricated. The project was so unique that all of the contractors had to be top-notch, and the expense of these, the molds, the fabrication, and the shipping and other logistics would require a substantial capital investment.

To offset some of the costs, Kai and Martin proposed forming a company that would promote and develop Roger's visionary architecture. Joining Kai, Martin, and Roger in the enterprise were Henk Rogers, a computer-game entrepreneur whose interests range from virtual reality to environmental recycling, and who has provided much of the company's financing; Tim Ryan, an English civil engineer and gunite expert; and Martyn Dean (Roger's brother), an industrial designer and photographer who built several stage sets for Yes in the 1970s. They called their new company Curved Space.

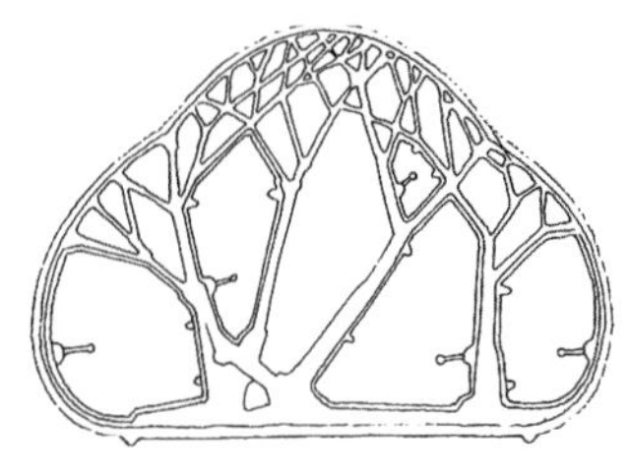

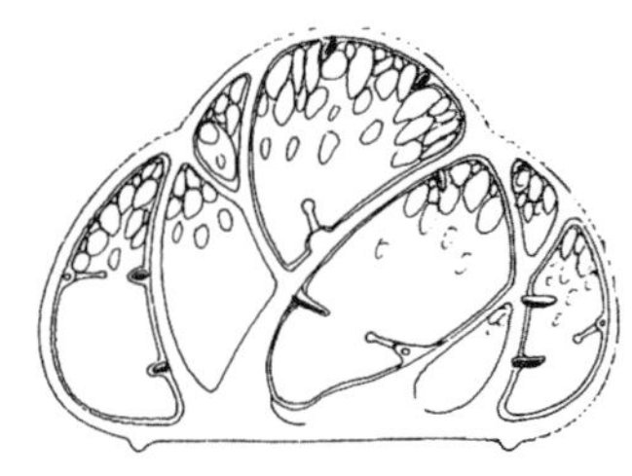

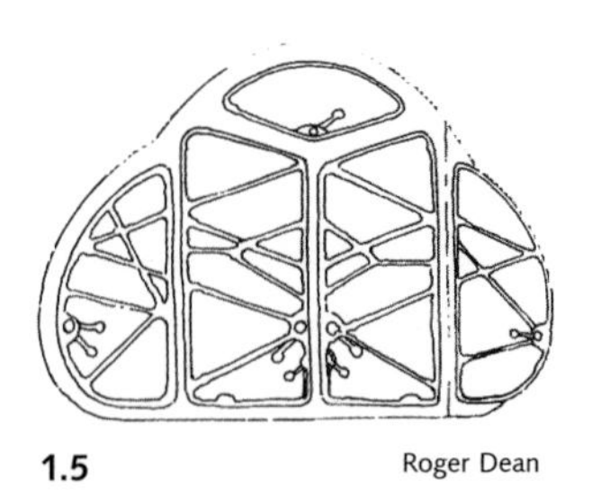

1.5 Roger Dean

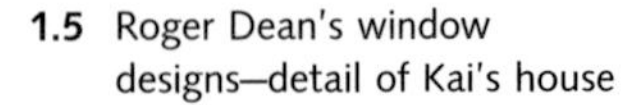

1.5 Roger Dean's window designs—detail of Kai's house

Just when they thought they had it all figured out—a great location, a great design, and a great company—their plans began to falter. Based on a change in its ridgeline rules, the California Coastal Commission rejected their original proposal to build on the site, thus requiring Kai and Martin to submit an alternative proposal. That proposal involved a redesign, aerial photos, drawings, scale models, and other requirements, as well as a reduction in the house's size from 10,000 square feet to 7,500 square feet. It took a great deal of time and effort, but they did it. In 1989, three years after the design process began, they were able to secure approval from the commission.

The problem then was that the concept, design, and approval cycle had taken a very long time. Meanwhile, Kai and Martin were engrossed in other projects and ventures. "The details for a project like this are so time-consuming," Martin told me. "It would have required hiring the best contractors and then supervising at the job site a great deal of the time. Neither of us had the time to focus on it." Most recently, Kai's and MetaTools' late 1994 relocations to Santa Barbara delayed the project further. But Martin did not rule it out completely; with the right set of circumstances, he hinted, they might one day bring this unique design to life.

And Curved Space still exists today, with one project under development in Turkey and others pending. Meanwhile, Roger continues with his painting while working on two architectural projects that are in advanced stages of development. With any luck, even more of Roger's incredible structures will come to fruition.

But their best-laid travel plans would go awry. During the two years he and his friends worked out the trip's details, Kai applied for a year-long exemption to the mandatory German military draft. It was an exemption for which he was eligible, so he thought the application process would be little more than a formality.

But the wheels of bureaucracy didn't stop for Kai. Shortly after taking the mandatory examination for draftees, while still attending Gymnasium, he received a notice saying that his application for exemption had not been received in time and that he was now part of the elite bomber-pilot squadron in the Netherlands. Although Kai was given the option to reapply for the exemption from within the German military, he was apprehensive, because he had sent his application four months before the deadline but was still considered late.

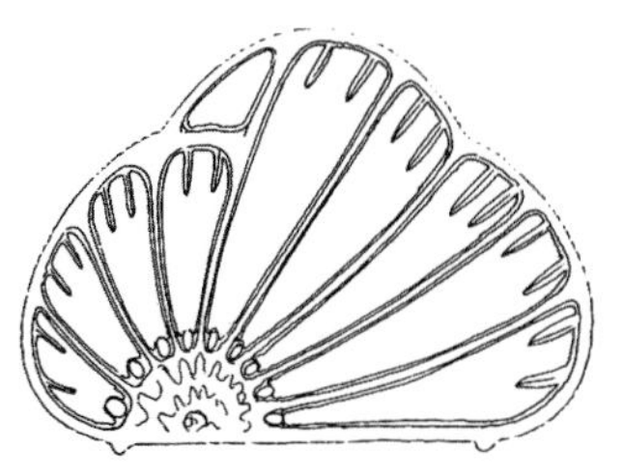

"The trip was down the tubes, and I had just days to make up my mind what to do," Kai told James Watson. "I sold everything I owned, convinced Barbara and Martin to leave—he was lucky, missed the draft by a few months—and in August '76 we left. I had tried to gain time—told them I was sick. And, if you can believe this, hours after I left a huge army truck-ambulance pulls up to get me…and they showed up on that exact day each year for 10 years! In the end my mother knew them by name, and they'd come in and drink cognac and look at pictures of me in L.A."

So Kai, Barbara, and Martin arrived in New York on August 17, 1976, with about a thousand dollars each, carrying all of their possessions in their backpacks. In just a few weeks, they left the New York YMCA and made their way west to San Francisco. Being new to the San Francisco scene, as well as the United States, they didn't have a clue as to the significance of their new address: the corner of Haight and Ashbury. They stayed there for six months, surviving financially by renting rooms in the seven-room flat out to five other people, which covered their rent with $10 to spare.

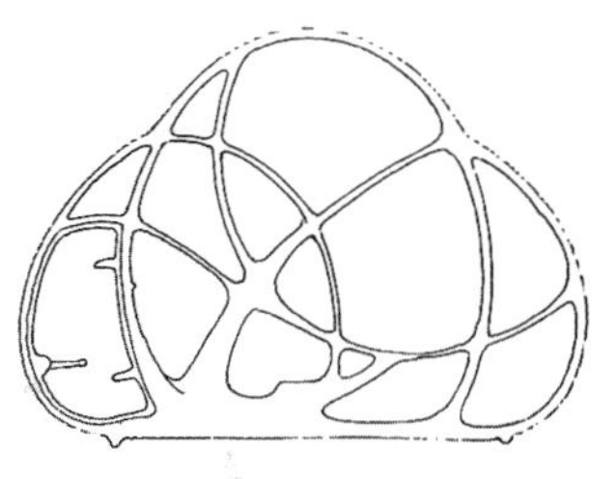

Then Martin bought a van, and they left San Francisco planning to tour the western states, still looking for the perfect piece of land to build a house on. They ended up in Los Angeles, and began working on jobs and projects that centered on one of the true passions in Kai's young life: electronic music.

In early 1977, shortly after arriving in Los Angeles, Kai and Martin started a digital design company called Prototype Systems (Figure 1.5). For the next six years, Prototype would serve as the base for many of their projects—consulting, sound effects, and electronic component design among them. "Prototype Systems is something Martin and I made up very quickly after arriving in L.A," Kai told me. "It was really self-taught digital design—trying to take electronic music and expand the machines that I used to have."

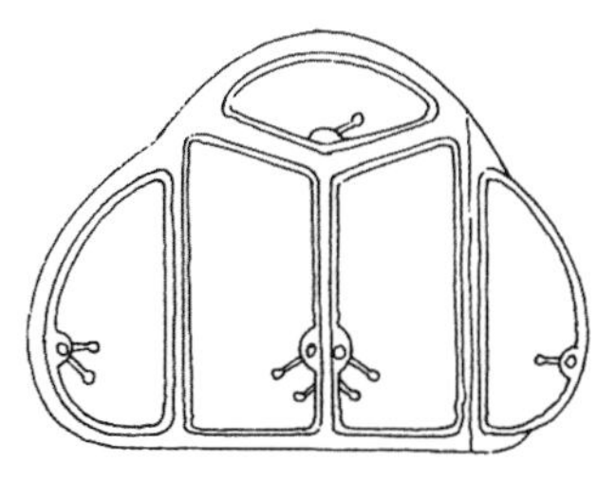

Kai described the development of Prototype's first commercial product: "I used to pay $8,000 for the first early, early, early synthesizer. It had three oscillators in it, and when I found that you could buy an oscillator chip for 10 bucks…the naive

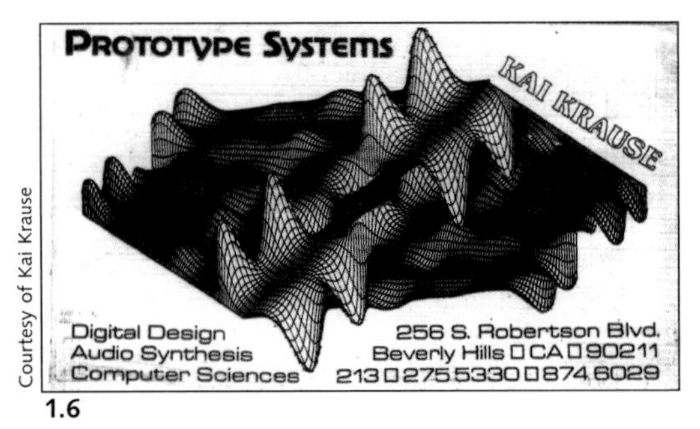

Courtesy of Kai Krause

1.6

1.6 A business card from Kai's and Martin's first company, Prototype Systems

assumption is that I can put 10 of those on a board, and stick them inside, and have a killer system for a fraction of the money." The digital waveform generator was the result of these explorations. It was designed with a slider metaphor that allowed very complicated waveforms. They had ordered and received the components for the first 3,000 generator boards when a flood hit their basement production facility, destroying much of the raw material for the boards. It was a discouraging turn of events, and rather than rebuild, they decided to shift their focus.

Going Digital

In 1978, after the disastrous basement flooding, Kai and Martin bought their first computer for Prototype Systems, an 8KB Compucolor, and began writing programs in BASIC. These programs explored their growing interest in fractals and chaos theory.

(*Fractals* are mathematical formulas that produce repeating forms that unfold in infinite detail. The stunning visual presence of fractals are enhanced by the paradoxical nature of the designs: No matter how closely one zooms in, details continue to emerge. *Chaos theory* is the science of randomness, and it specifically looks for patterns emerging from random actions. Kai's and Martin's explorations took the form of programs that generated repeating, random waveforms. Randomly generated waveforms and swirling fractal designs have held Kai's interest to this day, as evidenced by the Fractal Explorer module of Kai's Power Tools. (Figure 1.7.)

Further explorations came after Kai bought the 64KB Corvus Concept computer in 1982. In that year, Prototype Systems and Corvus began work on an ambitious project that was in the early stages of development. Corvus wanted to develop an interactive video game that featured components of virtual reality in a multiplayer, networked environment. Players would move around a maze, see each other, and face off in battle. Kai and Martin spent months writing the software, but the project ran into some snags due to networking-support problems with the Corvus machine.

1.7 Kai Krause

1.7 Kai created this homage to M. C. Escher using the KPT Vortex Tiling, whose repeating patterns parallel those seen in fractals

Sound Design

While Kai and Martin were developing their first product, Kai began experimenting with the Sennheiser Vocoder, a sound-effects system at which Kai became something of an expert. In addition to selling the systems to such artists as Herbie Hancock and Neil Young, Kai taught courses and seminars on the techniques and theory of the machine, primarily at San Diego State University.

"The Vocoder stuff got me around a lot," Kai said. "The University of Berlin had all these courses going on, and I wrote 40 or 50 pages on how the principle of Vocoding synthesis works. I wrote these examples that were printed by Sennheiser in Germany...Those notes and the teaching notes got around quite a bit. They were kind of a precursor to the [Photoshop] tips that I did later. They were unusual ways of putting things together."

Kai also began specialized in electronic music and sound effects during this period. Over the years, he became quite successful at it; his audio credits include such artists as DEVO, Joni Mitchell, Kenny Loggins,

Courtesy of Clio Awards Ltd.

1.8

and Keith Emerson. He created sound effects for movies as well, working with Disney Studios on projects such as *Black Hole* and *Tron*. This stage of his career was topped off by winning the Clio award in 1980 for his work on the advertising for *Star Trek: The Movie*, which he did for the London agency CIC (Figure 1.8).

"I did a whole bunch of things in those days," Kai said. "I was going back and forth between doing the sound library at Disney, and sound effects and specialized effects." The Clio award, he said, was for the Best Use of Sound in a Worldwide Commercial. "I made a commercial that used 12 different aliens talking about the movie in various voices, and they talked back and forth with each other with this whole script, and each one of those was done with the Vocoder and special sound effects. It sounded rather cool."

Despite his success, Kai decided to leave the music and entertainment business because he didn't have creative control over the projects he worked on. "It just drove me nuts to mix something as close to my heart as music with simply paying the rent," Kai explained to James Watson. "And while you sit in these leather couches in the most expensive studios in the world, you get frustrated because it's their project on their time, their creativity, and you just can't meddle with it." So on September 26, 1982, Kai sold all of his sound equipment to musician Neil Young, using the money to purchase a Corvus Concept 64KB computer.

While they waited for Corvus to fix the problems, Kai and Martin gave Prototype Systems a new name, DDD Software, and began a different exploration. They created a rotating-cube display program based on the idea of nesting cubes. Within three months, the nesting cubes had become 3D bar charts, and the program became DDD Software's first commercial software success. Corvus bought the rights to the software and bundled it on each of their systems, resulting in quite a payoff for DDD Software. Today that same software, which Kai and Martin named DDD.Graph, is the charting engine for software applications such as Adobe Persuasion, CorelDRAW!, and Quattro. (Martin took sole ownership of DDD Software after Kai joined HSC Software in 1992.)

Meanwhile, Kai and Martin also considered starting a business in which they would use computers to create high-end imaging for use as special effects in television commercials and films. They

1.8 Kai won a Clio award in 1980

would write custom programs that would enable them to produce these images and then sell their services to clients. They wrote custom programs because no commercial software programs existed then for image editing—there was no Adobe Photoshop or Live Picture, for instance.

Before they could decide, they met the founders of Pacific Data Images (PDI). PDI had a little one-room shop in Los Angeles and, using a Chromatics computer system, offered services similar to those Kai and Martin wanted to provide. In the end Kai and Martin decided against the plan; Kai felt it was too similar to the client-artist relationship he had just left in the music business. Pacific Data Images went on to become the premier computer-graphics special-effects house in Hollywood, specializing in digital morphing and other broadcast effects. PDI's credits include Michael Jackson's "Black & White" morphing video, as well as commercials such as the Schick shaving commercial, in which different faces morph with each razor stroke.

In 1985, Kai and Martin formed yet another company, Three D Graphics, that was separate from DDD Software. They initially wanted to publish retail software applications rather than selling programs to computer makers. In 1986 their first release, a graphics program called Perspective, won *PC Magazine*'s award for Best Graphics Software. Shortly thereafter, Boeing Aircraft seduced Three D Graphics away from the retail market when it hired Kai and Martin to develop a program, Boeing Graph, for its new computer division. Kai and Martin developed the program, giving Boeing a worldwide exclusive license. But later that year, Boeing Graph met its end when the company's computer division ended; during a round of budget cuts, Boeing decided to get out of the computer business and stick to building airplanes. Although Three D Graphics still exists today, Kai and Martin withdrew from its day-to-day operations in the early '90s, with both remaining stockholders.

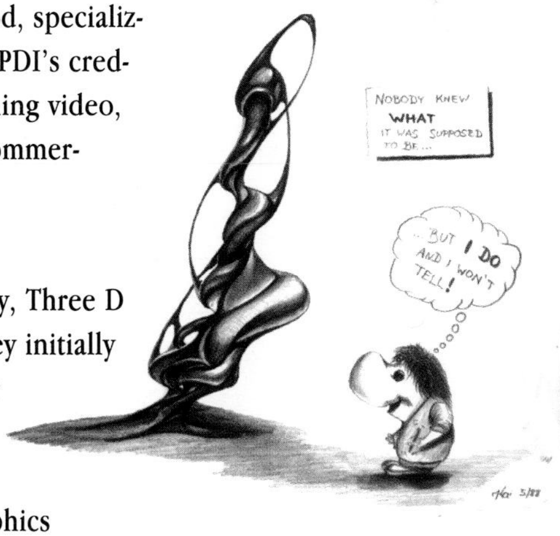

Kai Krause

1.9

1.9 Kai's varied interests extend to drawing "Schnuffis" a cartoon which originated in his Gibert Jeune notebooks

Throughout the '80s, DDD Software wrote and developed software programs for the rapidly expanding computer industry. This kind of custom software was big business at a time when there were relatively few commercial programs available. Their projects included the development of software, such as paint and charting applications, for the likes of Honeywell and Epson, which would bundle them with their products, and Aldus and Corel, which integrated DDD's charting engine for Persuasion and CorelDRAW!, respectively.

Martin's Projects

Kai Krause and Martin Schmitt have been inseparable friends since they met in Essen, Germany, more than 25 years ago. As Martin and Kai stepped away from the day-to-day operations at Three D Graphics in the late 1980s, they each began to pursue projects on their own—Kai with online Photoshop techniques and eventually HSC Software/MetaTools products, Martin with explorations in artificial intelligence (AI).

Working under the umbrella of DDD Software, which superceded Prototype Systems in the early '80s, Martin began by researching AI theories, with the goal of applying sophisticated AI techniques in consumer software. In the following essay, he discusses his cutting-edge projects and accessible approach.

1.10 Courtesy of Martin Schmitt

1.10 Martin Schmitt

I usually shy away from the artificial intelligence label since it has a permanent curse attached to it: As soon as we get "there," it's not AI anymore. It's like magic: As soon as you explain it, it's just a "trick."

Every advance in the field raises the bar; what was once the work of an "electronic brain," a jaw-dropping calculation, or a conclusion that no human could duplicate, soon gets trivialized as just an inference engine, a goal-seeking genetic algorithm, or some other "mechanical" process. In a similar vein, Kai had an amusing experience once when he demoed Live Picture to a competitor who was puzzled about the program's tremendous speed. After asking many questions, the competitor finally exclaimed, "Oh, it's just a bunch of math!"

AI is a thankless field to be in, trying to achieve something so ill-defined and fleeting. But I look at it from another angle: Why not use these powerful techniques and apply them to everyday tasks, such as helping people make better decisions?

In my years of creating graphics tools, I found that there seemed to be an inverse relationship between the power of the tools and the quality of the output. Just as in the early days of desktop publishing—or in the fad du jour, World Wide Web home pages—more freedom of choice typically meant freedom to make the wrong choice.

A similar phenomenon is happening in electronic publishing: More and more data is becoming available, but less and less of it is being properly applied; that is, turned into information. By its very definition, data itself is useless. It becomes information only when it resolves uncertainty and aids decision making.

I found that instead of feeling empowered, many people get overwhelmed by the wealth of available data. What was missing was a methodology that would put it all in context.

Based on my knowledge of evaluation theory, I developed a set of decision-support tools that allow you to explore, analyze, and compare any type of product or service in a fun, graphical user interface.

The question then became what to apply these tools to. Should I do a Web site that structures a discourse about presidential candidates, or one that helps an investor choose a mutual fund, or an interactive buyer's guide for home buyers? Where to start?

I finally settled on something that sounds very trivial: new cars. Being a serious car buff (I've owned some three dozen cars, ranging from a VW bus to an Aston Martin), I knew enough about the industry to realize the potential: Here is a $300 billion business that is run like a Turkish bazaar. Millions of people every year make the decision to buy a highly complex and expensive piece of machinery based on slick advertising, sales pitches, the opinion of the guy in the parking lot, and those red and black circles in *Consumer Reports.*

With the help of some outside investors, we will soon revolutionize this archaic process and keep people from making the second-biggest mistake of their lives: buying a Buick Ninety Eight Regency Elite.

A separate side project based on my software is a Web site that will recommend—and play samples of—new music CDs. The project is being funded by a large telephone company and is still very hush-hush.

Should anyone wonder, I continue to live in the hills of Malibu, California, with my girlfriend, Sue, and our Irish Setter. When I'm not thinking about decision-support software, I'm trying to decide between cycling and ocean kayaking—or I'm pondering the big one: Is it time to get married?

Kai Online

As Kai stepped away from Three D Graphics in 1991, he became interested in online services. In the early '90s, few realized the growth potential of this new medium, but Kai instantly recognized it as a way to communicate his thoughts and ideas with the growing digital-imaging community. Online services allowed him to build and significantly enhance his reputation as a visionary and imaging guru.

Kai Krause/Courtesy of *Wired* magazine

1.11

When he joined America Online (AOL) in 1992, online services were not nearly as popular as they are today. AOL, Prodigy, and CompuServe each had a subscriber base that numbered in the thousands, rather than the millions it currently has. But Kai saw its potential, and he became active in trying to develop the medium. "In '92 I joined AOL, which was a fledgling thing," Kai said. "The Photoshop forum had just been formed, and I remember writing letters complaining that there isn't enough stuff up there for material and content. I started to wildly post pictures and comments and tried to sort of rattle people up to make something of the potential....So they basically said, 'Well, do something,' and I did. I turned around and started to make my own content as I went."

Kai's first "postings" were examples of what could be achieved with digital imaging. "I posted the first picture purely because the pictures I saw in the Photoshop area were so lame," he explained. "So I put up a couple of [rock band] Yes logos, and after the description of that I wrote, 'Oh, by the way, I didn't use any of the [Photoshop] tools; it's all algorithmically computed.' And those files got downloaded 50 times, 100 times, 200 times, 300 times. People would send me letters asking how I did it, because I referred in the note that I did not draw anything. Then I wrote the first files—which then I did not call Power Tips; I called them Tech Notes or something like that. I put it in the

1.11 Recognizing Kai's widespread and loyal following, Absolut Vodka and *Wired* magazine asked him to create this Absolut Kai advertisement in 1995

Photoshop forum itself and, after it got downloaded several hundred times, I wrote another and another and another. When I had four or five of them, then AOL made me an area and said, 'Why don't you put all of these over here, and we'll call it Kai's Power Tips.'"

From these online tips, Kai's reputation grew, largely because he was offering something of value at no charge—literally sharing it with the digital community. Kai said, "I had come across these techniques literally 10 years before that, during the Corvus thing. I mean, the same program that I wrote there dealt specifically with how to put things together, with brushes that have feedback on themselves, and so forth....All the logical combination modes between two or three layers of pictures, and what all can happen with brushes that invert things underneath it as you pass over stuff. Having found these really cool ways to do things, I thought it was disappointing that nobody else knew them."

This sent a significant message early on about the kind of person Kai was. It also got him more attention than he could otherwise have garnered using more conventional means. It was the beginning of a relationship between Kai and the digital community that could not have been launched through the mail, newsletters, or any other form of distribution. And as online services grew in popularity, so did Kai Krause.

So by 1993, after being in this country just 17 years, Kai had established himself as an expert in the digital arena. He had developed a broad base of knowledge and skills, while fostering a great relationship with the digital community. To move ahead, he needed a product and some marketing savvy, and those were just around the corner.

Chapter 2

The Wizards of MetaTools

2.1 Courtesy of MetaTools

2.1 John Wilczak, founder, CEO, chairman of the board, and president of MetaTools, Inc.

In 1978, at about the time Kai and Martin bought their first 8 KB Compucolor computer, a Columbia University MBA student named John Wilczak discovered software development (Figure 2.1). In his last semester, John completed a course in programming—and knew immediately that he was *not* destined to be a programmer. But the course did expose him to the concepts and processes of software development. After graduating that year, John honed his business skills developing and implementing marketing and business strategy, first as a corporate consultant to the executive offices of General Electric and then, beginning in 1982, as senior management consultant at Touche Ross & Company. Yet his interests in computers, sparked during his undergraduate days at Brown University, and in software development never waned.

So while Kai and Martin were writing charting programs for the Corvus Concept, John was 3,000 miles away, invariably becoming involved with computer systems as they affected business operations. At Touche Ross, for instance, he led projects related to large-scale computer systems for Dean Witter's global commodity-trading operations, and he worked with a beta version of Software Arts' VisiCalc, the first desktop spreadsheet application (his ongoing practice of working with beta versions has always kept him a step ahead of the pack, he says). John also had the dubious honor of working with the first portable computer, an Osborne, which he described as "seriously truck-able." "I recognized that the computer provided me with a tool that at the time replaced the calculator, manual spreadsheets, and [hard-copy] documents," he said in an interview.

The origins of John's interest in and enthusiasm for digital imaging and computer graphics can be traced to his work with two Touche Ross printer clients. In 1983, he helped Newhouse Publications start up a major rotogravure printing plant in Nashville, Tennessee; later, he assisted Diversified Printing, which handles the production of *Parade* magazine, in setting up its first electronic prepress operation. Through his work with Diversified, he discovered Scitex workstation technology and realized the potential impact of digital page layout and design capabilities on the printing industry.

The Early Years

In 1985, John left Touche Ross and the East Coast and headed to California. With his soon-to-be-wife, Kelly Burke, he settled in Pacific Palisades, where he set up a business and marketing-strategy consultancy and quickly established his reputation. Early contacts at Xerox introduced him to the Xerox Star workstation, a predecessor of the computer publishing systems used today. Soon Revlon, American Honda, Citicorp, and other major corporations were requesting his electronic publishing expertise. In 1987, John decided to specialize in this area, so he formalized his business as Harvard Systems Corporation, which provided consulting and systems integration services (Figure 2.2).

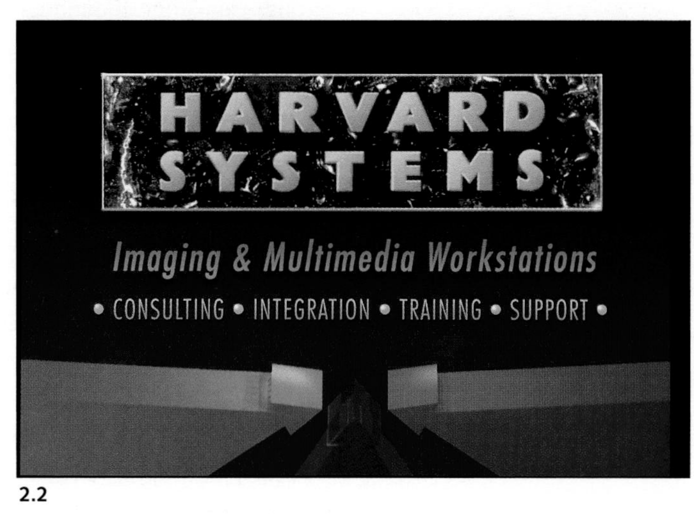

2.2

Courtesy of MetaTools

2.2 The Harvard Systems Corporation identity

In the next two years, as John slowly built the company, he reevaluated the opportunities and needs of this changing market. In 1989, he abandoned systems and hardware and concentrated on his primary interest, software development—specifically, computer graphics, imaging, and multimedia software.

The first problem John tackled was the rapid proliferation of incompatible graphics file formats on the PC and Mac platforms; the solution he came up with was a utility that would provide correct and rapid conversions between file formats. As he traveled the trade-show circuit, he met several developers who had pieces of the puzzle. Then he met James Alexander, a talented developer based in Georgia who had been working in this area. Together, they agreed that Harvard Systems Corporation would publish what became The Graphics Link Plus+ (TGL+) program, the first graphics conversion utility. Competition grew, and by August 1990, *PC Magazine* had deemed the new category important enough to do a round-up review of products, and it gave TGL+ its 1990 Editor's Choice award.

As Harvard Systems gained attention in the software world, it also gained the attention of another software company, Harvard Graphics. Harvard Graphics approached John and asked him to change his company's name, arguing that its similarity to Harvard Graphics caused confusion in the market. John agreed to modify the name to HSC informally then, and he formalized the change in summer 1992.

The year 1990 was a busy one for Harvard Systems. It released two more products: SunScan, a DOS-based scanning utility, and Image Tools, a conversion program similar to TGL+ but updated to support the latest file formats. It also started its Digital Beach design group, which would prove to be significant for the company's future. Digital Beach developed software tools customized for client projects, creating exceptional multimedia and animation presentations.

Scott Hawthorne, now MetaTools' business development manager, was one of the original members. "The [Digital Beach] multimedia production company did very well from the outset and provided a solid base for John to launch into software," Scott said in an interview. "We did some very advanced things for those days; we were the first to mix 3D studio animation with 2D traditional film animation, using the individual 2D animation cells." Digital Beach has since evolved to become MetaTools' in-house multimedia production company, and it also serves as MetaTools' ad agency. The group develops everything from computer graphics to digital video to software-demo CD-ROMs for MetaTools products.

Also in 1990, John began working with another brilliant developer, Ric Minicucci, and by midyear they had developed the DOS-based SantaFe Media Manager, the first multimedia database product on the market (Figure 2.3). The program enabled users to link multimedia objects to Borland Paradox database records, so they could track and locate photographic images, animations, and sound and video files. Alas, Windows 3.0 was about to ship that year, and Ric, like many other developers at the time, wasn't interested in programming for Windows. After a lot of soul searching, John decided that publishing provided the best opportunities for the future of his software business. He realized, though, that to build a world-class company, he would need a partner who had the technological vision to complement John's business expertise.

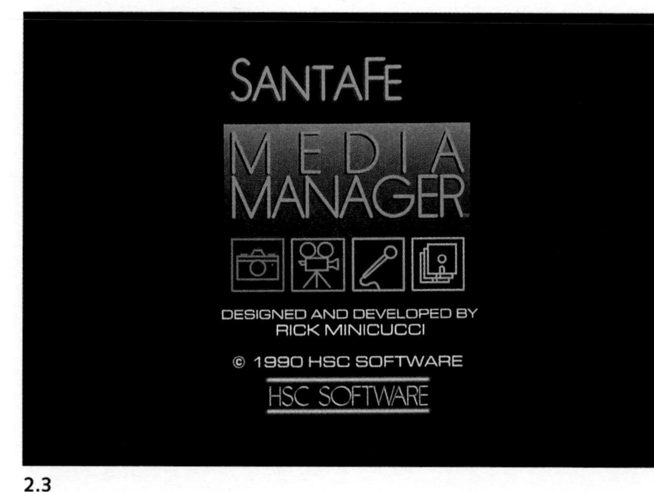

2.3

Courtesy of MetaTools

2.3 The SantaFe Media Manager logo

A Company in Search of a Product

Among John's business acquaintences was Uwe Maurer, who is considered a top electronic publishing consultant in his native Germany. One day in 1991, Uwe approached John and offered to set up a meeting between John and Kai Krause, who was a long-time friend from Germany. "His line to me was, 'This guy is great with software, and you have the business acumen to build a great company,' " John explained. " 'You should get together and do it.' "

And so John and Kai met and spent some time getting to know each other. In late 1991 an opportunity came for them to work together. Sony Corporation approached John about developing a video-editing product that would be called Sony Videoware. "Sony approached me about developing a consumer-level, cross-platform video-editing system that could be shipped on a floppy with every camera and [videotape] deck they produced throughout the world," explained John. "We decided to collaborate on this project, and within just a few months Kai had designed, and we had programmed, a PC- and Mac-based solution for this opportunity (Figure 2.4). But Sony later reported substantial losses on their business and this opportunity didn't pan out." Even though Sony Videoware never saw the light of day, it was apparent to John and Kai that they worked well together. Uwe later said, "It was almost fate that John and Kai ended up in Los Angeles at a time when they could get together."

Courtesy of MetaTools
2.4

2.4 The Sony Videoware product

Beginning in 1991, Kai posted images and tips on America Online's Mac Graphics and Adobe Photoshop forums. By early 1992, the popularity of Kai's side project prompted America Online (AOL) to give Kai his own area, called Kai's Power Tips and Tricks, which Kai and John rapidly expanded. Then they decided to put some of Kai's online Tips and Tricks on CD-ROM—but what started out as a casual project turned into much more. "It was a complete side thing," said Kai. "I decided that I'll make some of the tips on CD-ROM, and I invited other people to send me filters and curves and whatever else, to just make the CD a whole happy, full package. And all the stuff I received was so amazingly lame that I decided to go back in and write my own."

With the Sony losses putting the Videoware project on hold, Kai and John decided that building a powerful set of filters for Photoshop would be the perfect vehicle for getting into retail software development—something both had long considered doing. In April 1992 the two officially became partners, and HSC Software was born (Figure 2.5). "Kai and I joining forces was in essence a refounding of the company," said John.

2.5 The original HSC Software logo

Soon after, as Kai was working on the filters, John walked into Kai's lab, turned a white board away from Kai, and wrote the product name on it. After Kai showed John what he had come up with so far, John said to Kai, "I've named the product; want to see it?" When Kai answered yes, John turned the white board around, and Kai had his first look at the words Kai's Power Tools. "Oh, no. I don't think I want my name on a product," Kai said. But John persuaded him of the marketing wisdom in the name, and Kai's Power Tools went on to put HSC Software on the digital imaging map (see Chapter 5).

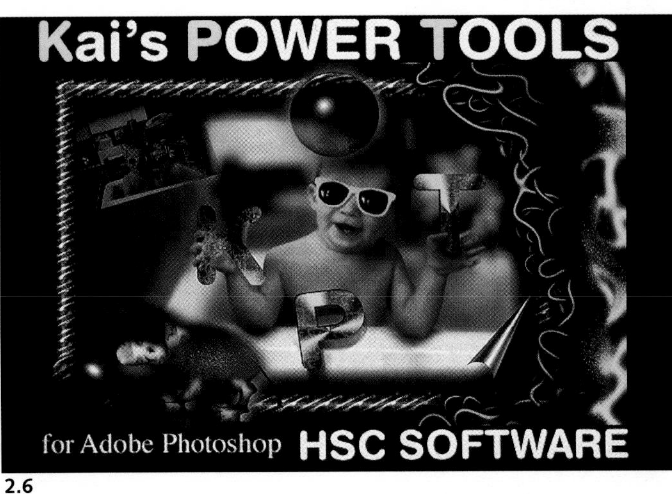

Courtesy of MetaTools

2.6

Kai's Power Tools would not have been possible without the work of Ben Weiss (see page 55), then a 19-year-old college student. Ben was referred to John by Jim Dudman, who at the time was producing multimedia and generating business opportunities for the company. Ben was willing to sign on as an unpaid summer intern, but John saw that Ben was no average intern or programmer. "His mathematical capabilities and inventiveness, coupled with Kai's vision and user interface development, quickly began to mold the product," John said.

It all happened very fast, according to Kai. "Early on I hooked up with Ben, and right away we became a very nice team. And he and I, we basically ducked under and in four months we wrote all of KPT. We started in the early summer of '92. By September we had it done, tested in October, and had it on floppies shipping at CyberArts [imaging conference] in November. And the official box, printed and everything, was in January in [MACWORLD] San Francisco in '93" (Figure 2.6). John's marketing instincts paid off in spades: List priced at $199, Kai's Power Tools became an instant best-seller, and direct and bundled sales have since topped 1 million copies.

KAI'S POWER TOOLS

Courtesy of MetaTools

2.7

Although KPT was very successful when it was first released, it did have its share of critics. Some in the industry complained that it was too different, that it strayed too far from the design standards that had been set up on the Mac. But the majority embraced the new look and feel of Kai's Power Tools, which in turn positioned Kai as an innovator and reformer in the area of interface design. With his more than 15-year perspective in programming and designing interfaces, Kai would say that the new look of his interface is the simple progression of technology. "I maintain that what we have here is a case of a lot of completely new problems that we've never had in the entire history of the earth," Kai said at a June 1995 San Francisco conference, "and they require totally new solutions. They require something unique, different, and totally for that task."

A Sense of Community

What Kai provides in creative and technical skills, John contributes in marketing and business savvy. Both men have the ability to see what's ahead—Kai in the realm of interface design and software development; John in the global marketplace and in understanding how Kai's creations can fill the needs of MetaTools' customers.

But they also share similar business philosophies. Kai often talks about the early days of desktop computers, when Apple was going to change the world and the industry eagerly awaited every new Apple or Macintosh system. Then, Kai says, everyone got jaded. Advances in RAM and storage became old news, and huge jumps in processor speeds were taken as a divine right instead of in amazement. The joy and excitement were gone from the computer industry, and it settled into becoming a business.

Except perhaps in Santa Barbara, California, where MetaTools continues to carry the torch. In fact, one of MetaTools' objectives from the very start has been to rekindle that sense of excitement and wonder. "That's what I cling to," Kai explained. "More than anything else that's what I'm trying to do here—not just to sell boxes, but to sell a spirit."

And he and John have clearly managed to maintain that energy (Figure 2.8). "'Psychic income' is one way of describing part of the relationship and payback that we each receive from working

Dan Giordan/Courtesy of MetaTools

2.8

at MetaTools," John said. "It is a wonderful feeling to get up in the morning and look forward to your work, because it is more than that—it is a love, a passion, something you enjoy doing."

Their common approach is also evident in John's unique management style. He believes in four guiding principles: (1) always exceed the customer's expectations; (2) develop advanced levels of technology while providing employees with an exciting, dynamic work environment; (3) provide the company's shareholders with value; and (4) give back to the local and national communities. The company appears to be succeeding on all counts.

MetaTools is adept at giving its customers what they want, before they want it, and at affordable prices. As for shareholder value, the privately held company's revenues have grown by more than 100 percent in both 1993 and 1994, and Computer Reseller News rated it as one of the top 10 multimedia companies in the nation. The company's talk about community means a lot, too. After MetaTools relocated its California headquarters from Santa Monica to Santa Barbara in September 1994, it wasted no time in reaching out to its new neighbors. MetaTools participated in the August 1995 MacSummit at the University of California, Santa Barbara, whose math and graphics departments also benefit from strong relations with the company.

John has also cultivated the relationship Kai had established with the digital community via the MetaTools forum on America Online (AOL) and the company's new World Wide Web site (see page 28). The AOL forum began as a way to gain exposure when advertising dollars were scarce, but it has since blossomed into a meeting place where the MetaTools staff can communicate with the artists who use MetaTools products. "It's all about community," John said, "whether it's the local community or the worldwide digital community."

2.8 John's and Kai's sense of fun is reflected in the company's 1994 New Year's postcard

MetaTools Online

Although Kai was successful before his association with America Online (AOL), it was only through AOL that he gained notoriety and exposure to a wider audience (see Chapter 1). MetaTools President and CEO John Wilczak recognized early the significance of Kai's online relationship with his fans, so he developed an AOL forum for the company (Figure 2.9). But true to form, this was no ordinary company forum. Beyond the usual content—software updates, product announcements, and order forms—MetaTools, as HSC Software then, turned its chat area, where AOL members can exchange short messages in real time, into a true meeting place. Each week, dozens of people log on to chat and exchange information about digital imaging technologies. Likely as not, they'll find themselves chatting with Kai himself—or John, or one of the product managers, or a MetaTools programmer. In essence, the people behind MetaTools have become completely accessible to its customers, making them feel like they are part of the company's planning process. And in fact they are—MetaTools receives instant, real-world feedback about what its customers want, and it moves quickly to implement changes. But it's also part of MetaTools' unique and sincere reaching out to its customers, who have responded with a loyalty that often borders on devotion.

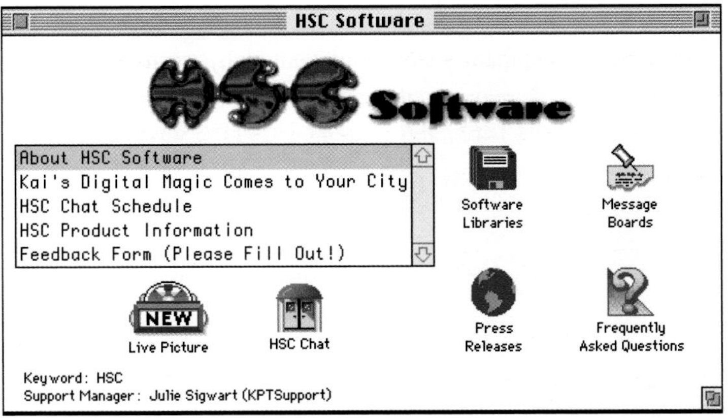

2.9 Courtesy of MetaTools

Gradually, chat-area topics expanded to include get-togethers at various trade shows, tips and ideas on how to use the applications, discussions of the newest Macintosh hardware, and other points of interest—much like a real community. Meanwhile, the company added image galleries and encouraged its customers to post images showing what the applications, as well as the artists, could do. MetaTools also set up folders on the

2.9 The HSC forum on America Online

forum to accelerate beta development for programs such as Live Picture and KPT Convolver. And all along, Kai posted his tips, along with his thoughts and ideas on the state of design and imaging today (for a taste of Kai's ruminations, see Chapter 3).

The MetaTools forum on America Online is a richly textured resource for thoughts, ideas, encouragement, and support for the MetaTools product line, as well as for imaging in general. It is hard to imagine MetaTools improving on such a format, but now there is another MetaTools forum that pushes the envelope still farther.

That forum is MetaTools' World Wide Web site, which went online in September 1995. The MetaTools Web site is an imaging meeting place that is entertaining as well as informative. When you visit, you are greeted by an impressive MetaTools logo featuring the advanced filters and effects that have made the company famous (Figure 2.10). And each time you visit, the logo changes—MetaTools has found a way to rotate through a library of different versions of the logo for a new look with each visit, even if they're just minutes apart.

The Web site also contains image galleries where you can check out images created by Kai and other artists who use MetaTools products. You can view high- or low-resolution images there, and you can read descriptions by the artists about the techniques they used. With the goal of providing a club atmosphere, the site features profiles of selected members of the imaging community, such as artists and employees.

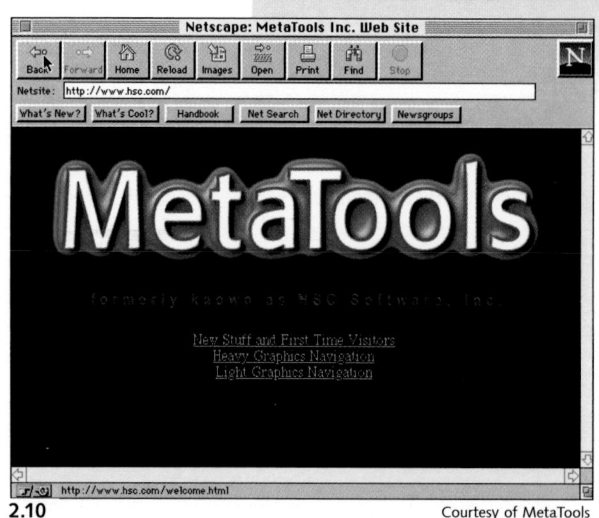

2.10 Courtesy of MetaTools

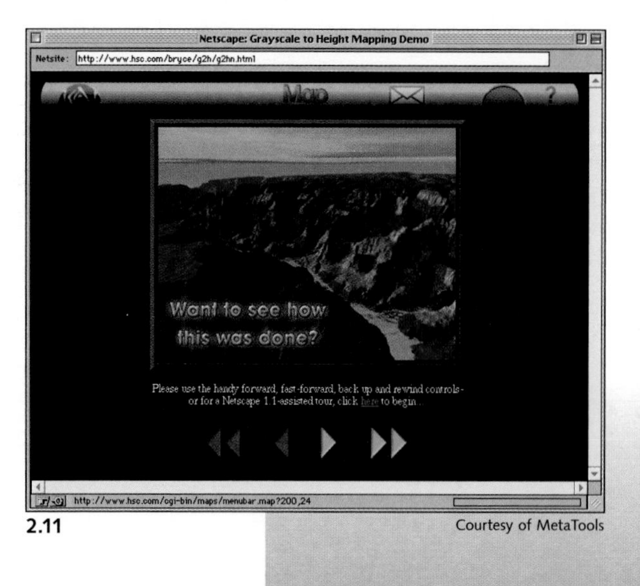

2.11 Courtesy of MetaTools

2.10 The MetaTools home page

2.11 KPT Bryce demo on MetaTools' Web site

Informative demos show you how to use MetaTools software and answer frequently asked questions (Figure 2.11). Here, you can find out how to configure and optimize your system, and find explanations of controls hidden deep within the applications. Curious about how to create a terrain in KPT Bryce? Clicking on a step-by-step slide-show link will take you through each part of the process.

The Web site is adaptive as well. If you have a slow modem and don't want to wait forever for graphics to download, click on a button and the Web site will download smaller graphics.

MetaTools' goal is to create a central resource on the Web for imaging and graphics. With its interesting, informative, and visually appealing site, MetaTools has set a new standard for Web site development. That shouldn't surprise anyone—they've been at the cutting edge of both graphics and online services for a long time. The MetaTools Web site's address is http://www.metatools.com.

Encore Products

MetaTools product development is usually led by both a development team, headed by Kai at the conceptual and programming end, and a product management team, which coordinates all of the marketing details, from manuals to packaging and press releases. Within the development group, Kai usually dictates direction and procedures. His vision is the guiding force in the development of new ideas and products at MetaTools. "Well, it's kind of the design-democracy thing [see "Interface Illusions" in this chapter]," said Kai. "It is very much a design rulership. I design the whole thing from A to Z, and it's a kind of team [at MetaTools] that will accept that and actually look forward to that."

Interface Illusions

Interface design is Kai's passion; it is his art as much as the swirling digital images he creates. Many think Kai is a visionary who sees the future path of technology. While this may or may not be true, when it comes to the software interface Kai is a visionary in a literal sense, because he has a clear vision of what the interface is and how it should be designed.

"I'd like the first hours to be totally sucked away," he has said, "and I'd also like to think that [users] stare at the glowing phosphor with a smile or a smirk. I want them to have fun with it, and realize that we are having some fun with it too."

The interface is the means by which the user interacts with the computer, harnessing the power of today's souped-up processors. How do you control the computer? How do you get it to do things? You do it all via the interface.

The interface is also a structure, a framework that lays out all of your options in a logical, intelligent fashion based on the way you work. A good interface seems to anticipate your next move, while a bad one only seems to get in your way, always underfoot, distracting you from your work. Therefore, the interface must be designed with an unwavering focus on the task at hand, and it is only successful when it facilitates that task.

And Kai feels strongly that the best interfaces are created by one person. "I sometimes get quoted on this where I say, 'Design is not a democracy,' " Kai said in his keynote address at the June 1995 Viscomm West Conference in San Francisco, "and of course they overquote me...But I mean something serious about it. I mean that you can't have 15 cooks in a room to try to do anything. There's something positive about one person mapping out an entire problem in one brain, and trying to put their arms around it in its entirety." He likened the interface designer's role to that of a master chef. You can't invite a chef like Wolfgang Puck to prepare your wedding banquet, for instance, and then tell him, 'Yeah, I think a little more pepper...How about a little more onions?' " Kai explained. "You're going to have to leave the guy alone and do it. Either you like it or you don't."

Kai's interfaces stand out because they facilitate the task at hand with little regard for software standards or norms. "Sometimes standards can be very stifling," Kai said. "If you try to express everything in terms of a commonality, in terms of metaphors that you're trying to cling to, you're kind of stuck in that entire vision of looking backwards to what you already know."

Kai has made a conscious decision to innovate rather than emulate. Examples of Kai's innovations are color pickers that allow color selection without a dialog box, and

Courtesy of MetaTools

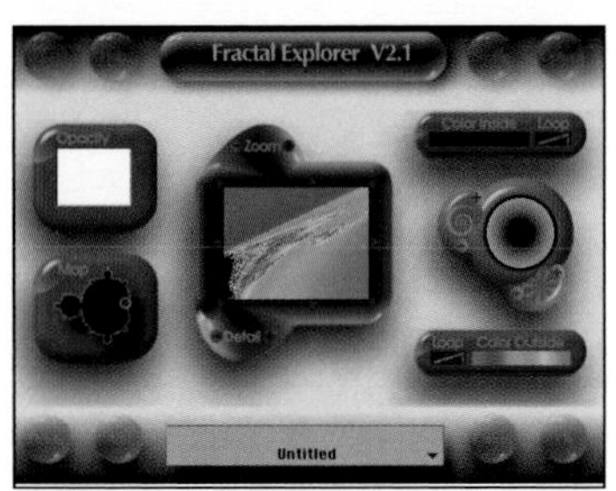

Courtesy of MetaTools

Courtesy of MetaTools

Kai's interface design evolves in versions 1.0, 2.0, and 3.0 of Kai's Power Tools intuitive atmospheric controls in KPT Bryce that update their results in real time. Kai's latest offering, KPT Convolver, takes interface design to its fluid, flexible extreme—at least for now. All of the tools in Convolver are intuitive and accessible from the main interface, increasing the user's ability to communicate by offering a greater sense of control. These things had never been done in the previous 10 years of Macintosh software development, and even though they were not significant as individual achievements, their cumulative effect on the industry was substantial.

Kai drew an analogy between these implementations and the development of automobile design. "I'm looking for things that are obvious in hindsight," he explained. "There are some things that happened from the Model T to the Lexus 400 SCXBZ whatever, and it wasn't some guy named Bob coming and inventing the 15,000-cylinder engine. It wasn't like one quantum leap; it was a lot of little, teeny-tiny things that actually happened. And you wonder sometimes where or when somebody invented the first rear-view mirror. Wouldn't that be amazingly obvious to put a mirror on there to see who's behind you? And yet it took a long while before that happened. You look back in automotive history, and suddenly there it was. And before that nobody ever had it—it was a patently nonstandard thing to use a mirror; you were supposed to turn around and cramp your neck muscles. Obvious in hindsight. I think there's a lot of things still missing [in software design], where you'd go, 'Yeah, yeah, it's supposed to be that way.' "

In his San Francisco keynote, Kai drew a parallel between the piano interface and the software interface. "What I find interesting, from an interface standpoint, [the piano] is the most simplistic, noncondescending interface. It doesn't say, 'C-sharp here,' with a little arrow pointing to it...If I had brought out Piano 1.0, [from reviewers] I would have gotten, 'The unlabeled black-and-white keys are nonstandard.' . . .

"It's true, but the point is that you have to invest a little bit to find out what the piano's all about and what comes out of it. I mean, until you sit down and go through X hours of discipline, nothing will come out. On the other hand, if you do, then a lot can come out. And what I try to do with the tools—all the tools that you've seen me use so far, and a lot more really sick stuff that's brewing in the lab—is trying to give tools to people to do things that nobody's ever done before...And I love that idea of giving the little kids the ability—that some 10-year-old will be the first person on the planet of 5 billion people, the first little kid to make that particular kind of picture."

But for the two products that followed on the heels of Kai's Power Tools in 1993—KPT Bryce, an innovative Macintosh 3D landscape generator (see Chapter 7), and Live Picture, a Macintosh image editing program that handles large files with amazing speed (see Chapters 4)—MetaTools worked with outside programmers. KPT Bryce was developed in tandem with Eric Wenger, a French artist and programmer, and Live Picture with FITS Imaging. (FITS Imaging, at the time a France-based company headed by Bruno DeLean, is now Live Picture, Inc., which is based in Soquel, California, and led by former Apple Computer CEO John Scully.

These were two of the most difficult programs to develop in the company's entire product line—largely because they were not produced completely in-house. With Live Picture, for example, Kai said, "I have no regrets about finding it, no regrets about taking it, no regrets about bringing it on the marketplace. If I have any regrets, it's that it wasn't really in-house, it wasn't really my baby. See, with KPT we controlled everything. As I usually say, design is not a democracy. It's our little benign kingdom; we can do whatever we like. With some of these collaborations it's not that way, and it tends to be much more complicated." As for KPT Bryce, despite these kinds of problems, there was no question in anyone's mind that it was a unique and powerful application. It became another best-seller and created a whole new audience for 3D imaging.

KPT Bryce

Courtesy of MetaTools

Live Picture was difficult to market because it was completely different from any other MetaTools (then HSC Software) application—and any other image editing application. Its pricing also set it apart; while the other flagship programs cost $100-200, Live Picture's initial price tag was nearly $4,000 (in early 1995 MetaTools brought the price down to $995). And although its interface was streamlined and elegant, again it was not what people were used to. Last and perhaps worst, some in the industry billed it as the Photoshop killer—inviting direct comparisons to Adobe System's popular image editing application, when in fact the two are complementary. "We've been trying so hard to get away from that [comparison] stuff from the very beginning," Kai said.

Courtesy of MetaTools

In late 1994, the company went back to its roots and released KPT Convolver, a $199 image enhancement Photoshop plug-in for Macintosh and Windows/Windows NT (see Chapter 6). It was developed entirely within Kai's "little benign kingdom," and the results are pure MetaTools—and pure Kai. The interface is intelligent and sleek, at times linear, at times circular and intuitive. And its functionality is unique as well, giving you new, kinetic ways to alter color and contrast and apply multiple effects at once, Gaussian blur to large images, and unsharp masking in real time, among other things. It wasn't long before the industry took notice: In March 1995 KPT Convolver won the Seybold Award for Excellence.

KPT Convolver™

Courtesy of MetaTools

In addition to the flagship products—Kai's Power Tools, KPT Convolver, KPT Bryce, and Live Picture—the MetaTools team has continued to offer multimedia applications in the Windows arena. These products include InterActive, a multimedia authoring tool, and Digital Morph, special-effects software that generates Hollywood-style warping and morphing (MetaTools' Suite Imaging bundles InterActive, KPT for Windows, and Digital Morph). And MetaTools has moved into animation on both platforms. Among its animation products are Gradient Designer fx plug-in for Autodesk's 3D Studio, which offers 3D Studio users the functionality of the KPT Gradient Designer module; KPT Final Effects, an Adobe After Effects plug-in for Macintosh for creating video and animation special effects; and KPT VideoWare for Alias\Wavefront Composer, special-effects extensions based on Kai's Power Tools.

A Company on the Move

MetaTools has always moved fast, but since late 1994 the pace has turned frenetic. Here's a rundown of the company's recent accomplishments and events.

- In late 1994, the company moved its California headquarters from Santa Monica to Carpinteria, near Santa Barbara (Figure 2.18). The new location, situated on cliffs overlooking the Pacific Ocean, has plenty of room for growth. In addition to increased physical space, the new offices have full high-speed fiber communications lines, which were instrumental in allowing MetaTools to develop its new World Wide Web site.

©Clarke Merritt/Tony Stone Images

2.18

2.18 Santa Barbara, California

- Also in late 1994, Vulcan Ventures, a Seattle-based investment firm owned by Microsoft cofounder Paul Allen, purchased a minority interest in MetaTools (then HSC Software). Vulcan Ventures' stake in the company is less than 20 percent of equity, and a representative of the firm fills one seat on MetaTools' seven-member board of directors.
- In a move that will affect MetaTools indirectly, Eastman Kodak licensed IVUE technology, the backbone of Live Picture, in January 1995. Kodak plans to incorporate IVUE in future generations of Kodak Photo CD and other digital imaging products.
- The company dropped the list price on Live Picture, from $3,995 to $995, in February 1995. Live Picture now sells at a street price of

around $600, making the revolutionary image editing program available to a much wider audience.

- From 8 employees at its 1992 beginnings, MetaTools topped the 80-employee mark in 1995.
- In June and July 1995, the company sponsored Kai's Digital Magic, a series of seminars and presentations at seven locations across the country.
- MetaTools launched its World Wide Web site in September 1995 to a flurry of activity. The Web site allowed it to expand the online service and support it pioneered on America Online (see page 23 in this chapter).
- In a bold move, HSC Software changed its name to MetaTools, Inc., in September 1995.
- Also in September 1995, MetaTools acquired Final Effects from Sweden-based UDAC Multimedia and rereleased it as KPT Final Effects.
- Since late 1994, major MetaTools product and upgrade releases have included KPT Convolver, Gradient Designer fx, Live Picture 2.0, Kai's Power Photos I and II, KPT Vector Effects, KPT Final Effects, and Kai's Power Tools 3.0.

2.19 Courtesy of MetaTools

Released in 1995, Kai's Power Photos I and II move MetaTools into the content-provider arena (you'll find 10 sample images on the CD-ROM included with this book). A boon to designers, each $199 Power Photos package ships with several CD-ROMs containing hundreds of royalty-free RGB TIFF images. Kai's Power Photos I includes five volumes on 10 CD-ROMs: Natural Backgrounds and Textures; Food Basics; Urban Textures and Backgrounds; Sky, Water, and Landscapes; and Sports and Recreation. Kai's Power Photos II: The Elite Series features five themes on five CD-ROMs: Kids' Toys and Backgrounds, Hot Rods, Bugs and Butterflies, and Fall and Winter Holidays. All images were photographed specifically for this series and have been sharpened and color corrected, so they have a consistent look and feel.

KAI'S POWER Photos™

Courtesy of MetaTools

Introducing KPT Vector Effects

MetaTools' latest product, released in June 1995, is a venture into the otherwise-alien world of vector graphics. KPT Vector Effects brings KPT-like capabilities to Macintosh and Windows versions of Macromedia FreeHand and other vector-based graphics programs in a set of plug-ins or "extensions" that dramatically increase their special-effects capabilities.

FreeHand and similar programs ship with a core set of plug-ins for manipulating paths and creating special effects. But the plug-ins are not as creative or intuitive as Kai's Power Tools filters for Photoshop are. KPT Vector Effects aims to fix all that. Its extensions allow you to interact with your vector image in a smooth, intuitive way. Many of the effects are standards, such as Resize and Reposition or Point Editor, while others are new and unique, such as Sketch and Neon.

Here's a list of the 13 Vector Effects extensions and their capabilities:

- KPT 3D Transform: for rotating artwork along three axes in true 3D space; extruding or beveling artwork; and changing depth, perspective, light-source location, or other aspects
- KPT ColorTweak: for adjusting colors in real time; tweaking brightness and contrast; adjusting color saturation, color inversion, and grayscale properties; rotating colors; and adjusting CMYK color tints (these functionalities are standards in pixel-based imaging but are new to vector art)
- KPT Emboss: for creating hard or soft embosses
- KPT Flare: for creating a lens-flare or "star" effect similar to a bright light reflecting a smooth surface
- KPT Inset Path: for increasing or decreasing the size of the paths in the artwork

- KPT Neon: for creating a neon tube effect
- KPT Point Editor: for making explicit changes to artwork points and curves using selection points and Bézier curve handles
- KPT Resize and Reposition: for resizing and repositioning artwork
- KPT Shadowland: for creating soft, halo, and zoom shadow effects
- KPT Shatterbox: for creating artwork that looks like it was struck, dropped, crumbled, and so on
- KPT Sketch: for giving artwork the appearance of being hand drawn in a rough manner
- KPT Vector Distort: for creating distortion lenses that twist, bulge, or otherwise misshape portions of selected artwork
- KPT Warp Frame: for creating "envelope distortions"—alterations to the shape of artwork—by attaching points and Bézier curve handles to a bounding box (envelope) around the selected object and then manipulating them to reach the desired effect (Figure 2.21).

Nearly all the extensions can be run using keyboard commands of the "host application," and KPT Vector Effects automatically detects what that host application is. Several extensions allow the precision of numerical input as well as visual adjustment, and numerous presets are included. And both the KPT Vector Distort and KPT Warp Frame extensions implement their effects not by automatically adding multiple points—which increases file sizes and complicates PostScript printing—but by mathematically adjusting the curve locations, adding points only where necessary.

2.21

Courtesy of MetaTools

2.21 The KPT Warp Frame extension

In addition, Vector Effects remains true to the KPT standard in that each extension allows for a broad degree of variation and user interaction. Some effects allow you to click and drag in the window and update your design in real time—a new concept in the vector world.

Don't look for a fantastical interface in KPT Vector Effects, though; it's about as far removed from Kai's Power Tools as it can get. The turquoise spheres and shaded buttons of KPT are all gone, replaced by black-and-white boxes with text—though very nice looking black-and-white boxes. The Vector Effects interface puts all of the buttons well within reach, without getting underfoot.

With Vector Effects, MetaTools has demonstrated that its design prowess is not exclusively pixel-based. It saw a need in the market for an implementation of vector-based special effects and once again responded with a solid, affordable product.

A Glimpse of the Future

It has been said that MetaTools gives its customers what they want, before they even know they want it. That was true for both Kai's Power Tools and KPT Bryce, and perhaps for all of MetaTools' products. The software that Kai has developed and designed does seem to be slightly ahead of its time. Given that, how are we to take it when he says things such as this: "The trickiest part is that everything you've seen so far, I consider it just a preamble. It's hard for me to make statements on interface designs coming from a bunch of little dialogs stuck in a plug-in. That's not what I would like to be known for or about"?

Up to this point, Kai has either produced plug-in applications or codeveloped stand-alone applications with other programmers, who had their own ideas about how the applications should operate. What if he created a stand-alone application of his own? Given his background and experience, you would think that his new project would be a graphics application, or perhaps some new sound or animation program. Yet consider this statement, presented in his keynote address at the June 1995 Viscomm West Conference in San Francisco: "I maintain that whatever we do have in every category—from word processing, spreadsheets, databases, data graphics, you name it—it all has to be reinvented, given that the machines have gone 200 times forward since the first ones." Spreadsheets and word processing? You wouldn't think Kai would be interested.

In a recent conversation with him, I made the mistake of casually saying that I thought word processing was a limited area for developers. Kai shot back: "I swear to God, there must be completely new ways to create documents, create text, edit your stuff, explore different versions and variations of the potential way that a document may go, and go fluidly from one, to the next, to the next. It just isn't there right now. There's no such thing as true WYSIWYG. I mean, you should get a photograph of your page that looks just like your page. with all the anti-aliased text right in the middle of it. So I would venture to say that we're very far away from having anything near the ultimate in word processing."

In fact, Kai has his mind on something completely different from anything he has done so far. True to MetaTools form, it is not what you would expect, and when you get it, you will wonder how you ever lived without it. True to industry form, neither Kai nor MetaTools could talk about it in detail before it's announced. Kai described it as a "morphing tool belt" that is context sensitive to the tasks at hand. In the same way that you need a spatula in the kitchen and a screwdriver in the garage, this system would intuitively have a sense of which tool set you need, and when.

The potential of this project must be very significant, because even Kai is excited. The guy who created KPT and Convolver, and brought us the likes of Bryce and Live Picture, is so into this new project that he can't stop talking about how great it's going to be. As we wrapped up our conversation, I was full of questions. Though he didn't tip his hand, his final words were encouraging. "Don't worry," he said, "the answers are much more positive than you could ever dream about."

A Continuous Evolution

MetaTools will continue to grow, breaking the rules at times, and often setting new standards in the process. The visions of John Wilczak and Kai Krause have evolved in unexpected ways. First it was filters, then it was stand-alone applications—and who knows what it will be a year from now? Most likely even Kai and John don't know exactly how things will play out, although it's safe to say that as the MetaTools team grows, so does its possibilities.

Kai says that all of the success thus far has only been a preamble, and that the best part is only beginning. "It's the whole story of the company in fact: getting everything ready to really do something, to do a change," Kai said. "And it took a year and a half just to rev it up to that, which was actually lightning fast. The whole thing has only been a little more than two years."

Chapter 3

Kai's Dinner Party Keynote

In January 1995, Kai Krause reinvented the keynote address at MACWORLD San Francisco by inviting fellow visionaries from the computer and music industries to join him in a free-wheeling discussion of future trends. It was a controversial move, and the response prompted Kai to post a nine-part essay on America Online's MetaTools (then HSC) forum, an edited version of which follows. In an online folder he named Crimson Sky, Kai articulated the evolution and concept of the San Francisco event, but his ruminations also reveal his unique personality and philosophy. He has since held similar keynote discussions at MACWORLD Tokyo and the Apple Worldwide Multimedia Conference in New York City.

Courtesy of Mitch Hall Associates, MACWORLD Expo, 1995

3.1

3.1 Kai introduces his unusual keynote event at MACWORLD San Francisco 1995

Courtesy of Mitch Hall Associates, MACWORLD Expo, 1995

3.2

Courtesy of Mitch Hall Associates, MACWORLD Expo, 1995

3.3

3.2 Author Douglas Adams makes a point during the roundtable session

3.3 From left to right: Charles Fleischer, Herbie Hancock, Thomas Dolby, Todd Rundgren, Graham Nash, and Kai Krause listen intently as Douglas Adams (hidden from view) speaks

January 17, 1995

The keynote address at MACWORLD San Francisco '95 was really dear to my heart. I am very happy that it all came together the way it did.

For the last few years I have been part of many speeches and opening keynotes, and been in the audience for many more. Very often it's either a dry talking head, or a product sales pitch, or a row of chairs with industry pundits. At best they are entertaining or informative; at worst it can get to be utterly predictable, pragmatic, self-fulfilling PR, or just plain boring.

And I have perpetrated these myself, of course, too . . . . ;)

In the summer of last year I had a chance to sit in for Al Gore, who could not commit to the keynote for MACWORLD Washington, D.C. (Mandela in South Africa had just happened, I think), and I ended up doing that one solo for 90 minutes, and a panel following that (incidentally, with Steve Case from AOL).

"I am convinced that things have never been this great before on this blue planet and at the same time never this horrible either."

The topic was, of course, Mr. Gore's Information Superhighway (ISH), which I renamed Soup or Highway for the purpose of that day. Really, my own title to the speech was "Muse and Ponder," meaning "There are so many interesting realities to actual online communities, with many anecdotes to muse about" and "There are so many incredibly deep philosophical implications to ponder for each of us." And I meant that quite sincerely; both sides are important in my mind.

Only later that day did I get to meet several Washington figures, including some that are apparently on the panels and committees for what promises to become the ISH. And the reality of them being proud of just having received their first e-mail (!) drove the point home that those of us who have been brain-deep into these concepts for years now really do have a responsibility to transfer that knowledge and stand on our soapboxes, both cheering and warning of impending doom and gloom.

It's a very bipolar issue. I am convinced that things have never been *this* great before on this blue planet and at the same time never this *horrible* either.

My solo keynote must have gone well, because IDG MACWORLD offered me soon after to do "the big one" in San Francisco. I accepted, but had a slightly different concept in mind.

Throughout my many travels in the last few years (I've circled the globe a few times; 3,000 miles by car through Europe; multiple visits to Tokyo, London; and took my wife for what was the 18th visit to Paris (eeeeek), which incidentally was the first time we had been there in 19 years, and in the romantic mood we decided to go for child #3—"still in Beta") (classic example of me getting lost in happy anecdotes . . .).

So in the last few years, I have had the pleasure of meeting many incredible people scattered throughout the globe. Over so many dinners and teas and in planes and over pool tables or playing Go, I had engaged in conversations and heated debates, giggling storytelling, and deep mental fistfights. I treasure these moments; I live for that depth of exchange. Sometimes the partners in these meetings are old friends, sometimes big players, and other times random strangers, often onliners too.

I have worked with enough famous people to not be easily "starstruck" anymore, but there is something about these folks that really does distinguish them in many cases: they have lived through situations and experienced events that are simply not commonplace. They bring a level of extra seasoning, and their perceptions can often be quite different simply because the box of reference material is different—not necessarily larger, but often unique. I have no problem in recognizing that and readily admit to rather having tea with Leonardo or Galileo or M.C. Escher any day than their anonymous neighbors in the same house, smart and happy as they might be.

This can easily be regarded as something like "elitist" (sigh), and the mere mention of a lovely event will draw such comments from others, especially many who don't know me at all. I fall in these traps a lot.

For that reason, you *very* rarely find me posting here where I went the other night or who I had sushi with in Roppongi. Sadly so, because often there is real content, real newness and interest that accompanies the story. Amusing or deep, muse or ponder....

> "Well, the idea for me here was, 'Wouldn't it be great to be able to duplicate the fun and depth of a dinner conversation between good friends.'"

Well, the idea for me here was, "Wouldn't it be great to be able to duplicate the fun and depth of a dinner conversation between good friends," and that's what I set out to do in San Francisco.

I asked IDG to build me a round stage in the *middle* of the audience, circled by chairs on all sides. A table for six in the middle, good audio for each, and a cone of light from the top. Boxing-ring lighting, ideally, since my idea was that they would entirely forget the audience and just get into the topics themselves, and not in some polite "your turn, my turn, next in the round," but a free-for-all, a true "interrupt me ...What, are you nuts?...Hey, I have an idea ...Oh yeah, get *this* ...Oh, I have an even better one ..." *dinner* discussion. Close to a philosophical food fight!

And you know what? I think that's exactly what we got—or as close as one can get it at 10 in the morning with 3,000 watching. For the first time, a keynote done in an unknown format and with an audience expecting an Apple announcement of System 7.6 or something.

"If they leave with just one deep thought, one neat quote, one cool idea, one little crack in their belief system, or a gentle nudge to extend themselves ...then it worked!"

I was very happy to see that it could work ....

I have full empathy, by the way, for some folks who just weren't up to early morning philosophy or were there for a technical briefing. But I also do believe that the keynote *ought* to be more than a mere "one more panel session." There are dozens, if not over a hundred, separate technical seminars throughout MACWORLD, and all of them seem to get so deep down into the literal specifics, as they must, that really there is no one pausing to think about the deeper implications of it all. That's what I tried to set up.

I wanted the audience to first watch this discussion unfold, and then I walked around with a mike folding them right into it as much as possible. And my goal was simply stated right in the beginning: if they leave with just one deep thought, one neat quote, one cool idea, one little crack in their belief system, or a gentle nudge to extend themselves ...then it worked!

Judging by the feedback for me, and the others, afterwards and in mail and e-mail, phones, messages, it worked very well, even!

Yes, there are (and must be!) some that are offended by the format or the f-word or the topic or a speaker's opinions, but that almost comes with the territory. We would have done something *wrong* if it didn't upset a few; there is no staid and placid, safe way to appease every view out there.

I also wanted to bring together a round of not-always-seen people; in fact I had fun working to unite an interesting group. You can't blame me for not just picking six random smart folks; it's a pragmatic point to realize that the audience wouldn't stick around (sadly enough!), and IDG probably would not even give the floor just to a set of unknowns. There are *many* other people I would like to see on such a panel, though this one had a uniting flavor of musicians and performers to it. I hope to do it again and vary that theme.

> "I regret really only one thing, and that is that we were unable to get any women to be on the panel."

I regret really only one thing, and that is that we were unable to get any women to be on the panel. And it's not for trying hard: many e-mails went back to the organizers and my own office, as well as each of the participants as they signed up. And we got very close until the last day. There was Laurie Anderson, who was about to embark on her new world tour and had to decline; Jane Metcalfe, who founded *Wired* magazine, who had to launch the Japanese edition just about that very day. We tried Diane Sawyer (her office had no idea "what's a MACWORLD and she just doesn't do these things …") and a couple of surprise guests that I still would like to have come up next time around. It was frustrating to pursue these, getting close to deadline (holidays and all right in front) and end up with multiple "almosts."

On the upside, while IDG insisted that printing simply "surprise guests" would not fly with them, and therefore they printed whom we could confirm very early, I *did* manage to bring a surprise guest, and even they did not know who until the morning of the event. I am very thankful to Douglas Adams [author of the *Hitchhiker's Guide to the Galaxy* series and other science-fiction books] for flying in from London just for 24 hours to do this. And he was a great asset to have in the round.

It started with a 15-minute little micro version of my ISH speech, and ended in my definition of the whole topic; namely, that it really has nothing to do with mere zippy phone lines or

500 channels of dubious content or anything we currently know. The ISH, I said, may very well take much longer to come around than we would hope or Al Gore might wish, but make no mistake, when it finally *does* exist in full gear, it should be this: that every person on earth has access to the sum-total of all human knowledge.

And *that* will change everything.

> when it [the Information Superhighway] finally does exist in full gear, it should be this: that every person on earth has access to the sum-total of all human knowledge.
> And that will change everything.

It will change the entire species of Homo sapiens, and the blue planet right along with it. For many in the little room for 3,000 in a hotel somewhere on that planet, it may seem like awfully big words to hear at 10:38 in the morning, but I really do believe that someone has to say this! And repeatedly so! And where do they say it otherwise? Where can it be said if not in front of that choir of the techno-savvy?

There was great depth in the little salons in Paris of 1910, or the Vienna coffeehouses. No one had to agree with any one viewpoint there—one did not have to like any of van Gogh's paintings or follow Jung and Adler—but one should readily see that there *must* be some of these people to push the envelope of our bit of planetary dust here.

I may not be one of them, but in this field I had hoped to earn my spot to be able to talk about technology, Internet, online communities, e-mail communication, global connectivity, "digital" art and all those loaded words. That I do know a little something about.

An interesting angle also for me was that these things are moving away from the white-lab-coat-egghead cartoon character in front of some monster machine with a paper tape that reads "does not compute!" to the real lives of single mothers and senior citizens and children. And as such, the people on the panel were also representing that crossover from technocratic inner circles to wider penetration into totally unrelated (or so we thought) areas.

There was Herbie Hancock: jazz musician, for a long time wired to the gills, surrounded with equipment, hooked to the Net with private T1 line, recording CD masters at home, performing MIDI via satellites, using graphics as backdrops and sound driving visuals. And yet I remember clearly when I led him into a room at an AES show in '76 and he saw his very first CRT on the beta Synclavier I—and he was scared spitless! Ha! We had fond memories to relive.

He is a gentle man who has seen a lot in his life, traveling the globe with esteemed peers and unforgettable legends. And yet he remains an open, peaceful, and genuinely life-loving soul. A great man to have dinner with any day of the week or year.

Todd Rundgren: truly knee-deep in computers, early pioneer in computer graphics, videos, animation, interactivity, his CD-ROM with truly user-controllable pieces, touring with a stage full of gear—when he kicked that off at our Exploratorium party last year, the system froze multiple times, and he continued without dropping a beat with analog, good-old acoustic guitar ;). He has most certainly earned his spot in the scene not only technology wise, but being an outspoken individualist, unattached to mainstream or special interests, unrestrained free thinking and even stirring trouble when it has to be stirred. And there again he did his voodoo, giving me the jab or two that I know I deserve every time we get together. Perfect for this.

Next in the round was Graham Nash, another legend on the musical side, having left his mark many times over in decades of work, and also truly wired to the hilt: he founded an entire company, Nash Editions, to create special fine-arts-level digital printing on custom-modified IRIS printers—high-resolution, large-format prints from digital sources. He was also the winner of the Biggest Toys award with a gig-RAM Onyx, collaborating with Silicon Graphics on a project to let him surf his entire career in a real-time, live collection of clips, pictures, sounds—pushing the limits again on that front. And as he demonstrated in several press conferences I had, where he popped in to give very witty and spontaneous support, he is a no-nonsense kinda guy and will say what he feels, whether over dinner or onstage. Just what was needed... and he did it great!

"I just resent anyone calling them [the roundtable guests] "pop stars" as if they were up there for teenage girls to adore. They came as humans."

Thomas Dolby has been a veteran of technology, always on that bleeding edge, touring all alone with MIDI gear when it was not reliable or safe to do so yet, doing projects with unique people and special sounds and customized equipment, and venturing into whole new areas where he was almost always pretty much alone. Immersed in soundtracks for animation, his recent direct involvement with computers is an entire new system of continuous spatial soundscape design, where the visual interactivity of CD-ROMs finds a matching sonic component, bringing the metamorphosis of music and effects and images to a controllable composition level rather than mere cut-and-paste sequences. He, too, has been on seemingly endless tours, meeting minds all around the world, and has much to say about where we stand and where we go. Very happy he could make it!

Charles Fleischer may be the best example of these circles of technology invading unexpected places: who would think a stand-up comic, the voice of Roger Rabbit, to be developing visual graphics as one sideline and deep at work on CD-ROM comedy databases ("Romedy") as another? His take on the absurdities of life and his finding the sweet details on a human level, coupled with a very fervent mind to express the ideas, and lightning-fast if called for, makes him an ideal participant in any round of friends at any dinner, onstage or not.

These descriptions are mine, talking about them just as friends, as I feel about them. None of this appeared in the event, and we only touched upon many of these cool credentials in passing even. I just resent anyone calling them "pop stars" as if they were up there for teenage girls to adore. They came as humans.

And last in the round was the surprise.

This gave me great joy too: at the end of my intro piece, I proceeded to read a page of a book, where a race of beings creates a supercomputer that would finally come up with all the answers to the deep questions I had alluded to earlier. That computer was, of course, called "the Earth."

The two-minute segment from the *Hitchhiker's Guide* (Douglas was probably groaning as I read it, mangling the vowel-less names as I went) led me to the line I always wanted to use, from Woody Allen in *Annie Hall*, where he is arguing while standing in line with someone about Marshall McLuhan. And so in that same spirit I was finally able to say: "We know nothing of these questions; I happen to have Mr. Adams right here!!!!" And with that, Douglas came on stage first, to quite a thundering round of applause, and the others (all seated until then in the first rows all around the stage) came up all at once.

It was a lovely start.

And I *really, really* must hand it to the panel members, each and every one: they really got into the spirit of the event, as a dinner discussion between friends. No one got special billing (other than that minute for the surprise guest); no one talked about their latest CDs or projects or promoted anything at all. They made references where appropriate to recent works or experiences, but in a great, refreshing sense of just "stuff they are about," not something borne out of PR.

I tried to leave them alone for a while to find a rhythm, and pros that they are, no one needed to fill the space instantly or clamor for the right sentence right away. They took their time, a few minutes, to go around the circle and put connections on the table. Maybe with lesser people it could have been awkward *not* to have a set question or introductions or speeches or panel talk. No one was especially introduced or asked to describe things—it went right smack into the muse and ponder. Within 10 minutes Douglas, especially, started to curl off lovely thought constructs of the nature of communication, information being available to other information, book covers melting into homogenous glut, and before long they broached topics of security, netcash, education, equality of access, mankind's mutation, and on and on. An hour into it, which flew by, we had the proverbial food fight, lively debates, f-words and exclamations, many great lines and ideas.

"An hour into it, which flew by, we had the proverbial food fight, lively debates, f-words and exclamations, many great lines and ideas."

The audience was at times totally forgotten and then brought back into it directly: I tried to fade out and leave them be, then pulled up a chair and mused right along, and then ran to some random person to request input, questions, and comments.

Not as easy as it looks, that much I know. ;) Phew.

Maybe it looked like a cheap Donahue imitation—it's hard to do this and *not* broach that notion—but hopefully it at least achieved that mixture of having the audience be part of it without overwhelming it. It's not an easy balance to have six such complex personalities do a little dance and still allow that to be punctured with yet more variables.

Few will have noticed that, but I tried hard to fade into the background, and to not mention a single product of mine, or my company, or indeed *anything* I do in the business itself ....(The temptation is great of course, just as I opened with the line, "Do you have any idea how hard it is to resist the temptation to start with cheap Pentium jokes??")

This is a completely separate endeavor for me, and I stuck to the ethics of that dividing line very clearly (again, some naysayers might object that I do this as some cheap commercial, but that one really will not stick ....I even objected to the 30-second introduction calling me Exec VP, and will insist even *that* not to be there next time). Gotta be, oh, so clear ...being very vulnerable to them naysayers ....

Audiences can be at the same time like five-years-olds, giggling and following Simon, and then they can turn. Communally, they also are nearly omniscient!—as I pointed out in the beginning, when I wrote down 3.1415926 ...on an overhead projector and asked for the next number, knowing that *someone* would yell "5" within a second ....

That, by the way, is *exactly* the point of the computer = the Earth, and it plays right into the notion of the Internet and superhighway, connecting it all up from isolated groups into a coherent web (not that the World Wide Web is coherent yet; the term is meant as opposed to the unconnectedness of Earth in 1895, or 1638, or 1266, or 933, or any other date prior).

I think there were at least 20 questions woven into the flow from the audience; some with longer answers, some in short discourse (and I must have had twice as many whispered to me to be edited and selected on the fly—edited only in the sense that I had to stay the course and not allow the all-too-obvious mundane ones to take over; e.g., what's your last CD, Herbie?; why "42," Douglas?; and is CSNY reuniting, Graham? etc., etc.) (I was proud that that is exactly what did *not* happen here ….)

"Really, if you don't think this has anything to do with you and me and us all in this room and on this planet, then I don't know what does, I'm sorry."

There was hardly a five-second pause for nearly the entire two-hour period.

In the end, one woman was irate and just pelted me with furor: "All this talk about the meaning of life and the Net and the future—what does this have to do with MACWORLD???" And I gave her the mike (she didn't want it) and I stopped the discussion. And I said, "Really, if you don't think this has anything to do with you and me and us all in this room and on this planet, then I don't know what does, I'm sorry." And I truly felt that.

We had pretty much a standing O, rousing applause, and ended with that last bit of controversy, which again I thought was a good thing, too.

Earlier someone objected to the use of the f-word, and again, I really felt that this is almost our responsibility to escape the silliness of network-television-like contraptions. In a real dinner discussion, that's how people speak! I saw no reason (and no way) to censor *these* people, and I heartily support their right to say well-chosen words of any kind. This was not some random profanity thoughtlessly slung around; we were getting into topics that clearly warranted a personal outrage. This, of course, was itself one of the very topics: a country in which one can show a woman being shot in the face repeatedly on a Sunday afternoon, but a nipple will be edited out at midnight (unless it happens to be in mid-mutilation, I assume …). Yech! (another four-letter word?)

Again, I respect someone raising that as a point; that's at least valid criticism, whatever side of the argument one finds oneself on. I don't expect, surely, to please 3,000+ people with *any one thing*. Clearly, if someone came expecting new Macs or great future revelations by [Apple President and Chief Executive Officer Michael] Spindler, then I can only lose. I did talk to Mr. Spindler the day before and injected at least the quote that "Apple will indeed be around a decade from now!" And I surely did not mean to do the keynote instead of an announcement.

This was planned for months, and the people up there, I think, proved that they were not stand-ins as "pop stars" or irrelevant in the proceedings. Quite the contrary; I was very proud of them truly getting right down to the elusive big stuff, while making it entertaining enough not to end up looking like a bunch of monks in a monastery.

> As far as I am concerned, I would show up to such an actual dinner any old time.

The IDG group came and asked me to recreate the entire thing, full panel and all, in Tokyo and at the first MACWORLD Beijing in China even! The entire *crew* for lights and sound came and expressed their thanks and said that out of 100 events a year, this was the first time they actually paid any attention to the words being said! (No kidding.)

As far as I am concerned, I would show up to such an actual dinner any old time.

It was my pleasure to let several thousand participate in this one, and I would love to bring that to you again in the near future.

Kai

The Start of a Beautiful Friendship

Kai's nine-part Crimson Sky essay prompted these philosophical remembrances from MetaTools Software Designer Ben Weiss (Figure 3.4), who implemented coding and algorithms for Kai's Power Tools.

January 18, 1995

Let me tell you a story...the story of how I met and got to know Kai, all those many years ago. Has it really been two and a half years? Oh my...

I was 19 then, had just finished my sophomore year of college and was looking for a summer job to hold me over a few months 'til school started up again. One day in June, my father went out surfing at Topanga, and bumped into Jim Dudman in the water, and they started talking. The subject somehow turned to me looking for a summer job, and Jim mentioned that he worked for a small computer company in Santa Monica. He suggested that I might stop by for an interview.

So a few days later, I showed up at this small office in an old brick building in downtown Santa Monica—10 guys there, PC hardware bits and pieces everywhere. I brought some images of computer graphics stuff I'd been working on, just as a hobby on the side [see Figure 3.5]. They all agreed that my stuff looked interesting. The bottom line, though, seemed to be, "We do mostly PC multimedia; we're not really sure if there's a place for you here.

"But you should talk to Kai."

I gave them my phone number, not really expecting much. At that time I had never heard of Kai. The only Kai I knew was an Asian guy I went to high school with, so somehow I formed a mental picture of this wizened Asian computer geek playing with circuit boards up on a mountaintop somewhere.

So anyway, a week later, I got a phone call back. Kai and John wanted to meet me at the office and discuss the possibilities for a job. I went in to the office, did a double-take when I realized that the tall German guy wandering around the place was Kai, and we sat in the tiny conference room to discuss. I showed them my stuff again, they thought it was cool, and we signed a deal for $1,600 a month full-time summer work. I had no idea what to expect. They had no idea what to expect.

Finally, Kai needed a ride back up to his house in Malibu. I volunteered to drive him, thinking we'd sit together at his place for an hour and he'd show me all the work he was doing with Photoshop 2.0.1 on his new Quadra. After negotiating the winding hill up to his house, we found we had a lot in common: a passion for music, art, philosophy—and, of course, computer

David Weiss

3.4

3.4 MetaTools Software Designer Ben Weiss

graphics. So we went up to his studio, he launched PS, and my jaw dropped. When after a while it started getting light outside, it dawned on us that perhaps we were onto something bigger than just a summer job.

What happened to my life from that day forward would easily score a 10 in any professional gymnastics competition. From the academic duality of "this over here is your education, and this other thing over here is real life," I first began to really appreciate the "fundamental interconnectedness of all things," as Douglas Adams so eloquently put it. Kai taught me Go, the two-hour metaphor for life; just a week ago I inherited his well-worn Go board, passed down from his Go teacher 15 years back—an honorable tradition. We've been all over Europe—from Kai's hometown of Essen, through Paris and beyond—and sat for hours at his kitchen table drinking tea, playing Go, listening to obscure, brilliant music from his formidable collection, planning the future.

It hurts me to see the standardized, accepted vision of what "work" is defined to be in modern society: sit in a tiny cubicle from 9 to 5, never see the sun, hate what you do, "work 22-hour days down at the mill for a tuppence every five years." And yet so many people do just that, blindly accepting their work as "part of life."

In working with Kai, I've found that work being "part of life" has quite the opposite meaning. The distinction blurs; the creation of software takes on the same passion as surfing a 12-foot wave on a good day at Rincon. Slightly different time scales, to be sure, but the feeling is the same.

Sure, I could treat my job as 9-to-5 grunt work, do the minimum I can get away with, and then have a separate "life" when office hours are over. But I think I prefer things the way they are. Kai could have just as easily acted as my "boss," telling me exactly what to do and how to do it, and when to have it done by—but he didn't. Instead, the relationship we have forged over the past two and a half years is only in small part tied to MetaTools, or KPT, or even computer graphics. It's a rich fusion of all the variety of life itself, from taking time out from a deadline to play just one more game of Go to wandering around the streets of Paris looking for just the right crêperie. And we've gotten 10 times the amount of work done this way than we possibly could have otherwise.

What does all this have to do with Kai's keynote? Not microchips or megahertz, that much's for certain. ;)

Ben Weiss

3.5

3.5 Ben showed this and other images he created to John and the HSC staff on his first visit

Chapter 4

Exploring Live Picture

This chapter discusses strategies for making the best use of Live Picture's capabilities. The technical capabilities of Live Picture are not its most significant features; there are programs that are more complex and clever. But few combine processing improvements with creative tools as Live Picture does. Its most significant aspect is that it enables the artist and digital imaging professionals to do things they've never been able to do before. It empowers them to work with huge files with total flexibility in the creative process.

The next section shows the Live Picture interface, with the main areas, icons, and tools labeled and described. You can use it as a reference and a guide for the information in this chapter.

The Live Picture Interface

This section presents graphically the Live Picture interface and its elements (the layer stack, the Creative mode tools, and the Insertion mode tools), together with descriptions of key tools and icons for each.

The Environment

The Live Picture environment is made up of four components: the toolbar, the control bar, the layer stack, and the image workspace (Figure 4.2).

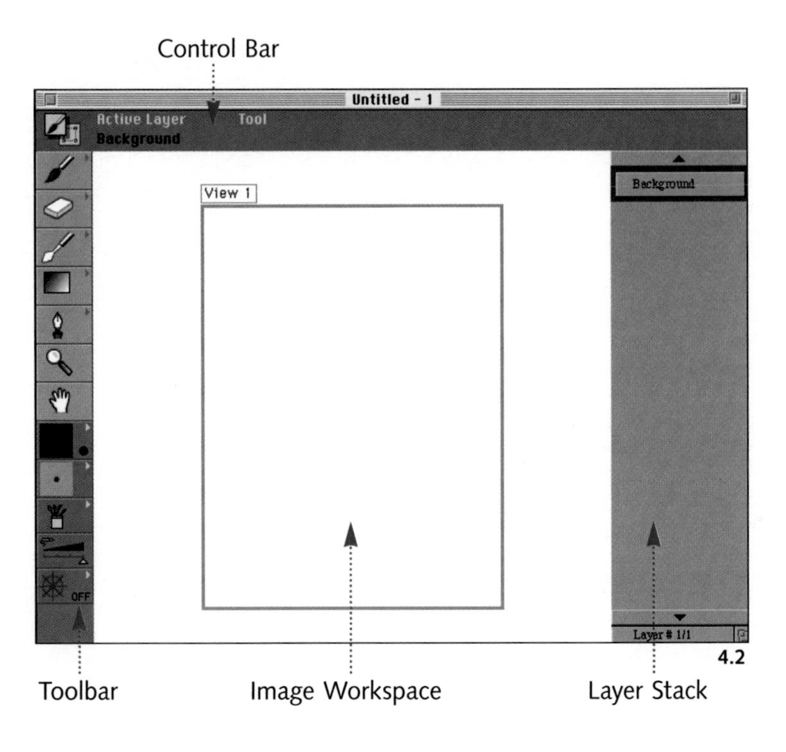

4.2 The Live Picture environment

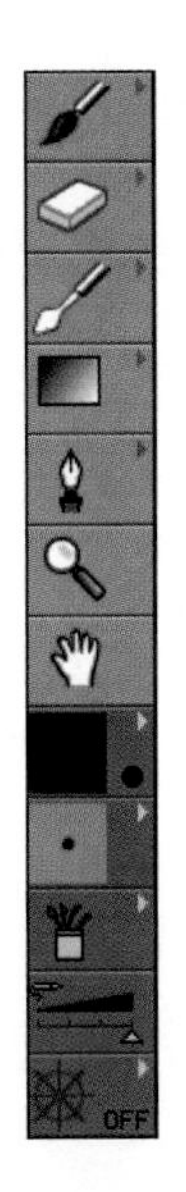

The **toolbar** provides access to Live Picture tools. Creative mode tools change with the active layer type, but the Insertion mode tools remain constant. The Creative/Insertion button allows you to toggle between the Creative mode and Insertion mode tool sets.

The **control bar** shows either the name or the statistics of the active layer in the file, depending on the mode. In the Creative mode, the control bar shows the active layer and the active tool; in the Insertion mode, it shows the X-point's location on the x-y axis and the image's size, as well as measures of scale, rotation, and skew.

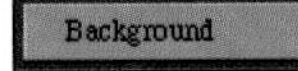

In the **layer stack**, you can shuffle the layers and turn them on and off.

View 1

The **image workspace** displays the image, shows the views that you have created for each part of the image, and allows you to perform image compositing and modification.

The Layer Stack

The layer stack is made up of layer bars, with new layers appearing at the top (Figure 4.3). The stack enables you to reorder and access layers, and you can collapse or expand the more informative layer panel by clicking on the triangle in the layer bar.

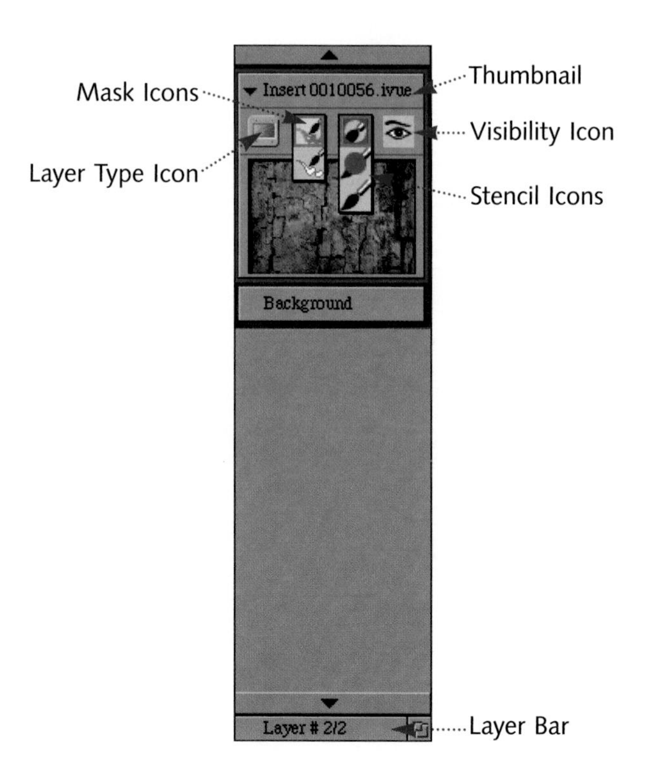

4.3 The Layer Stack

The **visibility** icon toggles between revealing (open eye) and hiding (closed eye) the layer.

The **stencil** icons control how a stencil works in the image:

Indicates a stencil with the **inside area active**

Indicates a stencil with the **outside area active**

Indicates no active stencil

The **mask** icons toggle between soft- and hard-edged masks and layers.

Indicates a **soft edge**

Indicates a **hard edge**

The **layer type** icon corresponds to one of the eleven types of layers in these four categories: Paint, Image, Filter, and Color Correction.

The **layer bar** shows the layer's title, which may be changed by selecting Get Info from the Layers menu.

Creative Mode Tools

The options for each Creative mode tool vary depending on the active layer type (Figure 4.4).

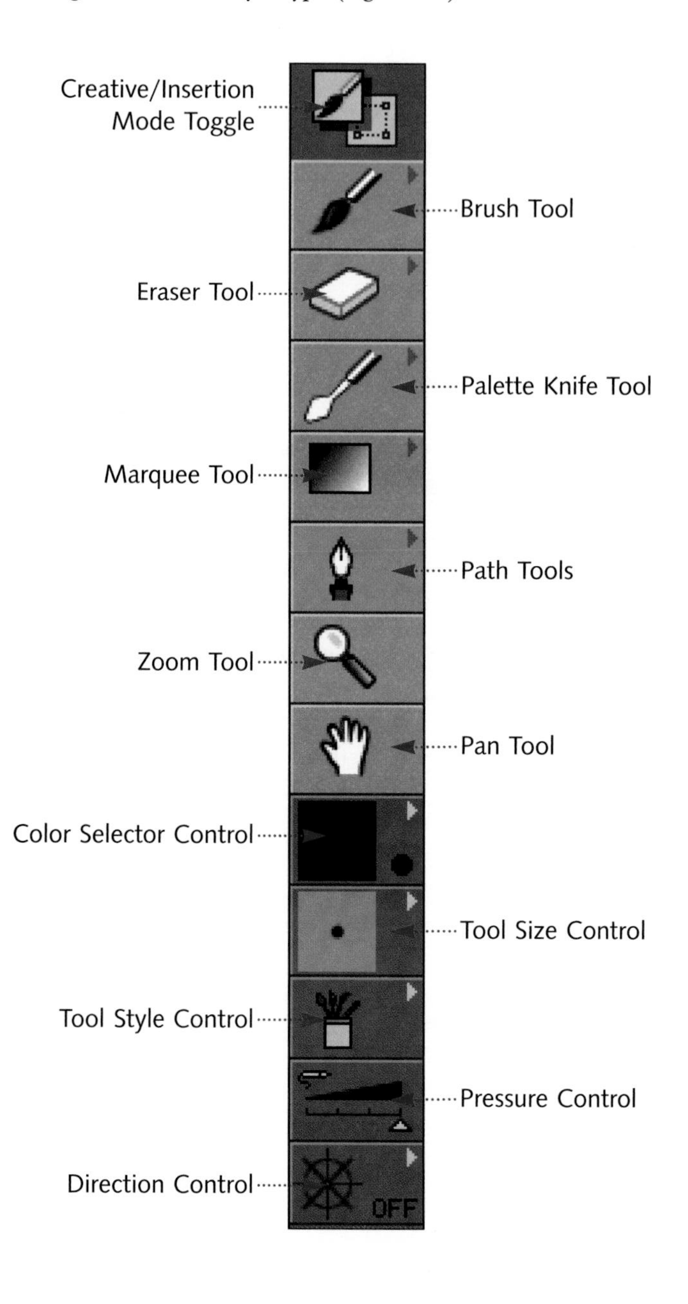

4.4 Creative mode tools

Use the **Creative/Insertion mode toggle** to switch between Creative mode and Insertion mode.

Use the **Brush** tool to paint, to insert images, and to apply effects such as blur and sharpen.

Use the **Eraser** tool to selectively remove paint, images, and effects such as blur and sharpen.

Use the **Palette Knife** tool to smudge, smear, push, diffuse, or blend paint, images, and effects.

Use the **Marquee** tool to fill a rectangular region with paint or images, or to create gradients or other effects.

Use five **Path** tools—freehand, marquee, oval, rectangle, and type—to create shapes called paths; other options are the scissors and selection tools.

Use the **Zoom** tool to magnify or reduce the onscreen view of the image.

Use the **Pan** tool to move the image around the screen.

Use the **Color Selector** control to access the color bar, the Live Picture Color Picker, the Apple Color Picker, or a Pantone Color Picker.

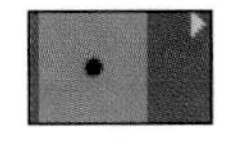

Use the **Tool Size** control to select a resolution-independent size for the Brush, Eraser, and Palette Knife tools; the side button toggles between large and small brush sets.

Use the **Tool Style** control to apply one of four textures (pastel, water, fiber, or granite) to the mask when using the Brush, Eraser, or Palette Knife tool.

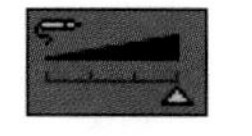

Use the **Pressure** control to increase or decrease pressure sensitivity when using the Brush, Eraser, or Palette Knife tool.

Use the **Direction** control to constrain tool strokes to one angle.

Insertion Mode Tools

Many Insertion mode tools (Figure 4.5) base their modifications on the X-point, a user-defined reference point for scaling, rotating, skewing, flipping, moving, and cropping numerically. Click and drag the X-point to change its location, or double-click on it and enter new coordinate values in the dialog box that appears. To move the image to a new location on the screen, simply type the new x-y coordinates in the control bar.

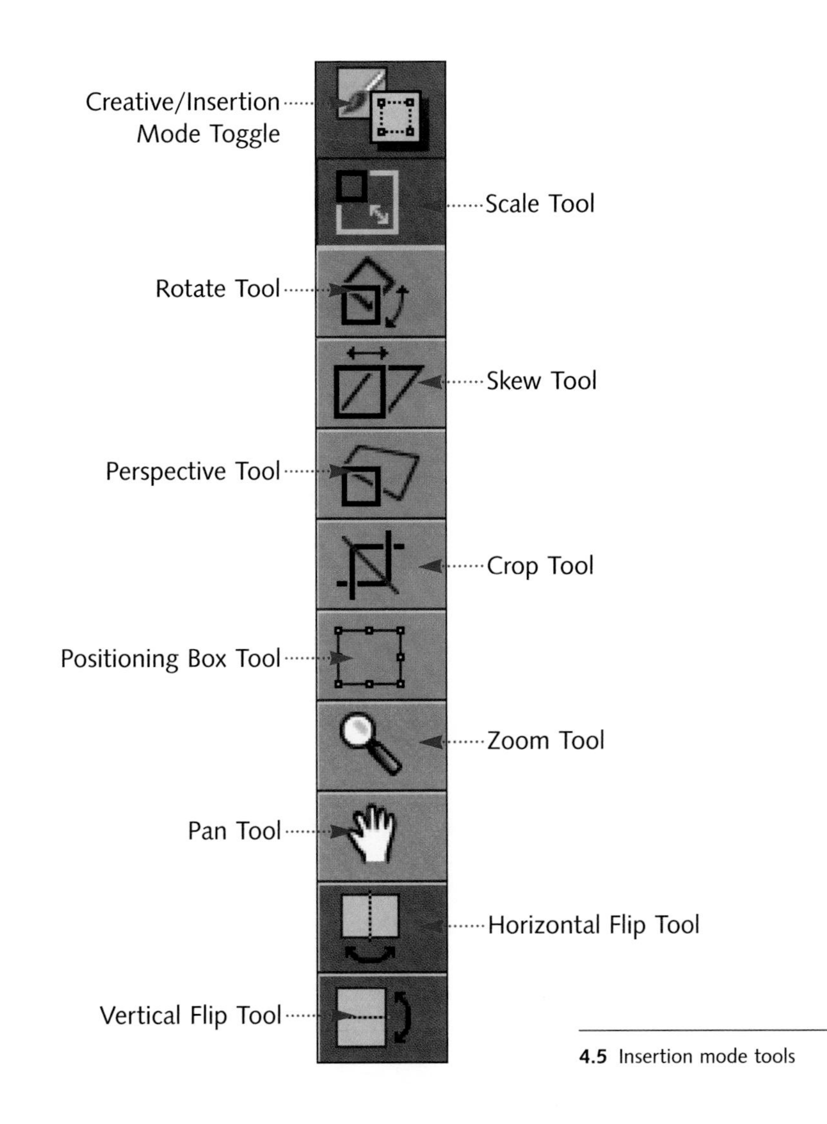

4.5 Insertion mode tools

Use the **Creative/Insertion Mode Toggle** to switch between Creative mode and Insertion mode.

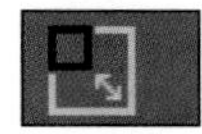

Use the **Scale** tool to change the dimensions of an object around the X-point.

Use the **Rotate** tool to rotate an object freely around the X-point.

Use the **Skew** tool to slant an object around the X-point.

Use the **Perspective** tool to change the vertical or horizontal perspective of an object.

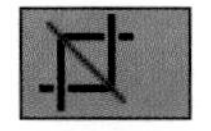

Use the **Crop** tool to select part of an image and discard the rest.

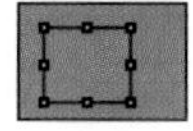

Use the **Positioning Box** tool to adjust the size of the positioning rectangle.

Use the **Zoom** tool to magnify or reduce the onscreen view of the image.

Use the **Pan** tool to move the image around the screen.

Click on the **Horizontal Flip** tool to flip objects horizontally; the X-point acts as a pivot.

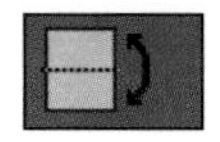

Click on the **Vertical Flip** tool to flip objects vertically; the X-point acts as a pivot.

Live Picture Components

Although unique file formats and types are central to Live Picture's capabilities, they are not the only resources employed. The components detailed below round out the unique image processing capabilities of Live Picture.

Layers

Live Picture structures different tasks in separate layers. Let me repeat that: *Live Picture structures different tasks in separate layers.* This is not a user-controlled option; it is inherent in the application itself. For example, each imported image is placed on a separate layer; paint effects are applied on a separate layer; sharpen/blur effects are applied on a separate layer; even color correction and distortion effects are applied on their own separate layers.

Layers are created within the FITS file. The great thing about layers is that they add very little to the size of the FITS file itself, because the FITS file is resolution-independent. You could add a hundred layers to a FITS file and still keep your overall file size under 5M. This is an important distinction vis-à-vis bitmap applications.

Interaction between layers is based on opacity, which is similar to acetate overlays in the predigital design process. An opaque object placed on one layer, for instance, would hide any objects directly beneath it on other layers. A transparent layer would partially reveal what was beneath it, depending on the level of transparency selected (Figures 4.6 and 4.7).

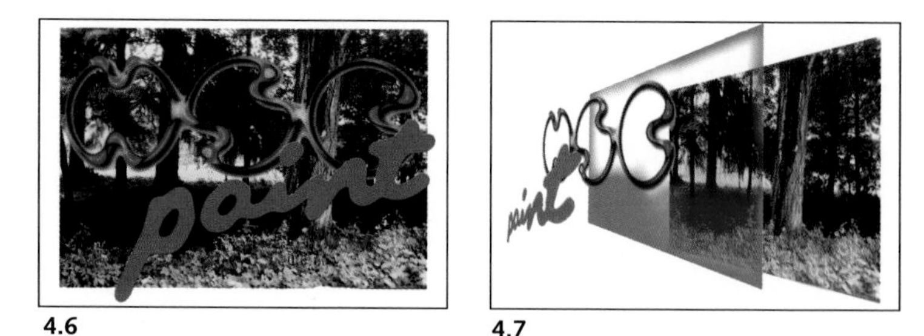

4.6 4.7

Layers can be named and grouped, allowing for greater organization as their numbers increase. They can also be turned on or off at your discretion, so that various design options can be considered. We will discuss strategies for using layers later in this chapter, but for now you should understand that everything exists in separate layers and that you maintain full control over each one.

Sources, Masks, and Stencils

Sources, masks, and stencils are the three components of a layer. It is the combination of these components that determines what is revealed within the layer itself and within the layers beneath it. The *source* component could be a paint color, an image, an effect such as sharpen/blur, or a color-correction curve. The source is linked to one or more layers and may be revealed using varying degrees of transparency/opacity as it interacts with the layers beneath it.

A *mask* component is a defined area that reveals the source. This is somewhat deceiving in that most people think of a mask as something that conceals (a mask conceals a thief's face, for example). Instead, imagine a window fogged over with steam: You apply a cloth to the window, and wiping away the steam reveals the view through the glass. In the same way, you apply Live Picture's tools to the surface of the layer, creating a mask that reveals the source.

4.6/7 Examples of Live Picture layers

A *stencil* is a specific type of mask that gives you greater control over what is revealed in the layer beneath it. You create a stencil either by converting a mask to a stencil or by creating a path that is then converted to a stencil. Once a stencil is created, the layer's active area is restricted to what's within the stencil's shape. The concept is similar to placing a cardboard stencil on a board before painting it; the cardboard protects the surface beneath it, and paint is applied only in the stencil's openings. A Live Picture stencil is also similar to an active selection in Photoshop: The selected area can be modified, but the inactive area outside the selection cannot be.

Masks and stencils are specific to the layers in which they are created, although they may be copied from one layer to another. Stencils can also be inverted so that the active area changes from the inside to the outside.

Creative Mode Tools

Live Picture offers a range of Creative mode tools, such as the Brush, Eraser, Zoom, and Palette Knife tools. All Live Picture tools modify the mask that conceals the layer's source component. The Brush tool does not apply paint; instead, it modifies the mask, which in turn reveals the source (the image, or color, or sharpen/blur effect). All of the Creative mode tools manipulate the mask that is associated with a particular layer.

Insertion Mode Tools

The Insertion mode tools appear in their own toolbar and provide control over the placement of layers. Here, *placement* refers to the way various layers interact and align with each other. These tools also allow control over the scaling and rotation of a layer. Insertion mode tools include Scale, Rotate, Crop, and Zoom.

Live Picture and Adobe Photoshop: Complementary Programs

Ever since Live Picture was first announced in 1993, there's been a lot of confusion about the relative merits of Live Picture and Adobe Photoshop. Because many of their capabilities are so similar, people wonder whether they need to choose one or the other. But in fact, the two programs are complementary. There are some tasks Live Picture performs better than Photoshop, and some that Photoshop performs better than Live Picture. And certain functionalities are available in one application but not the other. Here's a comparison of the two programs' features that will guide you in deciding when to use Live Picture, and when to use Photoshop.

4.8

Although Live Picture allows you to paint and use some texture effects, it is in working with continuous-tone images that the program's power—and its similarities to Photoshop—becomes fully evident. All of the tools in Live Picture lend themselves to photographic images. Cutting silhouettes and correcting color are easily handled in Live Picture, as are cleaning up dust and scratches. Photo montaging and abstract effects such as distortions and diffusions are also second nature for Live Picture. With Live Picture's raw speed well established, the decision to use Live Picture for minor tasks should be based on the size of the file. Files that are 100M or more justify using Live Picture for even the smallest tasks, such as image cropping or rotating.

The application of a filter can sometimes mask the image's limitations, and the use of filters can also reduce the need for high-quality, high-megabyte originals. Before version 2.5, Live Picture didn't know what to do with a poor-quality original. It could not mask its drawbacks with effects, other than sharpen and blur, and a poor-quality original is likely to be blurry already. Live Picture 2.5's support of Photoshop plug-ins is uniquely implemented to preserve the original layer or layers, while generating copies on the fly containing the filter effects. The process is longer than in Photoshop because Live Picture is actually building the file, applying the filter, converting to IVUE, and placing the image as a layer into the composite. If filters are all you intend to do on an image, Photoshop is still the answer. However, if you alternate between Live Picture and Photoshop as you work, you will appreciate not having to switch back and forth as often in the course of designing.

One capability found only in Photoshop is its layer modes and channel blending options (the latter is called Calculation Blending). Live Picture does not have similar capabilities, making it difficult to do some of the special effects that are often taken for granted in Photoshop. The latter's layer modes and blending options—Normal, Hard Light, Difference, and so on—are computed by comparing pixels that overlap in different layers or channels, which is why they are only available in comparative situations. The names for layer modes and blending options are derived from this pixel comparison (for example, in the Difference mode, Photoshop compares mathematically the difference in brightness between pixels on one layer and those on another). Because these modes and options can result in surprising and happy accidents, you'll still want access to Photoshop's capabilities.

With layers, however, Live Picture has the edge. The main problem with Photoshop's layers is that they are pixel-based. While this allows Photoshop to perform calculations between layers, it also causes the file size to expand quickly as more layers are added. Photoshop tries to compensate for this limitation by allowing you to collapse layers and flatten images, but the limitation remains. As a result, the Photoshop user tends to use layers sparingly. It comes back to the speed issue—the machines slow down substantially as layers are added. Live Picture is built from the ground up to handle layers deftly without sacrificing speed. The layer stack, layer options, layer types, and the ability to isolate effects on separate layers gives Live Picture users more creative freedom. While an absence of pixels prohibits a FITS file from performing channel blending operations, it does allow for fast, effecient handling of layers.

The type capabilities in Live Picture are also outstanding. Type in Live Picture is completely scalable, with no distortion along the way. That's because, as it is entered, the type is converted to a path, which then becomes a mask or stencil. The type resides in the FITS file at all times, and therefore is resolution independent and can be scaled indefinitely. (See page 77 later in this chapter for more information on working with type.)

So Photoshop works well for smaller files or for excursions into the world of altered pixels, and Live Picture is best for large images and type. The key is not to be too analytical about the comparison. Some people will respond more to one interface than another, or to the way one program indulges a certain way of working. Most people will employ both of these valuable tools, using them for the strengths each brings to the image editing process.

Getting the Most Out of Live Picture

Live Picture is a very complex and powerful application, and it is possible to understand all of its components without having a clear method for using them. The following strategies should get you thinking about ways to optimize Live Picture's capabilities, allowing you to work smarter and more intuitively.

Take Advantage of Views

You've created your first document and inserted your first image layer. You want to start adding more layers and moving colors and pixels around. Before you do that, however, you need to create some views, which will help you navigate through the image. This is not a casual suggestion; rather, it is a very important habit to get into. Views are user-defined zoom presets that allow you to navigate an image at varying levels of detail. Because Live Picture is resolution-independent, the zoom goes deeper than you're probably used to. And it's not like Photoshop, where you can just double-click on the Zoom tool to go back to a one-to-one ratio—you can get lost in Live Picture pretty easily. That's why the first view is already created for you when you open a new document; it's the home base that you can always get back to.

As you looked at your image, you probably noticed certain areas that you'll want to develop further; perhaps it's a face, or an eye, or a detail in the background. Create a view for each area you will be zooming to most frequently. Now you simply select the view by name from the Go To command in the View menu, and your view will nearly fill the screen. In effect, you've established a preset magnification of this area of the image. Using Views allows you to quickly hop from one area of the image to another without waiting for interim zoom levels to render onscreen.

There are several ways to create views in Live Picture, but the easiest is through the View menu.

1. First, select the Add/Edit command from the View menu. The toolbar now shows only three tools—View, Zoom, and Pan—and the control bar also contains different information (Figure 4.9).

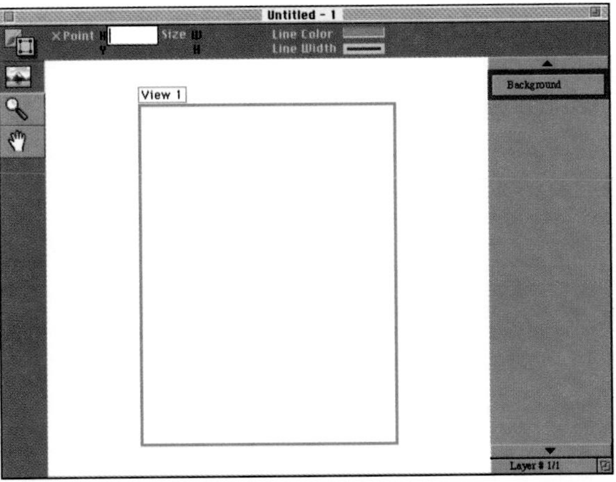

4.9

2. Click on the View tool; the cursor changes to a crosshair. Drag the crosshair across the workspace to make the rectangular view you want (Figure 4.10).

4.9 The toolbar after selecting Add/Edit from the View menu

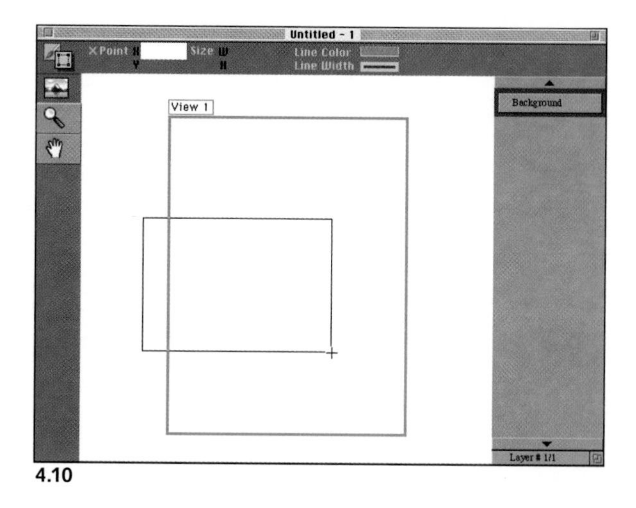

4.10

3. To change the view's name (in the box at the top of the view rectangle), click on it once to highlight it, then type any name you want (Figure 4.11).

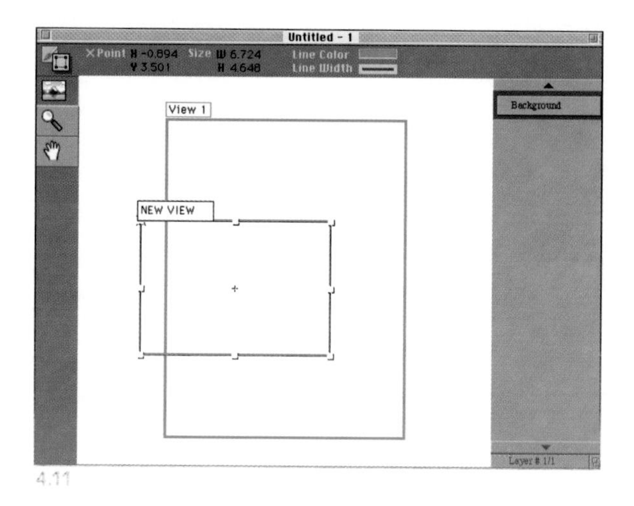

4.11

The color and width controls in the control bar allow those parameters to be modified as well. The Views menu provides many options, such as hiding or deleting views, that help you manage the views you create.

4.10 Click and drag the crosshair to define a view

4.11 Type in a new name for the view

Using Type Creatively

Ever since Apple released the LaserWriter in the mid-1980s, people have been trying to figure out how to get type to print smoothly and to avoid bitmapped "jaggies." This was especially true for people using Photoshop, because its bitmap/resolution-based nature didn't know how to handle the smooth edges of a typeface. People were always taught to do their imaging in Photoshop and add type effects in QuarkXPress or Adobe Illustrator.

Live Picture offers new possibilities in working with type because it is free from the resolution constraints that have always hampered bitmap programs. In Live Picture, type is converted to a path. It does not exist as a mask when it is created, and it is no longer associated with its point size once it appears in Live Picture. As a path, and as a native element in a FITS file, it is resolution-independent. This means you can create type effects and scale them up to billboard size and they will still look sharp and crisp.

Type is created in Live Picture much as it is in Photoshop. You select the Type tool, click on the location where you want to place the type, and enter the text in a dialog box. You can also set the font, relative size, and style of the type. Unlike Photoshop, however, Live Picture's Type tool creates outline paths with handles that can be modified at the user's discretion. Like any other path in Live Picture, the type path can be assigned to a layer by converting it to a mask or stencil. Once it is converted, you can incorporate the image, paint, or effect of that layer into the type design. It is generally a good idea to convert type to a stencil rather than a mask, because a stencil's edges cannot be modified to maintain the smooth shape of the type. To assign a mask or stencil to a layer, activate the layer and select Path—Stencil or Path—Mask from the Mask menu to convert the path.

Live Picture's ability to convert a type path to a stencil presents a wide range of possibilities, all of which yield smooth, clean results. The stencil acts almost like a selection in Photoshop, in that you are able to modify the type path's contents to create the effects. A photo can easily be placed in a word or letter by simply assigning the type-based stencil to an image layer. More interesting effects can be created by assigning the type path to a blur layer over an image, so that the image that runs into the type outline is blurred.

Drop shadows are easy, because you can apply the same stencil to both an image layer and a paint layer. To make a drop shadow, first paint a transparent shadow in the type-based stencil. Then switch to Insertion mode and offset the type slightly from the original position, and drag the paint layer beneath the image layer. The image layer then floats above the shadow. Another approach would be to create three layers containing the same image. Assign the same type path to the top two layers; give the path in the second layer a feather edge when you convert it to a stencil, and then offset the path from its original position. Then select Layer/IVUE Correction/Color Controls, and lighten the first layer and darken the second. By juggling this three-layer approach, you can achieve a wide variety of image and paint effects. For example, consider making the second (shadow) layer an Image Distortion layer, or modifying the texture of the paint or image that you apply.

Live Picture handles type so smoothly and easily that you have the freedom to focus on design. All of the type and color effects are resolution-independent, because they are stored in the FITS file. This allows you to scale, distort, paint, and tweak without fear of pixelization or loss of quality.

Guilt-Free Layering

It's only a slight exaggeration to say that Live Picture can handle 100 layers as easily as one. This is because Live Picture computes only the pixels required for display at any point in time. For any one pixel, the effects performed in each layer are described as mathematical equations, which are then combined and simplified into a single equation that describes the pixel.

The following exercise will give you a sense of the creative power of layers.

1. Create an IVUE image file, choosing an image with distinct elements in it.
2. In the Create menu, select Image Insertion to open the IVUE file in an Image Insertion layer and corresponding view.

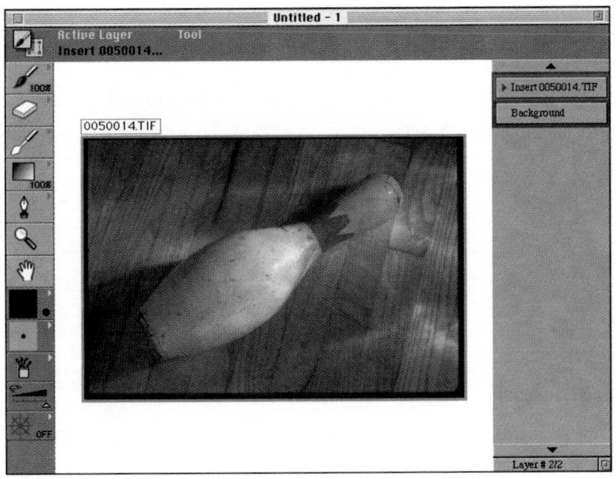

4.12

4.12 Open an IVUE file

3. Erase all but one element in the image (here, the bowling pin).

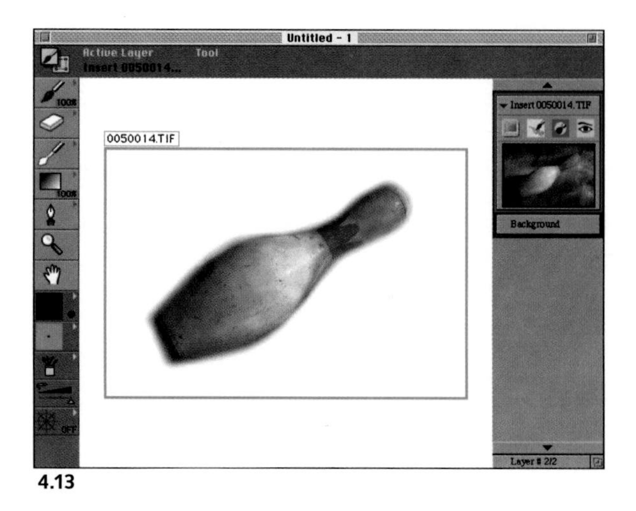

4.13

4. While holding down the Option key, click and drag the image's layer bar up in the layer stack to create a duplicate of the layer (Figure 4.14).

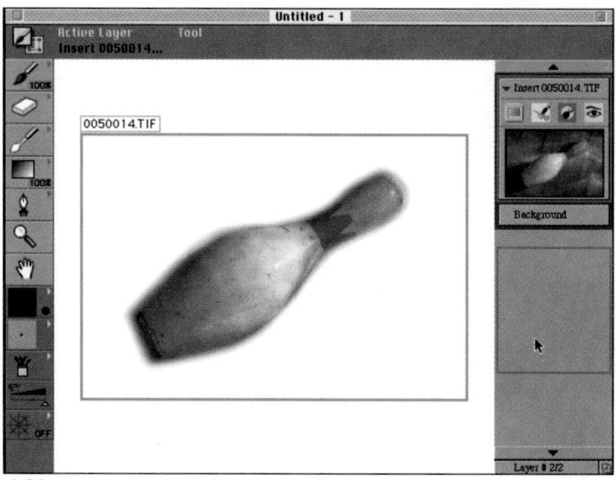

4.14

4.13 Erase the background

4.14 Duplicate the layer

5. From the Create menu, select Colorize to create a Colorize layer; activate this layer by selecting the Colorize layer bar, then choose Activate from the Layer menu (Figure 4.15).

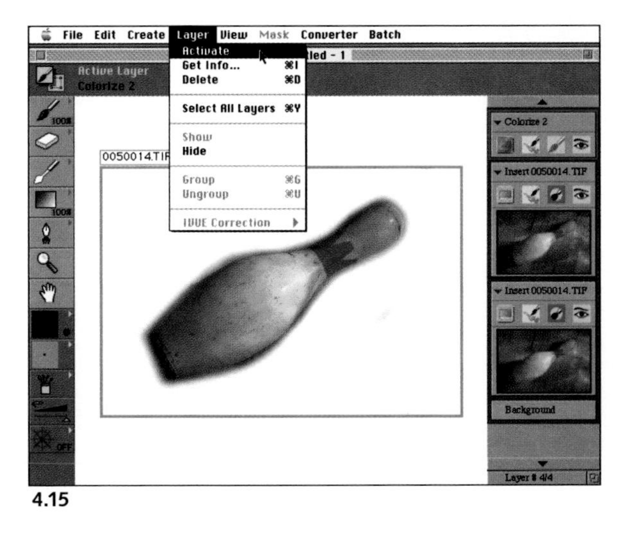

4.15

6. Create a 4-point gradient over the image. To do so, first click and hold on the Marquee tool, and select the Gradient option set to 4 Points (Figure 4.16).

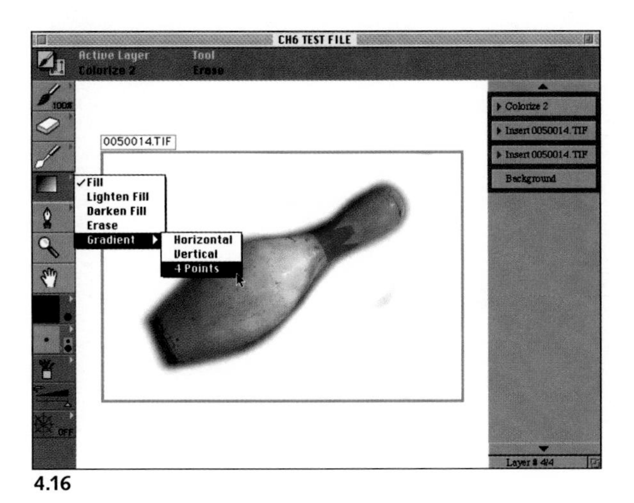

4.16

4.15 Activate the Colorize layer

4.16 Select a 4-point gradient in the Marquee tool

7. Drag the crosshairs to create a rectangle over the entire image layer/view (Figure 4.17).

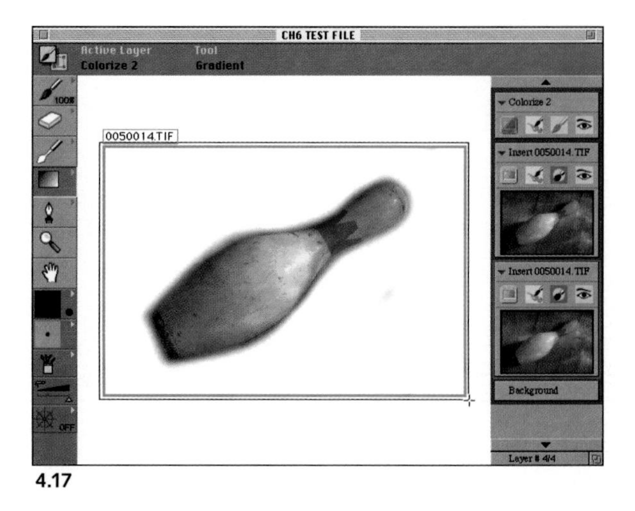

4.17

8. At each corner of the rectangle, click on the text box and type in a tint percentage, and then click and hold the color square and select a color (Figures 4.18 and 4.19).

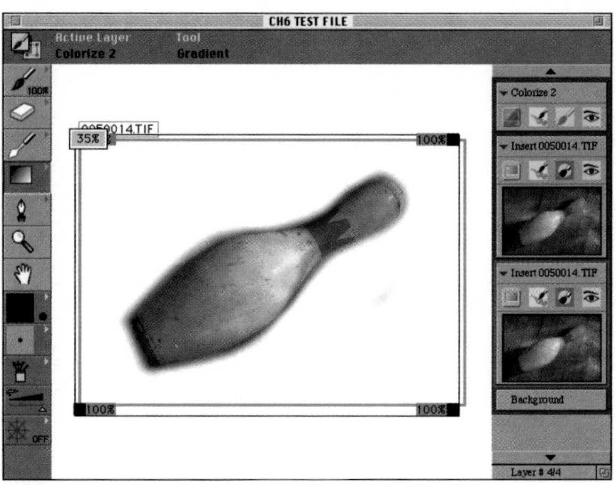

4.18

4.17 Marquee the entire image layer/view

4.18 Type in a percentage to set the tint of the color

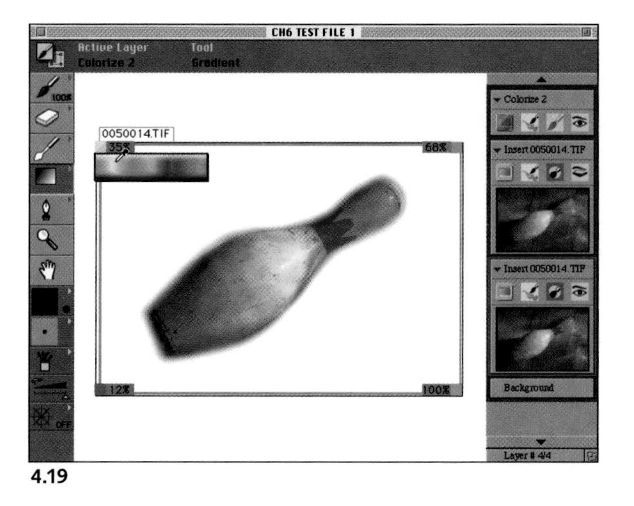

4.19

9. Click anywhere in the image area to apply the gradient (Figure 4.20).

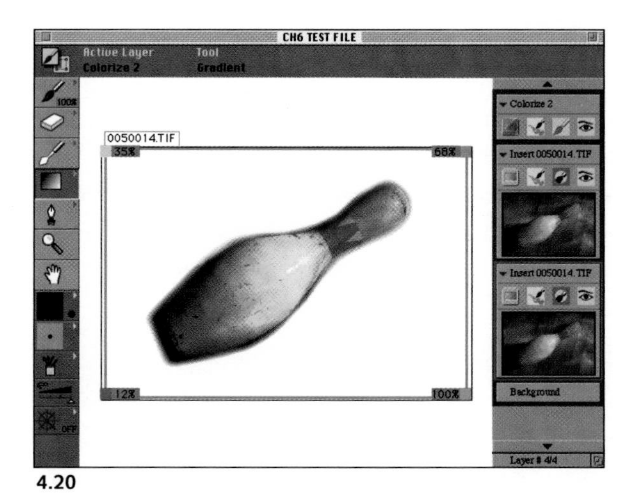

4.20

4.19 Click and hold the color square to access the color picker

4.20 The gradient applied

10. Activate the first image layer, and then select the Marquee tool, choosing the Fill option. Drag the crosshairs to create a rectangle over the entire image; this step restores the complete image (Figure 4.21).

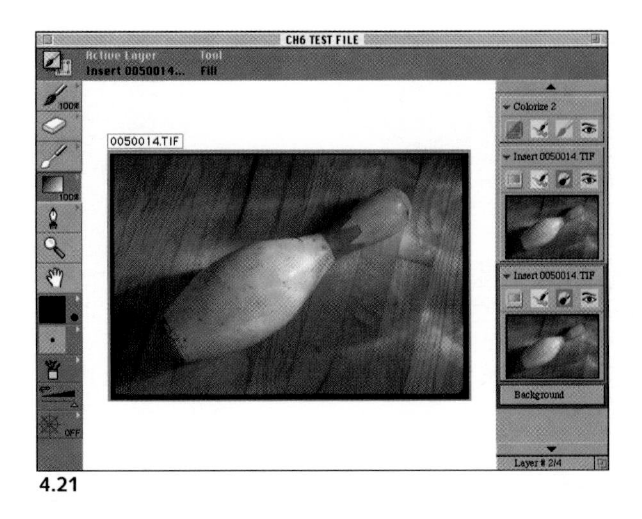

4.21

11. In the layer stack, click and drag the duplicate image layer of the silhouetted bowling pin to the top of the stack. Activate this layer to see the resulting composite, in which only the element you retained in step 3 is masked from the gradient application (Figure 4.22).

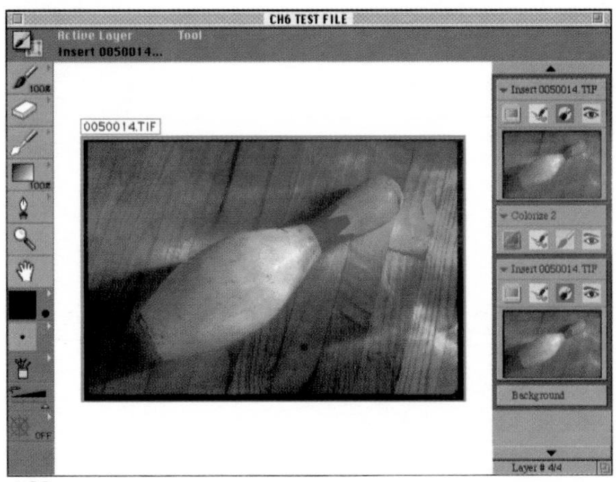

4.22

4.21 Restore the complete image using the Marquee tool

4.22 Drag the duplicate layer to the top to complete the effect

Experiment with multiple layers using the same source image as well as different source images. With a FITS file containing copies of the same source image in 25 different layers, you could change the order of each layer, as well as its size and scale. The image layers could also be distorted, silhouetted, or cloned. When these effects are combined with the power of IVUE Correction (see page 92), the amount of variation can be vast.

You can also experiment with changing the order of layers in the layer stack. Such layer types as Colorize and Sharpen/Blur can create interesting effects when moved out of sequence. Image layers modified with various levels of transparency also yield interesting results. Another approach might be simply to turn selected layers on and off without changing the stack order. (Note that a layer that has been turned off will not be included in the build process.)

Controlling Color

The color controls within Live Picture are very robust, and you should have a solid grasp of your options and when to employ them. The program's emphasis is on keeping the corrections separate from the image itself, which allows you to make continual modifications. Of the five color options that interact with the image, for example, four exist as separate layers and one is a correction that is made to the mask on the image layer itself.

The color controls in Live Picture are as follows:

- Monocolor layer
- Multicolor layer
- Colorize layer

- Color Correction layer
- IVUE Correction

Monocolor Layer

The Monocolor layer creates a mask that has just one color assigned to it; if a new color is selected, all of the color applied to that layer will change to the new color. You are able to paint, globally or in spots, with the one assigned color using the Marquee tool or freehand using the Brush tool. The Monocolor layer is useful for applying color tints to an image, correcting color, or applying color changes. This feature should not be used in place of the curves available in IVUE Correction (see page 92), but it is a good way to quickly get a sense of how a color shift can affect an image.

The following exercise will get you acquainted with the Monocolor layer.

1. Create an Image Insertion layer and then create a Monocolor layer on top of it by choosing Create/Monocolor (Figure 4.23).

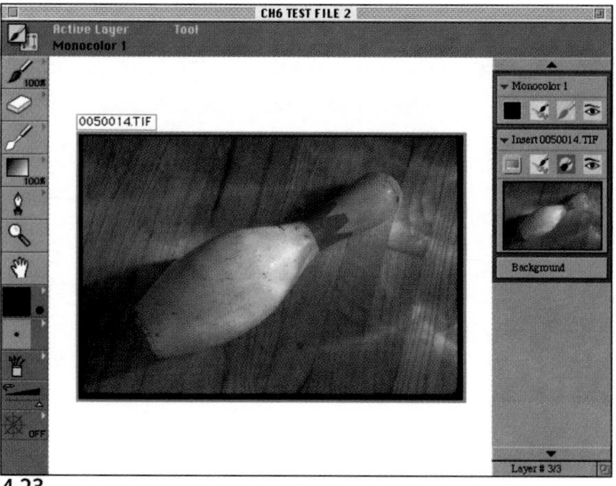

4.23 Create a Monocolor layer

2. Select the Marquee tool and drag its opacity slider to 15 percent (Figure 4.24).

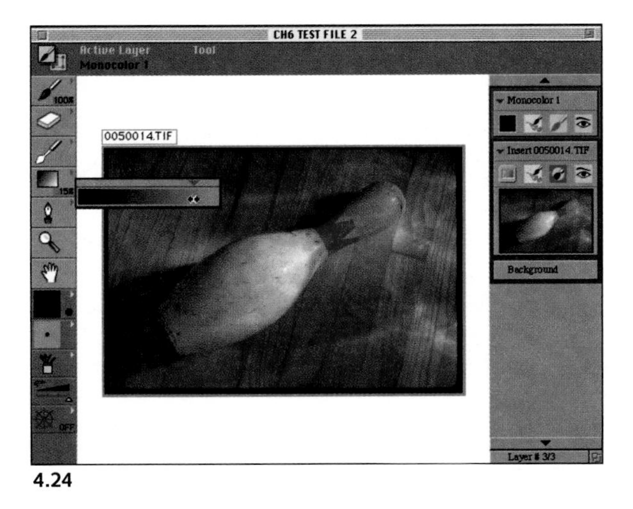

4.24

3. In the color selector control's color bar, select a color at random (Figure 4.25).

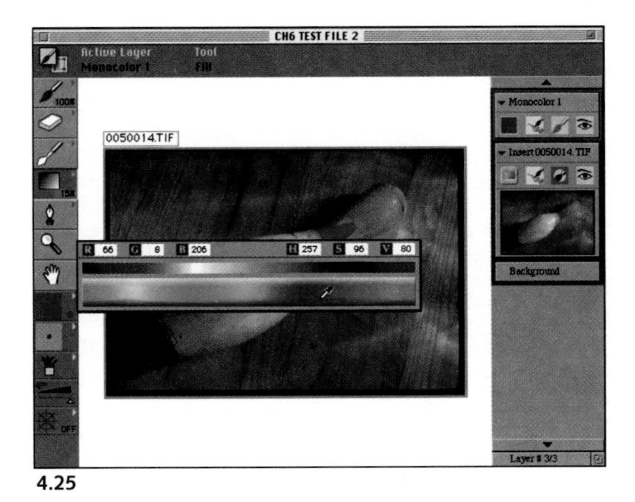

4.25

4.24 Set the Marquee value slider to 15 percent

4.25 Select a color

4. With the Marquee tool still selected, drag a rectangle over the entire image (Figure 4.26).

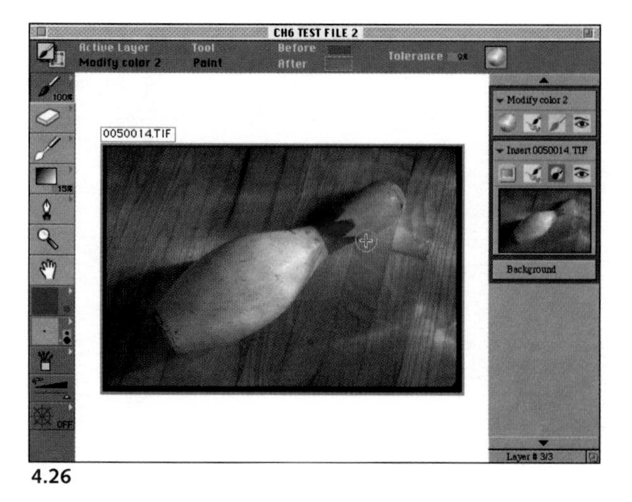

4.26

The picture takes on a 15 percent tint of the color you selected in the color bar. Now if you select a new color, the color in your entire image will shift as well. For these tints, keep the opacity slider as low as possible, never going above 15 percent. When you have a color you think is close, turn the Monocolor layer on and off in the layers palette for a before and after effect.

Another good use of the Monocolor layer is to quickly tone and darken an image. The technique is similar to the one shown above, but select black as your color and darken the image using the Brush tool (opacity also at 15 percent) rather than by dragging a marquee. This method allows you to "burn in" part of your image with a neutral color. It differs from the darkening method of the Colorize layer, which can oversaturate the image(s) beneath the active image layer.

4.26 Drag a marquee to fill the area with the selected color

Multicolor Layer

As the name implies, with the Multicolor layer you can work with multiple colors in the same layer. This is useful for general-purpose painting effects because you can switch colors in the color picker and go right on painting with the Brush tool. Use several colors and large brushes to create soft, misty vignettes over large areas.

The Multicolor layer also makes good use of the 4-Point Gradient option in the Marquee tool. This tool allows you to drag a marquee over an area and then select specific colors and opacity settings for each corner. Click and hold on the color square and the number percentage in each corner to access modification sliders for these settings.

In the Monocolor and Multicolor layers, the color cast dominates, sometimes at the expense of the highlights and shadows in the subordinate layers. As a result, the tonal range of the overall image is greatly reduced, which sacrifices the photographic qualities of the image. For this reason, you should not use these layers for hand-coloring effects; use the Colorize layer instead.

Colorize Layer

The biggest difference between the Multicolor or Monocolor paint layer and a Colorize layer is that the color in a paint layer is independent of any layers beneath it, while the color in a Colorize layer interacts only with those in the layers beneath it. Therefore, if you create a Colorize layer all by itself and try to paint, nothing would show up in the workspace. But when you place an Image Insertion layer beneath the Colorize layer, for example, the effects become visible.

The Colorize layer interacts with layers beneath it based on saturation. For instance, the layer's Paint option (Brush tool) adds saturation to the image while applying a color cast. Because it operates on saturation rather that as paint in a layer, the tonal range of the layers beneath it is not diminished.

The Colorize layer offers two other Brush tool options: Lighten and Darken. These options can be deceiving because they add no color at all, even though they are in the Colorize layer. The Lighten and Darken options emulate dodging and burning in photographic printing; they lighten or darken the image but add no color cast.

Color Correction Layer

Color Correction is a unique and interesting layer in Live Picture. The Color Correction layer allows you to select a range of colors that can be changed into another range of colors. The Color Correction layer, which appears in the layer stack as Modify Color, is similar to the Colorize layer in that it only reacts in relation to the image beneath it. If the Color Correction layer were by itself, then nothing would be visible, regardless of what effects you created.

The control bar in the Color Correction layer displays Before and After color fields. Click and hold on the Before field and select a color you want corrected, either from the color bar that pops up or by clicking on the color bar and dragging to sample a color from the image itself (Figure 4.27).

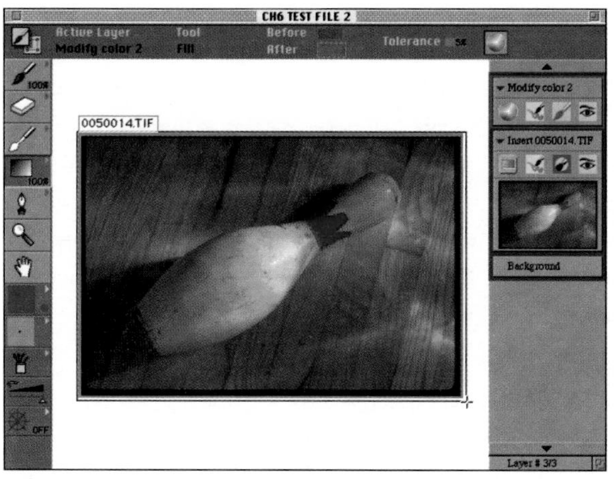

4.27

4.27 The Before and After color fields in the Color Correction layer

You can then select an After color in the same way. By carefully modifying the tolerance setting, you can articulate the exact range of color to correct. You can then apply the color correction either selectively, using the Brush tool, or globally, using the Marquee tool. Once the initial correction has been applied, you can then change color in the After field and see your image updated with the new color in real time. It is also possible to change the tolerance after the effect is brushed into the layer. This allows for real-time tweaking of the range of color modified, providing for clean edges and transitions (Figures 4.28 and 4.29).

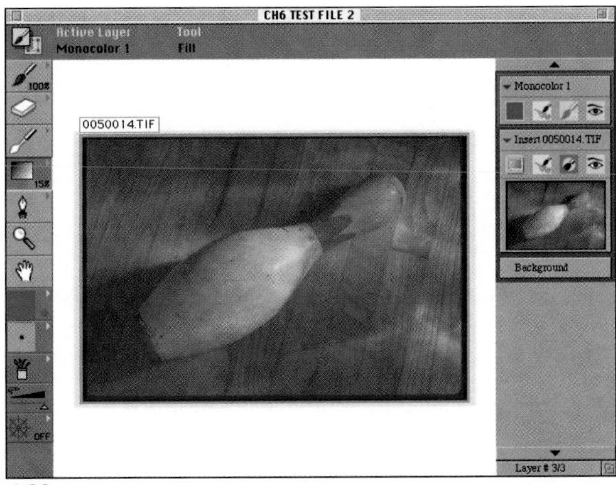

4.28

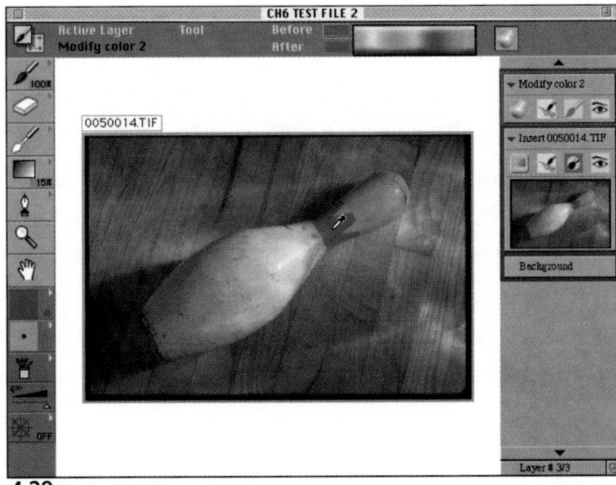

4.29

4.28 Painting the Color Correction

4.29 Results of the correction

IVUE Correction

Wouldn't it be nice if you could modify a Live Picture IVUE file in terms of RGB and CMYK curves, histograms, invert commands, and other precision color controls? It would be even nicer if the corrections made to the IVUE file were only evident in its associated FITS file, so that the IVUE file itself remained pristine and unchanged but the corrections were incorporated in the output file.

In fact, that is exactly what IVUE Correction does. Although it appears that you are modifying the IVUE file, in reality IVUE Correction modifies the mask in the selected image layer rather than the IVUE file itself. Because the mask is getting the color modifications, and the mask reveals the IVUE file, it acts as a filter that changes the appearance of the source image.

IVUE Correction is accessed from the Layers menu, where a pop-up menu gives you the following options:

- Brightness/Contrast (adjustments)
- Color Control (curves)
- Color Levels (histograms)
- Invert (to create a negative)
- Color Steps (to reduce the number of color levels)
- Color Shift (to balance colors)
- Presets (preset color corrections)

IVUE Correction is valuable when you want to make color and tonal changes to an image layer without modifying the layers beneath it. With some images, this task could be done using a silhouette, but silhouettes are time-consuming and in some cases yield unacceptable results. It is easier to highlight the target image in the layer stack and select an IVUE Correction option. When using these options, take advantage of the Preview button (and its zoom feature) so you can see the changes you've made to the layer as they will look in the full composite (IVUE Corrections works only on image layers, and only on one layer at a time).

Chapter 5

Exploring Kai's Power Tools

In the beginning there were filters, which Kai casually sought to put on a CD-ROM. And they were lifeless and void, not possessing an interface, limited in scope. With help from Ben Weiss, Kai poured his spirit into the program, and its form began to take shape. Kai said, "Let there be turquoise spheres." And they appeared. "Give me an intuitive color picker," Kai said. And it was so. Responding to his own ideas and interests, such as fractal and texture explorations, Kai breathed life into what would be called Kai's Power Tools 1.0. After four months of labor, Kai rested. Looking at his creation, he said, "It is good" [even if it was just a bunch of dialog boxes stuck in a plug-in. ;)].

The next section shows the primary Kai's Power Tools interfaces, with the main areas, icons, and tools labeled and described for each. You can use it as a reference and a guide for the information in this chapter.

The Kai's Power Tools Interface

What began as a collection of separate filter elements in KPT 1.0 has evolved into a more cohesive filter set in subsequent revisions. The release of KPT 3.0 unveiled the KPT Spheroid Designer and KPT Interform interfaces, as well as KPT Lens f/x, which combines all of the pixel-based "one-shot" filters found in prior versions into a single interface (see page 114).

Common Elements

There are many common elements in four key KPT 3.0 interfaces: KPT Gradient Designer, KPT Interform, KPT Spheroid Designer, and KPT Texture Explorer (KPT Lens f/x has a very different interface, as does the unchanged KPT Fractal Explorer 2.1; both can be found under their own headings in this section). Most can be found along the top and bottom of the interfaces. These elements are categorized in this section.

Title-Bar Elements

The four elements that run across the title bars of all four primary KPT 3.0 interfaces are Kai's logo, the Help button, the title, and the Options button (an exception: Spheroid Designer does not have a Help button) (Figure 5.1).

5.1

The **Kai's Logo** button, when you click on it, blacks out the KPT interface to show a full-sized preview of the image with the current effects applied to it.

The **Help** button activates the Kai's Power Tools help screens. In KPT Spheroid Designer (and KPT Lens f/x), help is accessed through the Options menu.

The **Title** identifies the active filter interface. Clicking and dragging on this area allows you to reposition the dialog box on the screen.

The **Options** pop-up menu allows access to various controls for the interface, such as Preferences, viewing options, and the About KPT screen.

5.1 Title-Bar Elements

The Lower Interface Elements

The five common elements found on the bottom border of all four primary KPT 3.0 interfaces are the Information Bar, the Delete Preset/Preset Manager icon, the Add Preset icon, and the Cancel and OK icons (Figure 5.2).

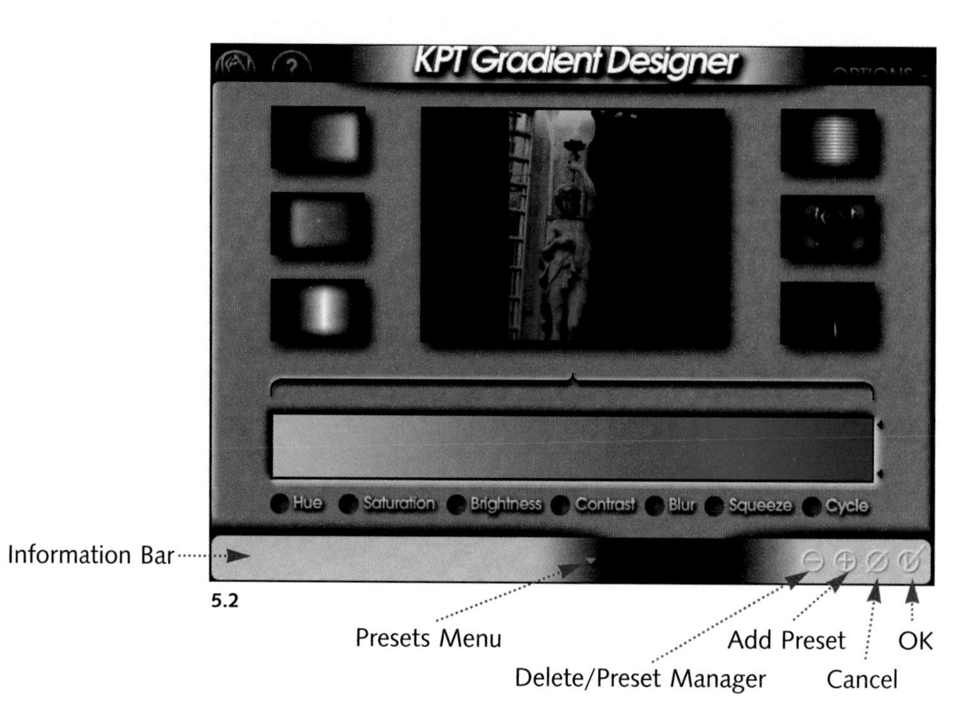

5.2 Lower Interface Elements

The **Information Bar** identifies the name of the tool when you pass the cursor over its icon.

The **Presets Menu** triangle provides graphical or pop-up-menu access to the presets available in each of the four interfaces.

The **Delete Preset/Preset Manager** icon activates the Preset Manager, where presets can be imported, exported, or deleted. In Spheroid Designer's Preset Manager, you can also manage bump maps.

The **Add Preset** icon allows you to add the current preset to the presets list.

The **Cancel** icon returns you to the main Photoshop interface without applying any KPT effects.

The **OK** check mark applies the current effects to the image and returns you to the main Photoshop interface.

KPT Gradient Designer

KPT Gradient Designer allows you to create and apply gradients to images; it generates blends of up to 512 different colors, with up to 256 levels of opacity (Figure 5.3). A wide range of presets are included in Gradient Designer, and these interact with other interfaces such as KPT Texture Explorer.

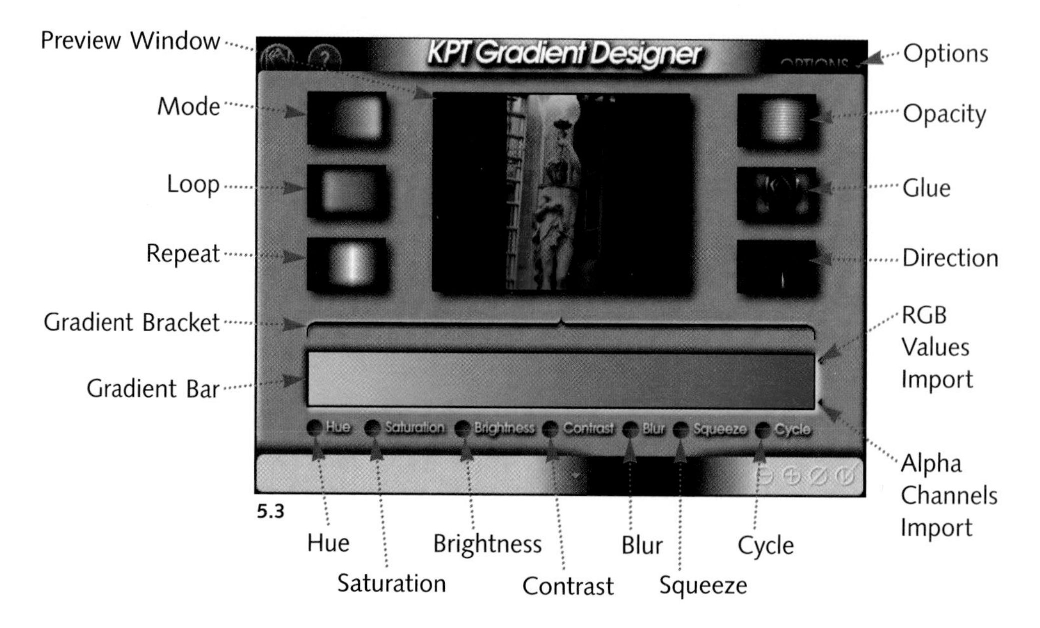

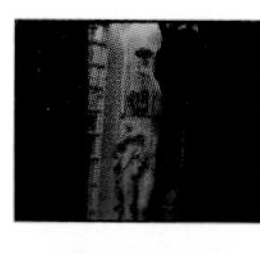

The **Preview Window** shows the cumulative effects of all controls in the Gradient Designer Interface, updating changes in real time.

The **Gradient Bar** allows you to add, by clicking and holding on it, any color to the current gradient via its pop-up color picker, which enables you to adjust opacity, grayscale, and color selection by dragging to the desired value (Figure 5.4). New colors are inserted at the point where you clicked, and then smoothly blended with adjacent colors.

5.3 KPT Gradient Designer

The **Gradient Bracket** defines the modifiable area of the gradient. Click and drag at its ends to resize the area; Shift-click to resize at "notched" increments; click and drag at the middle to move the entire bracket; or double-click on it to reset it to default size.

The **RGB Values Import** triangle allows you to import RGB values from other presets.

The **Alpha Channels Import** triangle allows you to import alpha channels from other presets.

5.4 The KPT Gradient Designer color picker

The **Hue** button allows you to cycle the gradient through the color wheel while maintaining the original distance relationships between hues (click and drag on the button).

The **Saturation** button allows you to increase color intensity (click and drag to the right) or decrease it (click and drag to the left).

The **Brightness** button enables you to increase color brightness (click and drag to the right) or decrease it (click and drag to the left).

The **Contrast** button allows you to increase color contrast (click and drag to the right) or decrease it (click and drag to the left).

The **Blur** button enables you to add blur to the gradient (click and drag to the right) or reduce blur (click and drag to the left).

The **Squeeze** button allows you to compress the gradient toward the right (click and drag to the right) or the left (click and drag to the left). (You can achieve the same effect by Option-clicking on the Gradient Bar itself.)

The **Cycle** button enables you to scroll the gradient through the Gradient Bar (click and drag to the right or left), effectively changing its beginning and end points. (You can also do this by Command-clicking on the Gradient Bar.)

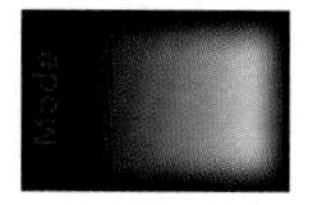

The **Mode** control swatch changes the type of gradient. The options in its pop-up menu are: Linear Blend, Circular and Elliptical Sunburst, Radial Sweep, Square and Rectangular Burst, Angular and Circular Shapeburst, Angular and Circular Pathburst, Grayscale Mapburst, and Gradients on Paths. Click repeatedly, or click and drag, to cycle though and view options in the Preview Window.

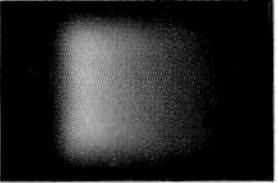

The **Loop** control swatch determines the way the gradient repeats in the image. Its pop-up menu options are Sawtooth, which repeats in a linear fashion with sharp drop-offs, and Triangle, which cycles from one end of the gradient bar to the other in a smooth transition. The A->B, B->A, A->B->A, and B->A->B options refer to whether the gradient is applied starting at the left or the right of the Gradient Bar. Click repeatedly to cycle through and view the options in the Preview Window.

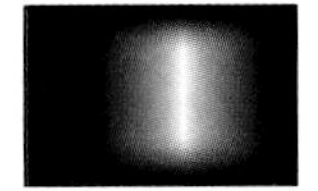

The **Repeat** control swatch controls the number of times the gradient is repeated over the image. Click and drag on the swatch to view gradient repetitions in the Preview Window. When you see an effect you like, click once on the Repeat swatch to apply it to the Gradient Bar.

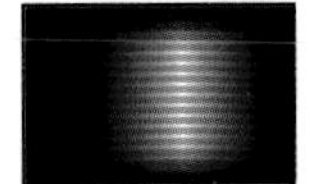

The **Opacity** control swatch controls the opacity and transparency of the effect. Click on it repeatedly to cycle though various backgrounds, and view the current effect against them in the Preview Window. Click and hold to access a pop-up menu of these same background options. Click and drag to change the opacity of the effect, using the image itself as the background.

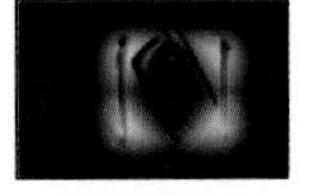

The **Glue** control swatch controls channel operations in the image, comparing the original image with the image after the current effect is applied to it. Click repeatedly, click and drag, or use the right and left arrow keys to cycle through and view your options in the Preview Window. Click and hold on the swatch to access a pop-up menu of these same options.

The **Direction** control swatch allows you to change the direction of the gradient (click and drag on the swatch).

The **Options** menu provides access to the Preferences dialog box and standard About KPT screen; it also allows you to modify the color-picker spectra and the feathering between gradient color transitions, as well as to enable and disable real-time linking between the gradient controls and the Preview Window.

KPT Interform

KPT Interform is a module that blends two "parental" textures to generate a third "offspring" texture (Figure 5.5). Both parental textures can be independently set in motion, crossing each other in various degrees of opacity as they create the offspring texture.

In addition to 2D filter effects, you can also create QuickTime movies by saving parental and offspring texture parameters in cells that can be used as frames in a movie. Totally new images and movies can be created by using the parental elements in varying degrees of opacity and combining them with the Glue apply modes, which allow variations of the image you're working with to show through.

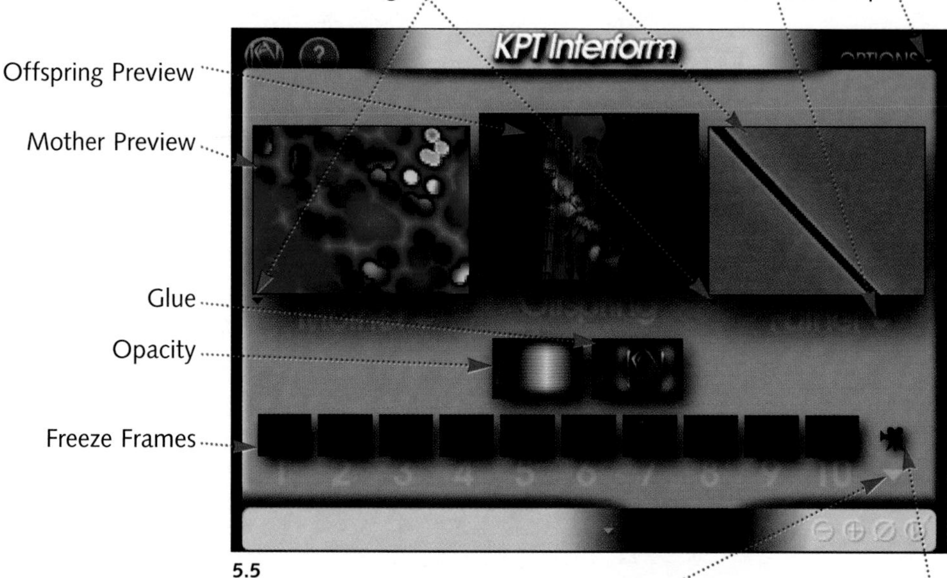

5.5 KPT Interform

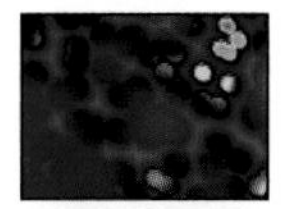

The **Mother Preview** window shows the active Mother preset texture, which is taken from the KPT Texture Explorer 3.0 presets.

The **Father Preview** window shows the active Father preset texture, which is taken from the KPT Texture Explorer 3.0 presets.

The **Offspring Preview** window shows the results of the interaction among all parental textures and motion algorithms, as well as Glue and Opacity effects.

The **Texture Presets** pop-up menus (click and hold on the triangles) allow you to assign textures from the KPT Texture Explorer preset menus to the Mother or Father Preview windows.

The **Motion Algorithms** pop-up menus (click and hold on the triangles) allow you to assign either a preset motion algorithm or the Manual Scooting motion to the Mother, Father, or Offspring Preview windows. With Manual Scooting, you click and drag in the relevant window to set the texture in motion.

The **Glue** control swatch controls channel operations in the image, comparing the current selection with the Offspring texture. Click repeatedly, click and drag, or use the right and left arrow keys to cycle through and view your options in the Offspring Preview window. Click and hold on the swatch to access a pop-up menu of these same options.

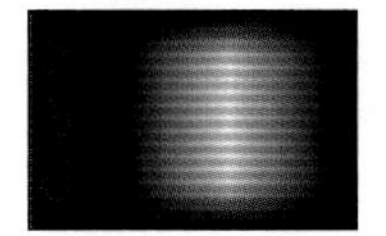

The **Opacity** control swatch controls the opacity and transparency of the effect. Click on it repeatedly to cycle through various backgrounds, and view the current effect against them in the Offspring Preview window. Click and hold to access a pop-up menu of these same background options. Click and drag to change the opacity of the effect, using the image selection as the background.

The **Freeze Frames** allow you to assign the current Offspring texture to a blank swatch. Click on an active Freeze Frame to reactivate the assigned effect, including all parental and animation parameters. Option-click a Freeze Frame to delete its contents.

The **QuickTime Camera** icon, with a click, allows you to record and save an animation sequence containing all Freeze Frames. The default transition between frames is fade-to-black, and the animation follows the parameters you set in the Movie Options menu.

The **Movie Options** menu allows control over QuickTime movie parameters, such as movie resolution, length, duration, and transitions. It also provides a preview of the current movie.

The **Options** menu, in addition to the standard Preferences and About KPT selections, allows you to choose from three movie-playback resolutions so you can optimize the trade-off between speed and quality.

KPT Spheroid Designer

KPT Spheroid Designer takes the idea of the original KPT Glass Lens effect and extrapolates it to an extreme (Figure 5.6). Here you create spheres (akin to lenses) and apply various light sources and ambient lighting effects to them. You can also apply textures to the spheres to simulate such effects as rough terrains, golf balls, or other types of relief. You can control the effects completely, or randomly generate them using a mutation tree.

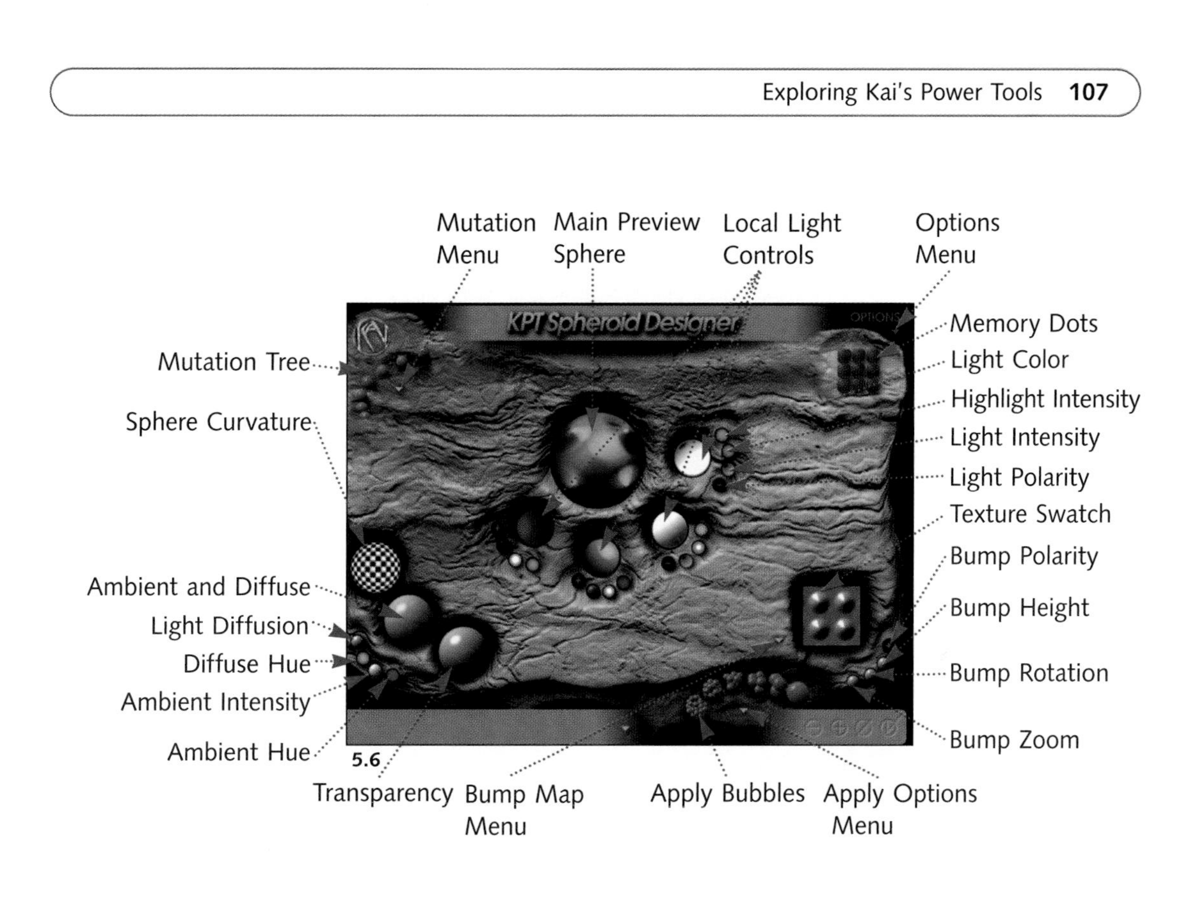

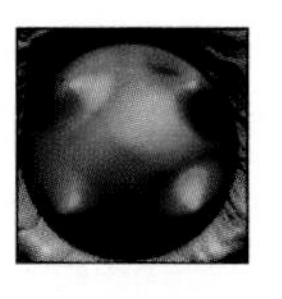

The **Main Preview Sphere** shows the results of all light and bump-map parameters. Click and drag to rotate the sphere.

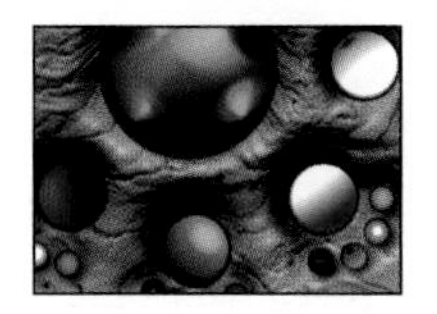

The **Local Light Controls** cast light on the Main Preview Sphere. Click on it to activate and deactivate; or click and drag to change direction.

There are four spheres for controlling the parameters for each Local Light Control:

5.6 KPT Spheroid Designer

The **Light Polarity** sphere's default is a positive setting, which shines light onto the image. Clicking on this control reverses the polarity for the associated Local Light Control, which has the effect of sucking the light out of the Main Preview Sphere. If the Local Light Control has a color assigned to it, reversing the polarity will apply the inverse of that color.

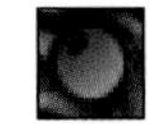

The **Light Intensity** sphere allows you to increase or decrease the amount of light, within the range of 1 percent and 200 percent.

The **Highlight Intensity** sphere enables you to set the highlight intensity of the Local Light Control, within the range of 1 percent and 100 percent.

The **Light Color** sphere allows you to select the light color for the associated Local Light Control; clicking and holding on the sphere activates the color wheel. The three spheres in the lower-left corner of the interface, and the four small spheres that accompany them, are global controls that can affect all other parameters.

The **Sphere Curvature** sphere allows you to modify the curvature of the Main Preview Sphere, from concave to convex, within a range of –100 percent to +100 percent; click and drag on it to control the modifications.

The **Ambient and Diffuse** sphere allows you to increase or decrease the ambient-light value by clicking and dragging it vertically, to make the Main Preview Sphere glow or become dull. Click and drag horizontally to add or remove diffuse qualities, which make the Main Preview Sphere more or less shiny.

The **Transparency** sphere, by clicking and dragging, enables you to increase the transparency or opacity of the Main Preview Sphere.

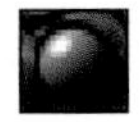

The **Light Diffusion** sphere, by clicking and dragging, allows you to increase or decrease the apparent glossiness of the Main Preview Sphere.

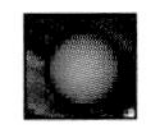

The **Diffuse Hue** sphere enables you to activate a color picker (click and hold) and change the color of the diffuse hue in the Main Preview Sphere. This global control will interact with, rather than override, the color of the Local Light Controls.

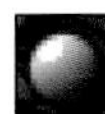

The **Ambient Intensity** sphere isolates the ambient-light component of the Ambient and Diffuse sphere; changes made here are updated in the other control, and vice versa. Click and drag to increase or decrease the ambient-light qualities, which control the Main Preview Sphere's self-illuminating qualities.

The **Ambient Hue** sphere allows you to modify the shadow color of the Main Preview Sphere; click and hold to access its color picker.

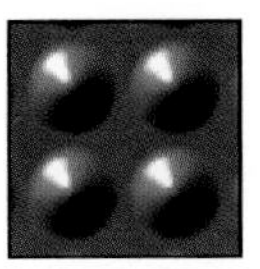

The **Texture Swatch** shows you a sample of the texture being applied to the Main Preview Sphere. The Bump Offset feature allows you to move the texture around in the Texture Swatch and apply the resulting portion of the bump map to the Main Preview Sphere.

The **Bump Map Menu** is a pop-up menu accessing bump map textures and the Bump Map Manager.

The **Bump Polarity** sphere allows you to alternate between positive and negative polarity by clicking on it; these make the bump map convex or concave, respectively.

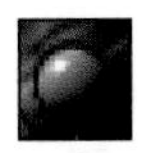

The **Bump Height** sphere, by clicking and dragging on it, allows you to increase or decrease the bump map effect.

The **Bump Rotation** sphere, by clicking and dragging on it, enables you to rotate the texture in the Main Preview Sphere.

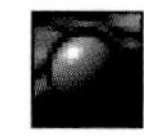

The **Bump Zoom** sphere, by clicking and dragging on it, allows you to increase the relative size of the texture, compared to the Main Preview Sphere.

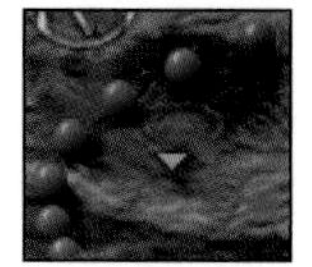

The **Mutation Tree** allows you to generate random spheres. It works like the Mutation Tree in KPT Texture Explorer; that is, clicking on the spheres that are higher in the tree creates a wider range of mutations, while clicking on the lower spheres results in minor modifications.

The **Mutation Menu** triangle's pop-up menu lists the mutation options, allowing you to select the parameters to be modified.

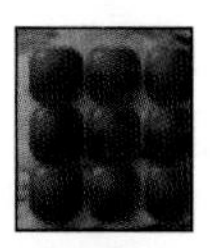

The **Memory Dots** grid, by clicking on it, allows you to save the current sphere effect to that dot. Option-click to erase the effect from a particular dot. Clicking on a saved dot activates its assigned effect.

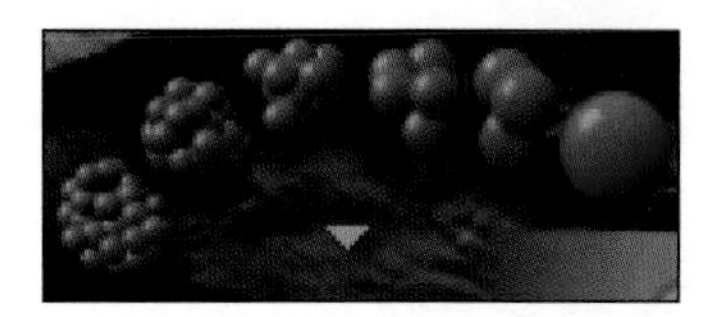

The **Apply Bubbles** buttons determine how many spheres will be created when you click on the OK check mark. The options are: 1, 10, 50, 100, 500, or 1,000 spheres. Rendered sphere sizes are determined by dividing your selection size by the number of spheres you want rendered.

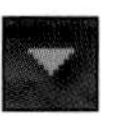

The **Apply Options** Menu controls the way numerous spheres are rendered. Options allow control over spheres vs. ellipses, overlapping, mutation controls, and pattern effects. The options available are: Apollonian Packing; Random Spheres; Random Ellipses; Spirals, Stars, Splatters, and More; Genesis Packing; Use Shadows; and Use Mutations. Consult the KPT manual for details on these apply options.

The **Options** menu allows access to the KPT help interface, as well as the standard Preferences dialog box and About KPT screen.

KPT Texture Explorer

KPT Texture Explorer 3.0 is perhaps the most advanced texture generator in the world, with the ability to generate infinite, complex texture fields (Figure 5.7). Version 3.0 introduced a new texture engine that eliminated the tiling associated with previous versions; the new engine also creates a smoother, more complex gradient. Its properties underlie much of the functionality in the KPT Interform filter as well.

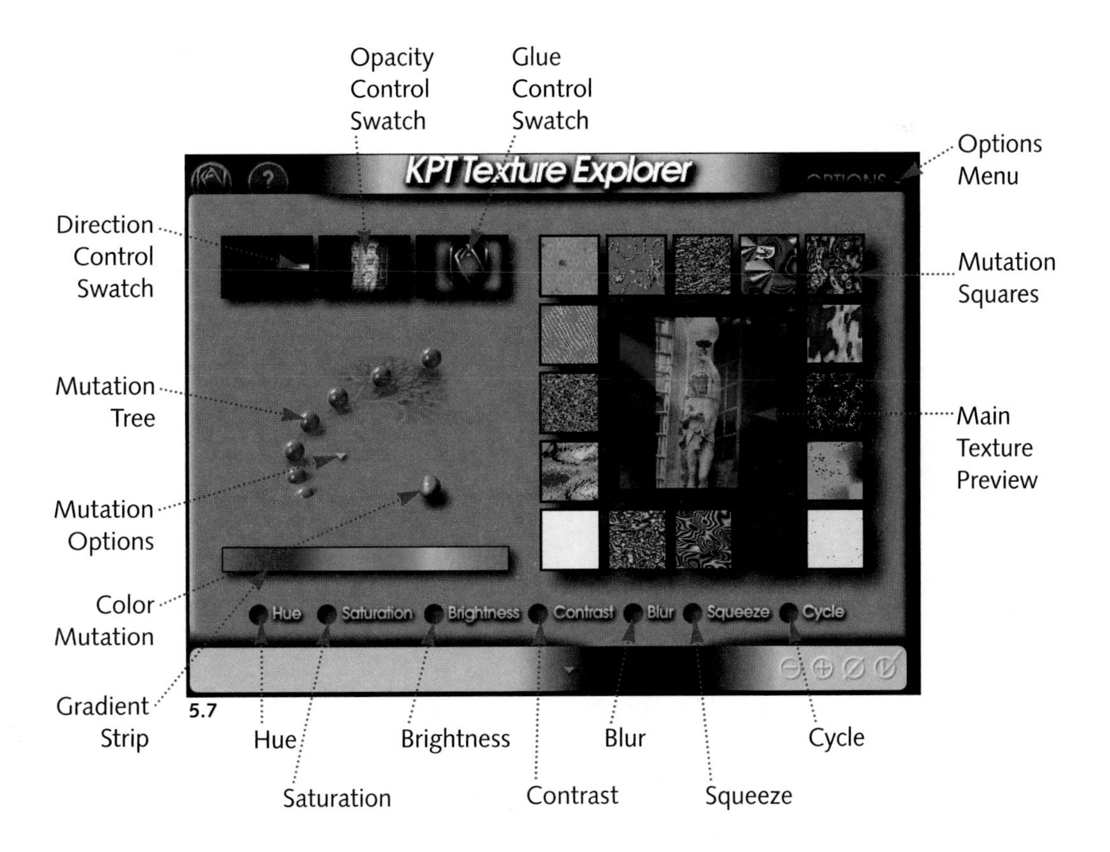

5.7 KPT Texture Explorer

The **Main Texture Preview** window shows the current texture, which is created by applying an algorithm to the gradient shown in the Gradient Strip. Click and drag in the window to pan through the infinite texture space. The plus (+) and minus (–) buttons allow zooming in and out of the texture.

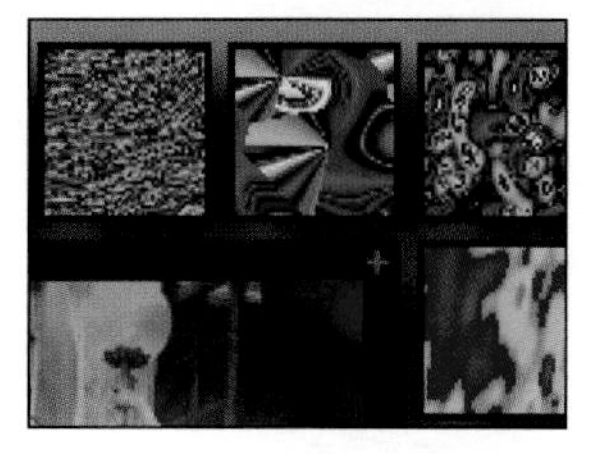

The **Mutation** squares surrounding the Main Texture Preview window show variations of the Main Texture. Click on a mutation square to place that texture in the Main Texture Preview window, where it becomes the current texture. Option-click on a square to protect it from being changed in future mutations. A red line around a box indicates its protected status.

The **Mutation Tree** allows you to generate mutations of the Main Texture and the associated Mutation squares. For subtle changes, click on the spheres closest to the bottom of the tree. Clicking on spheres higher in the tree results in more diversity in the generated textures.

The **Color Mutation** sphere shuffles the active Gradient Designer presets, changing only the color of the textures.

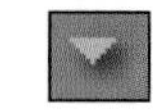

The **Mutation Options** Menu allows you to select the parameters to be shuffled when the Mutation Tree spheres are selected. Parameters include Panning, Rotation, Scale, Zoom, Color, Blending, Opacity, and Texture (click and hold on the inverted triangle to access the pop-up menu).

The **Gradient Strip** enables you to access the Gradient Designer preset pop-up menu by clicking and holding on the strip. The gradient assigned here is used as the color source for all generated textures.

The **Hue** button, by clicking and dragging it, allows you to cycle the texture through the color wheel while maintaining the original distance relationships between hues.

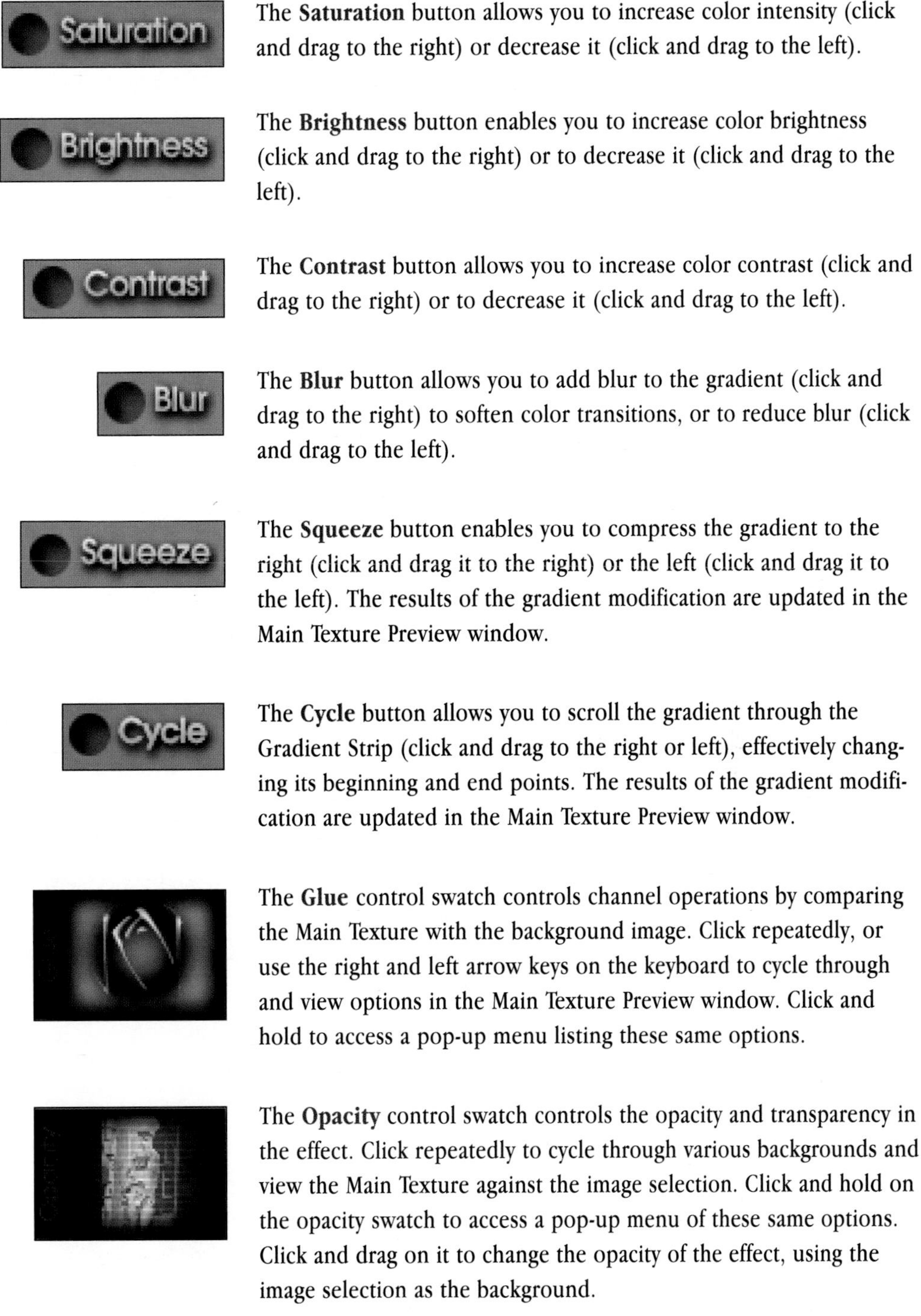

The **Saturation** button allows you to increase color intensity (click and drag to the right) or decrease it (click and drag to the left).

The **Brightness** button enables you to increase color brightness (click and drag to the right) or to decrease it (click and drag to the left).

The **Contrast** button allows you to increase color contrast (click and drag to the right) or to decrease it (click and drag to the left).

The **Blur** button allows you to add blur to the gradient (click and drag to the right) to soften color transitions, or to reduce blur (click and drag to the left).

The **Squeeze** button enables you to compress the gradient to the right (click and drag it to the right) or the left (click and drag it to the left). The results of the gradient modification are updated in the Main Texture Preview window.

The **Cycle** button allows you to scroll the gradient through the Gradient Strip (click and drag to the right or left), effectively changing its beginning and end points. The results of the gradient modification are updated in the Main Texture Preview window.

The **Glue** control swatch controls channel operations by comparing the Main Texture with the background image. Click repeatedly, or use the right and left arrow keys on the keyboard to cycle through and view options in the Main Texture Preview window. Click and hold to access a pop-up menu listing these same options.

The **Opacity** control swatch controls the opacity and transparency in the effect. Click repeatedly to cycle through various backgrounds and view the Main Texture against the image selection. Click and hold on the opacity swatch to access a pop-up menu of these same options. Click and drag on it to change the opacity of the effect, using the image selection as the background.

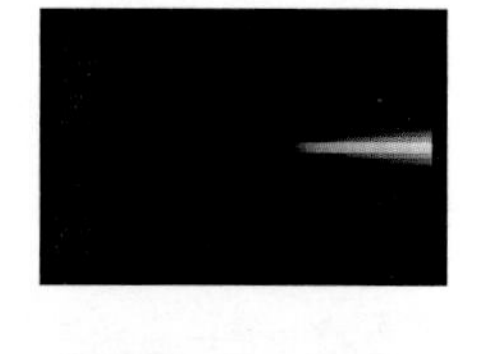

The **Direction** control swatch rotates the texture in relation to the background image. Click and drag on the swatch to see the texture rotate in real time in the Main Texture Preview window.

In addition to the standard Preferences and About KPT items, the **Options** menu also includes the Scale To Selection and Fill Selection commands. Scale To Selection ensures that the texture is applied to the selection in a true WYSIWYG manner. Fill Selection prevents the texture from scaling and applies it as it is seen in the Main Texture Preview window.

KPT Lens f/x

The smallest of the KPT 3.0 filter interfaces, KPT Lens f/x, delivers perhaps the most power per inch. Lens f/x looks and works like a magnifying loupe that printers use (Figure 5.8). You drag it around your image, looking through the lens at the image beneath it. Any changes are seen either at a 1:1 ratio, or at the magnification rate currently used in the image. Sliders control the effect intensity and opacity, and all of the apply modes are present as well. You will not find a KPT Lens f/x menu item; instead, you access it via the six filters that use its interface: KPT Noise f/x, KPT Gaussian f/x, KPT Edge Effects, KPT Intensity Effects, KPT Smudge f/x, and KPT Pixel f/x. Once you are in one Lens f/x filter, you can select any of the others from a menu in the interface; however, you can apply only one filter at a time before exiting the interface.

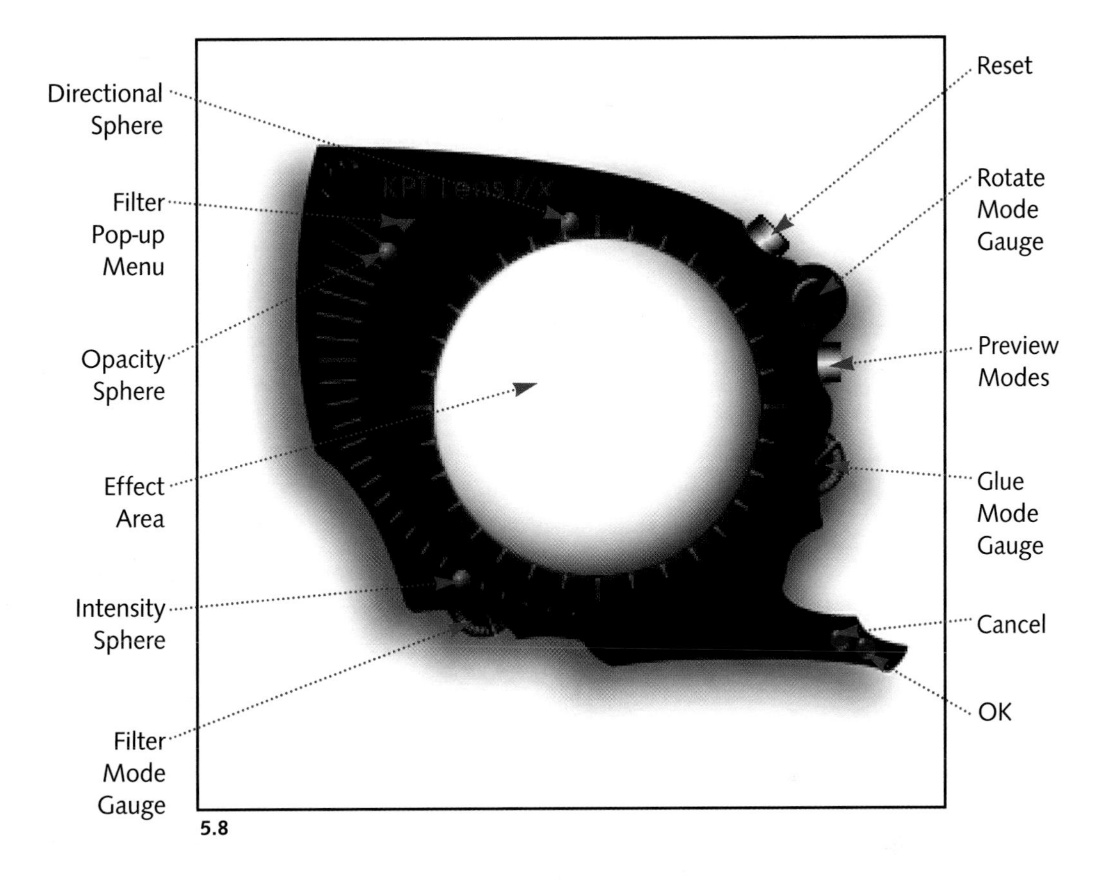

5.8

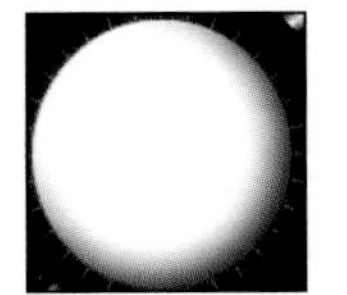

The **Effect Area** shows the selected effect applied to the image underneath the Lens f/x interface.

The **Intensity Sphere** slider controls the degree of the effect, from 0 percent to 100 percent. Drag up to increase the effect, and down to decrease.

5.8 KPT Lens f/x

The **Opacity Sphere** slider controls the degree of opacity/transparency. Drag up to increase opacity, down to increase transparency.

The **Directional Sphere** is available when effects are direction oriented. Drag around the perimeter of the Effect Area to change the direction of the effect.

The **Filter Mode Gauge** toggles between subfilters within a single Lens f/x filter.

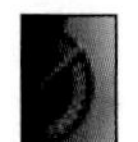

The **Glue Mode Gauge** offers a pop-up menu for selecting Glue options. Click repeatedly on this gauge to cycle through the options.

The **Rotate Mode Gauge** pop-up menu determines the properties of the Directional Sphere. It scatters pixels in a Unidirectional, Bidirectional, or Omnidirectional manner.

The **Reset** button sets all parameters back to their defaults.

The **Preview Modes** allow the image to be viewed at either a 1:1 Ratio or in Draggable Lens mode. In 1:1 Ratio, drag inside the Effect Area to pan through the image. In Draggable Lens mode, drag the entire interface around the screen to the area of interest.

The red **Cancel** sphere closes KPT Lens f/x, returning you to the Photoshop interface without applying any effects.

The green **OK** sphere applies the current effect to the image and closes the KPT Lens f/x interface.

Click and hold on the **Filter Pop-up Menu** to access all of the Pixel-based filter effects available in KPT.

KPT Fractal Explorer

KPT Fractal Explorer was left unchanged from the 2.1 version, perhaps because it was hard to improve on this elegant tool for exploring fractal designs (Figure 5.9). (It can be found in the TE & FE Classic folder on the KPT 3.0 CD-ROM.) Fractal Explorer allows you to select various fractal sets, with full zooming and panning on the endless details. You can apply gradient presets from Gradient Designer 2.1 to the inner and outer regions of the fractal to achieve stunning designs.

Because KPT Fractal Explorer is version 2.1, the buttons along the top and bottom of the interface do not offer the same functionality as their 3.0 counterparts. The Kai logo at the top hides the interface rather than applying a full-screen preview; the top Shuffle button generates random effects based on the parameters you've selected; and the Add and Delete buttons at the bottom offer control over the fractal presets list.

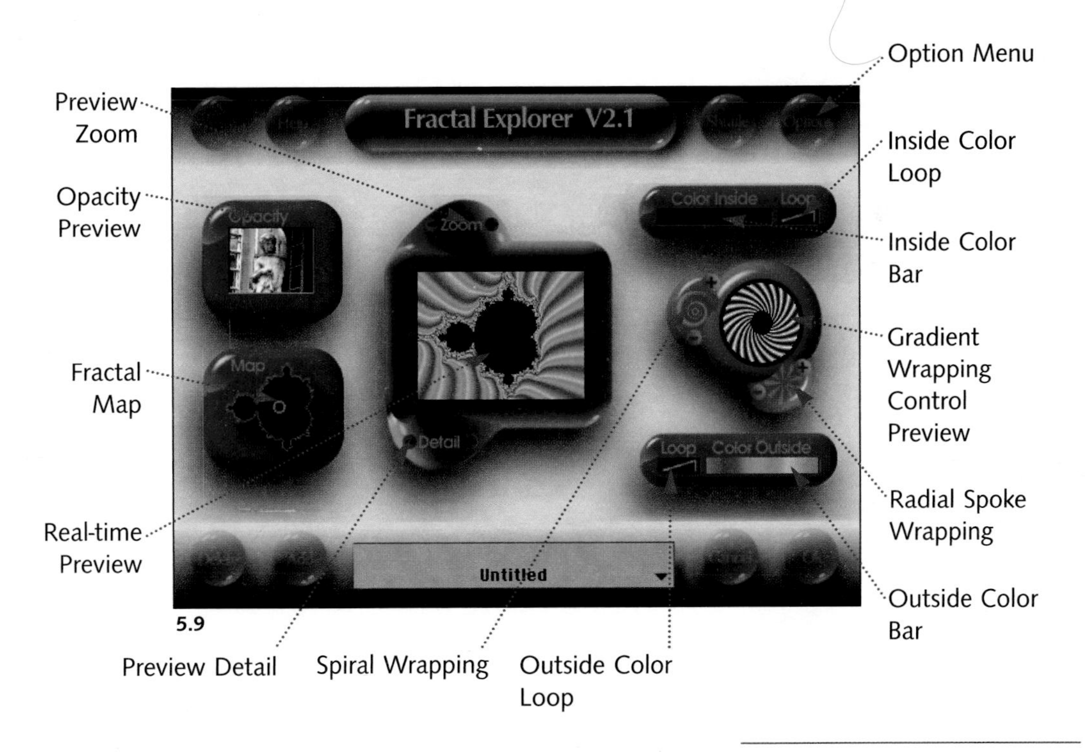

5.9 Fractal Explorer Interface

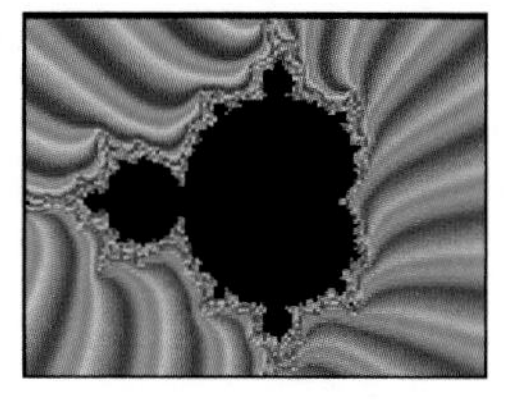

The **Real-Time Preview** window shows what the fractal image will look like, including any selected apply modes (referred to as Glue in 3.0 modules; see also "Understanding and Using the Glue Options" later in this chapter). Click the arrows around the edge of the window for directional panning, or click and drag in the window itself to pan in a more intuitive way. The cursor changes to a magnifying glass when it's over the preview window, so you can zoom to specific sections of the fractal.

The **Preview Zoom** controls allow centered zooming in and out of the fractal.

The **Preview Detail** controls dictate the amount of detail shown in the Preview window. Higher detail settings usually result in longer preview rendering times.

The **Opacity Preview** allows the selection of various background types against which to view the fractal image. Click and hold to activate a pop-up menu showing the available options.

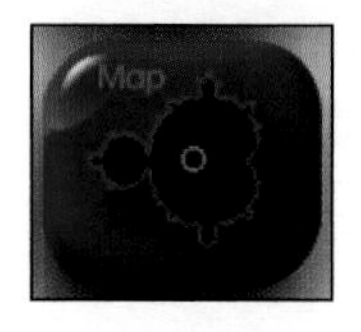

The **Fractal Map**'s pop-up menu allows you to select from several fractal formulas. Options include the Mandelbrot Set, Julia Set, M-J Hybrid 1, M-J Hybrid 2, Julia 2, and Julia 3. Command-click on the red circle in the Fractal Map to change the active coordinates in the fractal, thereby changing the current preview.

The **Inside Color** bar's pop-up menu allows you to access the Gradient Designer 2.1 presets, which are applied to the inside of the fractal design.

The **Inside Color Loop** button's pop-up menu enables you to control the direction and repeatability of the gradient in the fractal.

Spiral Wrapping controls how the gradient twists around the design as it spirals toward the fractal.

Radial Spoke Wrapping dictates how often the gradient is wrapped around the outer design, creating a zoom effect.

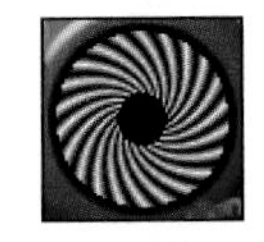

The **Gradient Wrapping Control Preview** is a graphic representation of your spiral and radial settings in the fractal, which are updated in real time.

The **Outside Color** bar's pop-up menu allows you to access the Gradient Designer 2.1 presets, which are applied to the outside of the fractal design.

The **Outside Color Loop** button's pop-up menu enables you to control the direction and repeatability of the gradient in the fractal.

The **Options** pop-up menu allows you to select the apply mode (now known as Glue in version 3.0). Apply-mode options include Normal, Procedural Blend, Reverse Blend, Lighten Only, Darken Only, Add, Subtract, Multiply, Screen, and Difference. There is also an option for wrapping the image instead of the gradient, as well as for numeric input (for fractal experts only) and Preferences for Fractal Explorer.

Individual Filters

These eight individual filters did not fit into either a full-blown interface or the pixel-based KPT Lens f/x, so each has its own, smaller interface (Figures 5.10 through 5.17). All eight interfaces have a similar look and feel, and their Opacity and Glue swatches work the same as they do in the more complex interfaces. In addition, the Options menus offer the usual items (About KPT, Reset to Normal, and Preferences), as well as controls unique to some.

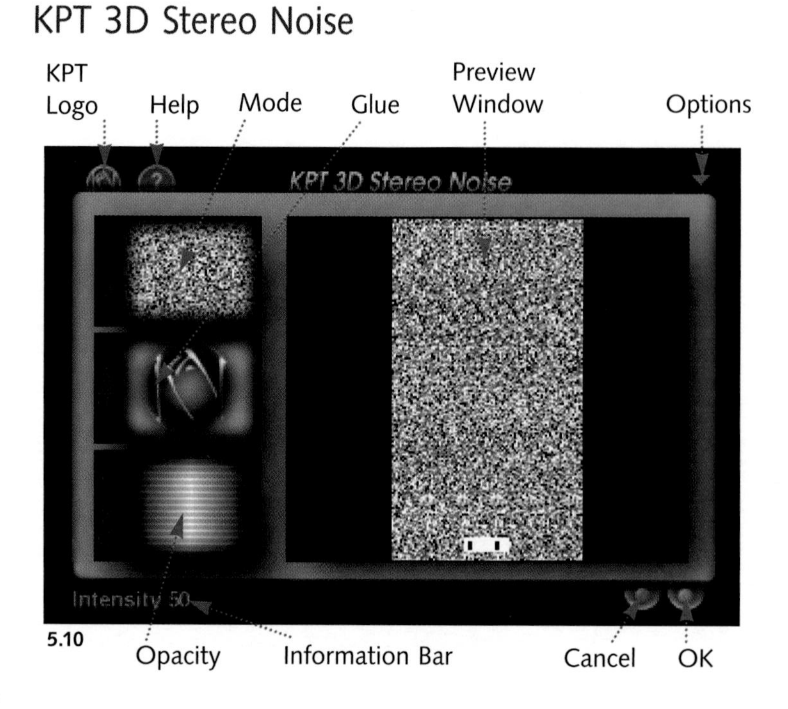

5.10 The KPT 3D Stereo Noise filter allows control over noise effects. You can adjust the effect intensity by clicking and dragging in the Preview window; the intensity level is reflected in the Information Bar. Click and hold on the Mode button to choose among Monochrome Noise, Color Noise, and No Noise

KPT Glass Lens

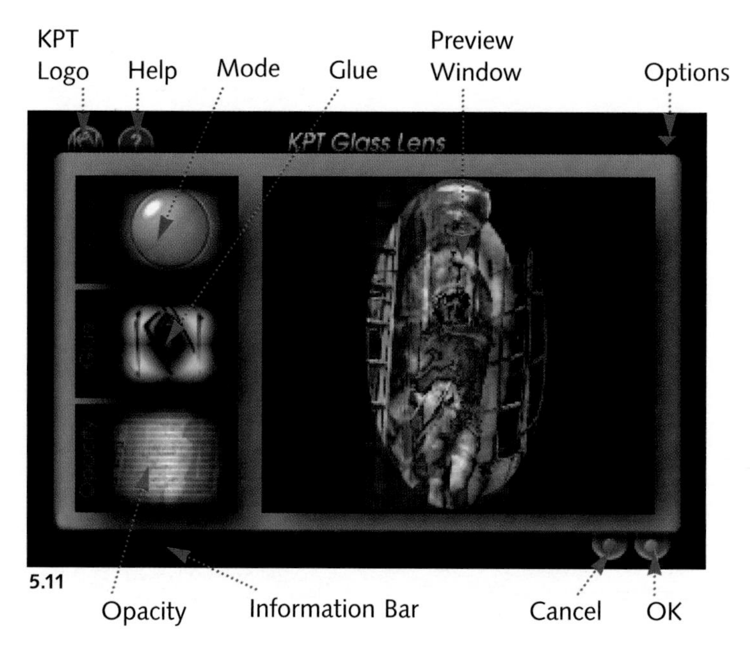

5.11 The KPT Glass Lens filter creates a spheroid shape of the image selection. Click and drag in the Preview window to move the coordinates of the specular highlight. The Mode swatch's pop-up menu allows you to select Soft, Normal, or Bright lens effects. The Options pop-up menu allows toggling the placement of the light source from front to back, and blacking out the background behind the sphere

KPT Page Curl

KPT Planar Tiling

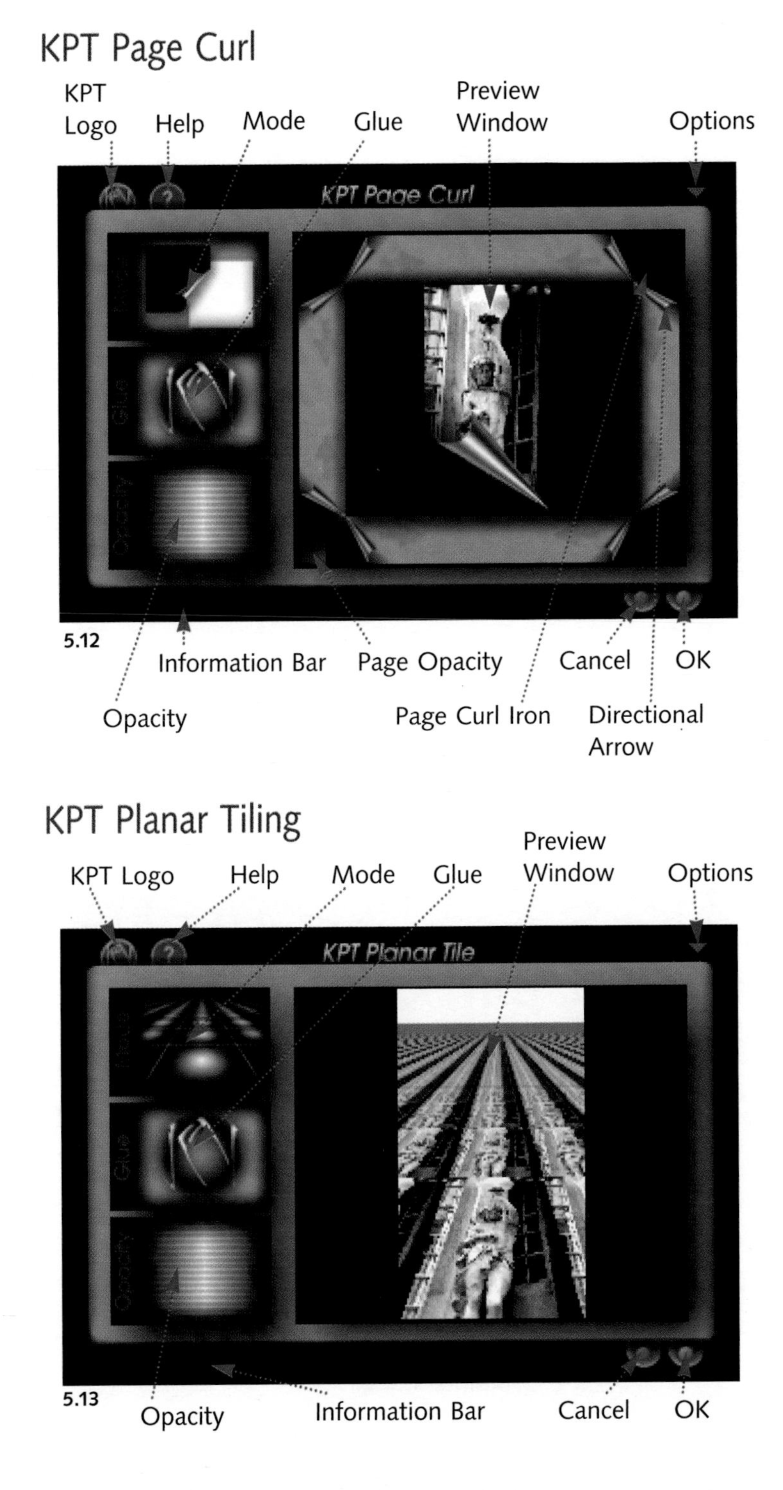

5.12 Click and drag on the Page Curl icons or their associated directional arrows in the Preview window to control the page curl direction and intensity. Click and drag on the Opacity swatch to control the curl's opacity, or on the Page Opacity swatch to control the background's opacity. Click on the Mode swatch (or select from its pop-up menu) to toggle between revealing the foreground or background color beneath the page curl

5.13 KPT Planar Tiling creates an infinite, repeating plane from the image selection. Click on the Mode swatch (or select from its pop-up menu) to toggle between Perspective and Parquet tiling of the image. In Perspective mode, drag horizontally in the Preview window to change the vanishing point, or vertically to raise or lower the eye-level (horizon) line. In Parquet mode, dragging horizontally in the Preview window rotates the plane, and dragging vertically zooms in and out. In either mode, the Option and Control keys each constrains one of the two modifiers

KPT Seamless Welder

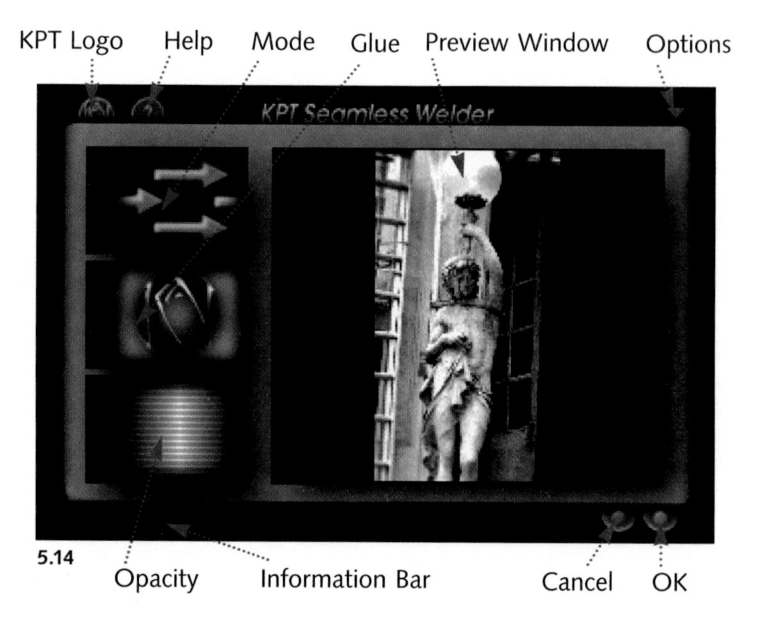

5.14

KPT Twirl

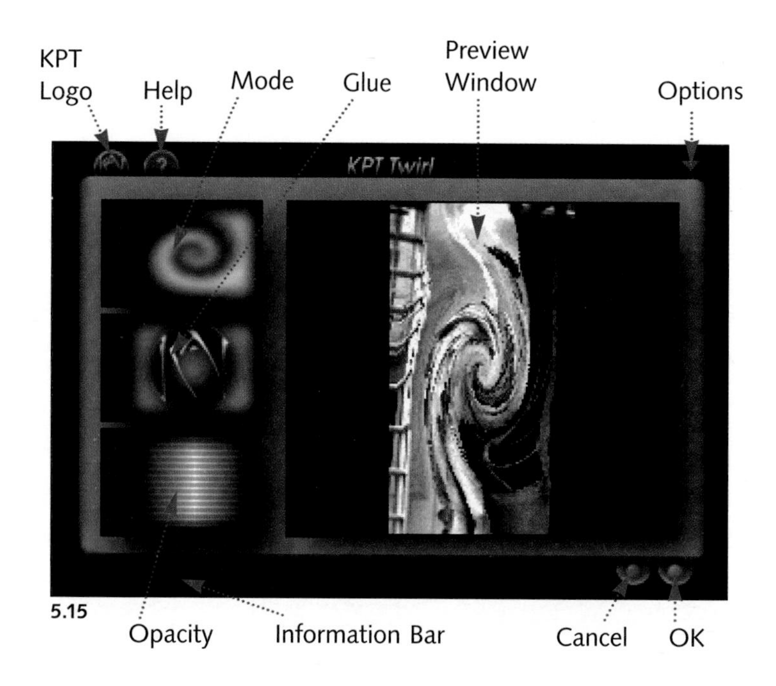

5.15

5.14 KPT Seamless Welder turns a rectangular selection into a tile that can be endlessly repeated with no abrupt edges. Click and drag in the Preview window to see the effect intensity. In the Mode swatch's pop-up menu, you can choose between Seamless or Reflective tiling methods

5.15 KPT Twirl applies a spinning effect to the image selection. In the Mode swatch's pop-up menu, you can select either Twirl or Kaleidoscope effects (or click to toggle between them). In Kaleidoscope mode, dragging vertically in the Preview window dictates the number of slices in the abstraction; in Twirl mode, dragging horizontally changes the twirl angle

KPT Video Feedback

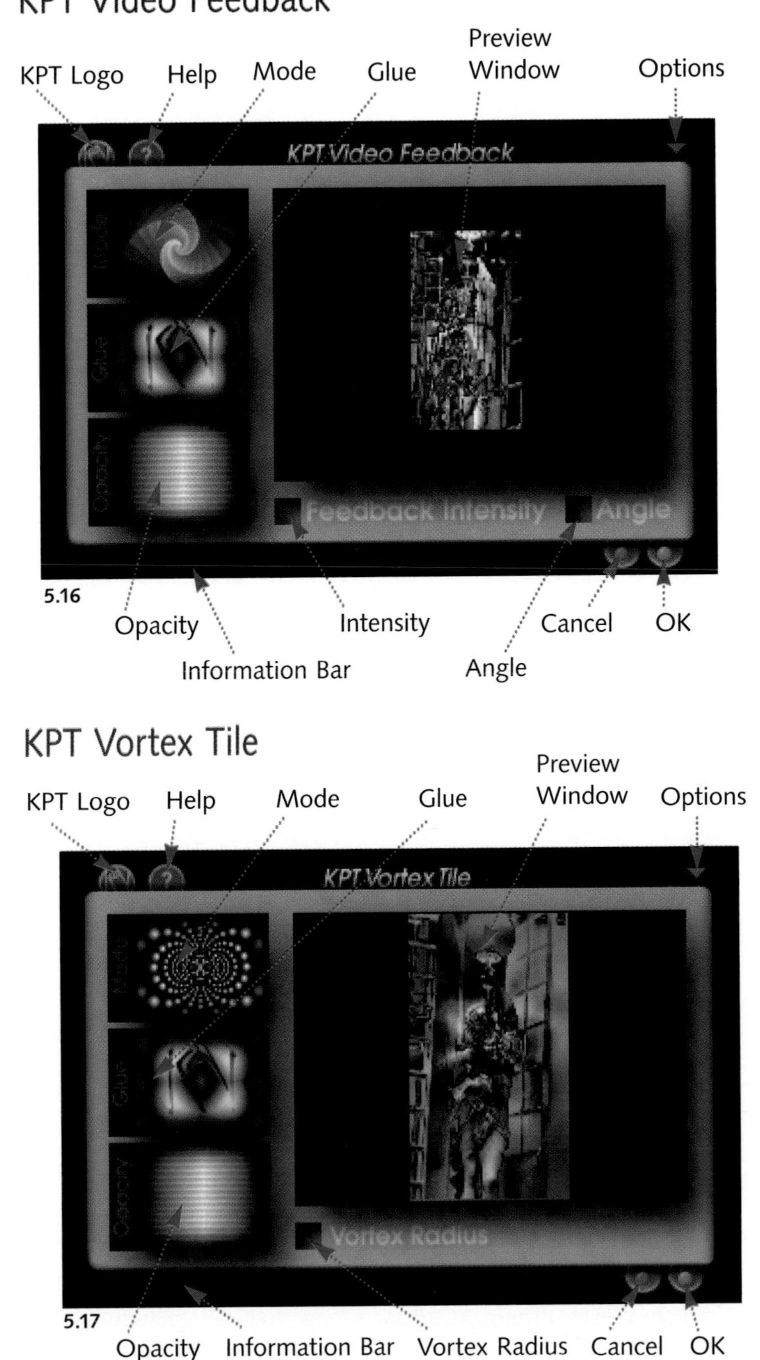

5.16 KPT Video Feedback creates an infinite repetition of the image selection in perspective. In the Mode swatch's pop-up menu, you can choose between Video or Telescope feedback (or click to toggle between them) to create elliptical or rectangular patterns, respectively. The intensity and rotation angle of the effect are controlled by clicking and dragging on the appropriate swatches

5.17 The KPT Vortex Tile filter creates an imaginary circle in the image selection, swaps the inside of the circle with the outside, and then tiles the result in an infinite pattern. Click and drag in the Preview window to move the center point. In the Mode swatch's pop-up menu, you can choose between Normal and Pinch tiling effects (or click to toggle between them). Drag the Vortex Radius swatch to control the size of the imaginary circle

The Basics of Kai's Power Tools 3.0

I can hear it now, as first-time Kai's Power Tools users click on their Filter menu in Photoshop and look at all of their options in the KPT 3.0 submenu: "There is so much here; there is just so much to explore." So they choose one or two filters, find some neat effects, and promise themselves that they will come back and go through it more methodically. But there is just so much there, and the filters seem like such a jumble at first, that they may never go back and cover all the bases.

Mastering KPT involves understanding KPT, and understanding KPT requires that you have a sense of how the various filters are related to each other. You can get a general sense of what's going on by taking a "one a day" approach to filter exploration, but it will not show you what's underneath the filter. To see that, you need to know how everything fits together, from the top down. Start by ignoring many of the flashy effects: The basic building blocks of KPT are gradients, textures, and bump maps. What follows is a quick tour of the key KPT 3.0 interfaces.

KPT Gradient Designer: The Presets Resource

KPT Gradient Designer is where much of the magic of KPT begins. Version 3.0 of the interface places so much control in your hands, it almost feels like a separate application. You create gradients by clicking in the Gradient Bar and dragging to the color picker or other places in the interface to pick up colors.

You can also add transparency to the gradient, which allows the gradient to interact with the underlying image. Once a gradient is exactly as you want it, you can add it to your gradient presets list by clicking on the Add Preset button, and you can access gradient presets through the Presets Menu triangle's pop-up menu at the bottom of the interface (Figure 5.18).

5.18

It is important to keep the image at the top of your mind when you're exploring with this or any KPT interface. It's easy to get sidetracked by all of the buttons and sliders, and the effects you can generate are quite impressive. But they are simply that: effects. Effects get boring fast unless you go beyond the mere generation of cleverly arranged pixels. The way to begin pushing past that is to keep the image in focus, to integrate the image with the effect. Some tools that facilitate integration are the Opacity and the Glue swatches. Try sampling the gradient colors directly from the image itself, or changing the opacity in a gradient so that the image shows through.

And since gradient presets are utilized by both KPT Texture Explorer and KPT Fractal Explorer to provide the color and blend references for the texture or fractal, the idea of basing the KPT effect in the image becomes even more compelling. Create a gradient by sampling the colors from the image, save that gradient as a preset, and make a texture out of it in Texture Explorer.

5.18 The KPT Gradient Designer presets

The Evolution of Kai's Power Tools

When KPT began as an outgrowth of Kai's idea to put tips on CD-ROM, plans for the design and marketing of the product were quite casual, to say the least. When the product debuted at the CyberArts show in November 1992, there was no official packaging; it shipped in envelopes with just a makeshift manual. When it was officially unveiled at MACWORLD San Francisco in January 1993, the box for version 1.0 sported a hip-looking baby with sunglasses juggling the letters K P T while surrounded by various KPT effects (see page 24). The floppy disks bore the Schnuffi cartoon characters Kai had been drawing since his days in Germany. Add to this the unusual interface, with its spheres and sliders. Taken as a whole, the nonstandard presentation caused many people to discount the value of the tools.

In a recent speaking engagement, Kai talked about the industry's reaction to the KPT interface: "I keep getting these people who are scared that I'm going to turn the entire Macintosh and Windows machines into little spaceships. That's not at all the idea. In fact, if you suffer from "turquoise sphere phobia," as some critics seemed to have the first time we did it, that's not what the interface is about. You could make them blue and round, or black and white. . . . And I still think that what comes through is that the interface design is about hiding complexity and about guiding the process."

As KPT was refined into version 2.0, the interface design was further developed, making the tools even more useful. The core set of 33 filters was enhanced by more intuitive fractal controls, better preview modes, and more accessible apply modes. In addition, the interface itself got a facelift, with the turquoise spheres getting gradient backgrounds and responsive toggle buttons.

With the release of version 3.0, Kai moved away from the radical design of previous versions, replacing the spheres and gradients with elegant grayscale controls. They show that Kai was serious about his idea that the controls should mask complexity while facilitating the process. For example, consider the apply modes. Before Kai began touting the powers of Photoshop's channel operations, they languished as just a poorly explained and seldom-read corner in the Photoshop manual. Kai renamed them ChOps and began promoting them in his Power Tips on America Online.

Given the emphasis he has placed on ChOps, both in his tips and in KPT, Kai obviously feels that much of Photoshop's power lies in these capabilities. In KPT 1.0, the modes were there, but previewing and forecasting the results were difficult. With version 2.0, Kai made sure the apply modes would be updated in the Preview window, which gave real-time feedback of the results. With version 3.0, Kai renamed them again, to Glue options, moved them out of a pull-down menu, and placed them front and center so you can click to scroll through the Glue options and see their impact effortlessly. Glue options are just one example of how Kai has refined Kai's Power Tools.

When KPT was released in the fall of 1992, there were certainly high hopes for success, but no one ever dreamed that KPT would be as successful as it has been. It has become a requisite for designers using Photoshop, as well as Fractal Design Painter and other imaging applications that support Photoshop plug-ins. It is popular on both the Macintosh and Windows platform, and is bundled with scanners, sound boards, and other peripheral products. Since then, direct and bundled sales have topped a million copies—a milestone for any software product. As Kai has said, "When [KPT] started out as a plug-in just for Photoshop, we put an emotional and psychological number on what [the sales volumes] might be. And we would have never, ever predicted that this would happen. It didn't make any sense."

Looking back, it is nice to see that KPT is an application that continues to evolve and improve. It is also nice to realize that in a world of conformity, excellence is almost always nonstandard.

KPT Texture Explorer: Infinite Variety

Beyond such flashy interfaces as Spheroid Designer and Lens f/x, it could be argued that the greatest benefit of version 3.0 is the improvement of the texture engine. Textures are far more advanced than they were in previous versions. They are now infinite, with no tiling, regardless of how large the selection is. In addition to being infinite, they are much more complex, and their structures more varied.

Just as you can save a gradient preset, you can also save a texture preset. This means you can create and save a number of textures based on the colors in the previous gradient preset, all of which were sampled from your image. The result is that the effect is integrated into the image in a very cohesive way.

Texture Explorer allows the smooth rotation and zooming of a texture, which makes possible the repeated application of the same texture at different angles and sizes. Throw the Glue options into the mix, and you are able to achieve a very high degree of variation within a very narrow space.

KPT Interform: More Than a Casual Diversion

You may have looked at KPT Interform and been amazed, or intimidated, or simply confused about what you are supposed to do with it. KPT Interform takes two textures from the Textures Presets menu and combines them to create a third texture. What's really amazing is that these textures animate as they layer over each other. This is possible due to the seamless-tiling aspects of KPT 3.0's texture engine.

With Interform, you are able to take the texture presets you created from the gradient presets, which in turn were sampled from your image, and combine them along with the image. At this point it begins to sound like The House That Jack Built, but these are not just a bunch of unrelated filters. There is a progression here, and everything builds on everything else. In Interform, for example, if you've already applied a texture to the image, you can animate a version of the texture against a static version of the same texture, which is itself present in the image. Again, the Glue options make this process even more interesting because of the way the options integrate the effect with the image.

Spheroid Designer

Spheroid Designer allows you to create complex spheres that are illuminated with various lighting and texture effects. The texture effects are created from grayscale bump map settings, which are loaded into the interface. (Bump maps are grayscale images whose light and dark portions determine the height or depth of each point in the texture.) The height, polarity, and position of the bump map are all modifiable. You can use any PICT image as a bump map, although its color characteristics are not used by Spheroid Designer. The Bump Map Manager, which you select from either the pop-up Bump Map Menu or the Presets Manager pop-up menu, allows you to import PICT images that you can use as bump maps in Spheroid Designer (Figure 5.19).

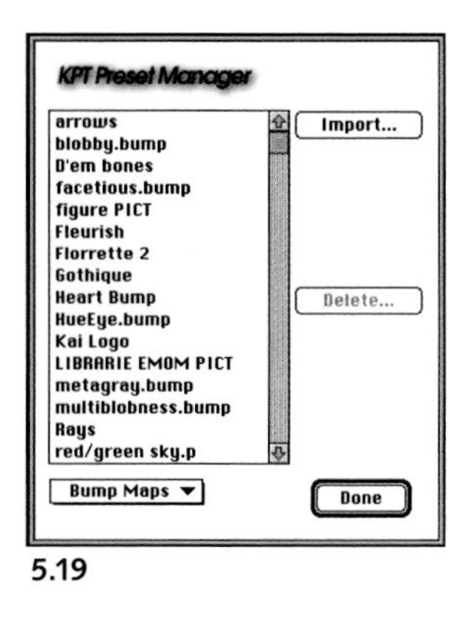

5.19

You can also import the image itself as a bump map, as long as it is a PICT file; the result is a sphere with the image embossed on its surface (see page 140 for step-by-step procedures). KPT Bryce PICT files can be imported as bump maps in KPT as well, and many of the PICT strategies discussed in Chapter 7, also apply to the bump map capabilities in Spheroid Designer.

These are just a few of the ways that thematic ideas about color, image, or pattern can be repeated and carried throughout an image. Once you understand how everything dovetails in KPT, you'll be bouncing back and forth from one module to another, customizing and swapping presets based on the image you're working with.

KPT Lens f/x: A Different Kind of Harmony

I remember the first time Kai showed me Lens f/x. He didn't have a name for it then; he just opened this module and a funny-looking thing appeared on his screen. At first it reminded me of some futuristic Batman-Ninja weapon. But when he started dragging it around the screen, I quickly abandoned that impression and began looking at it as some sort of designer's monocle or optometrist's gauge. When I started using it myself,

5.19 KPT Presets Manager allows you to import, export, and delete bump maps for use in KPT Spheroid Designer

I threw away all my analogies and saw it for what it was: One of the most useful tools available for Photoshop.

The KPT Lens f/x filter incorporates all of the pixel-based, "one-shot" filters found in KPT 2.1. Pixel-based filters calculate each pixel's values based on the values of the pixels around it (see page 174). Selection-based filters, such as Page Curl, are not pixel-based and so were not incorporated into Lens f/x. The filters that have been absorbed into Lens f/x are shown in Table 5.1.

Table 5.1. The Components of the Lens f/x Filters

KPT Noise f/x

KPT Gaussian f/x

KPT Edge Effects

KPT Intensity Effects

KPT Smudge f/x

KPT Pixel f/x

KPT Grime Layer

KPT Gaussian Glow

KPT Find Edges Soft

KPT Sharpen Intensity

KPT Smudge Darken (Left and Right)

KPT Scatter Horizontal

KPT Hue Protected Noise (Minimum, Medium, and Maximum)

KPT Gaussian Electrify

KPT Find Edges Charcoal

KPT Fade Contrast

KPT Smudge Lighten (Left and Right)

KPT Diffuse More

KPT Special Red Noise

KPT Gaussian Weave

KPT Find Edges Directional (new)

KPT PixelWind

KPT Special Green Noise

KPT Gaussian Blocks (new)

KPT PixelBreeze

KPT Special Blue Noise

KPT Gaussian Diamond (new)

KPT PixelStorm

Enhanced Color Control

Gaussian Blur Large Scale

As you look at Table 5.1, you'll notice that many of these one-shot filters were already related before being incorporated into Lens f/x. PixelStorm is an extreme version of PixelBreeze, for instance, with PixelWind falling somewhere in between. Gaussian Glow and Gaussian Electrify apply blurry haze effects that are applied to only the shadows or highlights, respectively. The Lens f/x filter allows you to customize the effect by applying the exact amount you want.

You can further develop these effects by using the Glue options (formerly known as apply modes) before applying them, as well as by combining several effects. The directional-based filter options, such as Pixel f/x, Edge Effects, and Smudge f/x, offer some especially interesting possibilities.

Strategies for Using Kai's Power Tools 3.0

The tricky thing about detailing a strategies section for a bunch of filters is that it can digress into a list of formal-based recipes for getting various effects. While there is some merit to providing this sort of information, it is not the end-all as far as KPT is concerned. Therefore, this section will begin with some effects that are blatantly labeled as recipes for getting some neat-looking results. It will then go on to show other ideas and methods of image processing.

Imaging Recipes

Any of these imaging "recipes" can be used at any point in the creation process. They are all performed on the same image (Figure 5.20) to show that they are not based on a particular image, but can be repeated with many types of images.

5.20

5.20 The original image

Neo-Digital Cubism

This technique will automatically arrange the image in the shape of an oval and begin to abstract the space.

1. Open the Twirl filter and set the Mode to Twirl.
2. Click and drag in the Preview window to modify the twirl effect. The angle in the image shown was set to 159 degrees.
3. Select Difference in the Glue swatch pop-up menu. The final image is shown in Figure 5.21.

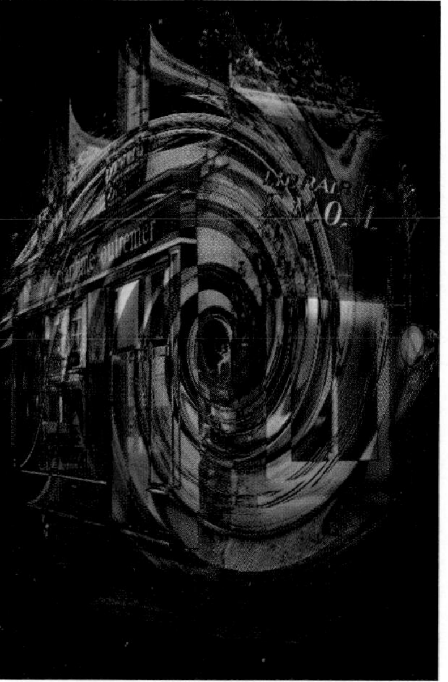

5.21

Color Casts

Color casts are not usually associated with the KPT Vortex Tile filter. This technique is effective because a low intensity level at the Vortex Radius creates minimal distortion. With minimal distortion, an overall color cast is created by the portion of the image that falls under the vortex center. In this case, a red cast

5.21 Neo-Digital Cubism

was created (when viewed in the Normal Glue option) by positioning the center over a small patch of neon lighting inside the shop in the image.

1. Open KPT Vortex Tile and set the mode to Normal Vortex.
2. Click and drag on the Vortex Radius swatch to set the intensity to a very low level. In this case, it was set at 4.
3. Click and drag in the Preview window to place the center of the vortex where it generates an effective color cast (Figure 5.22).
4. Try different Glue options to create the final effect. Difference was used in this instance, which introduced additional color casts (Figure 5.23). Click on the OK sphere.

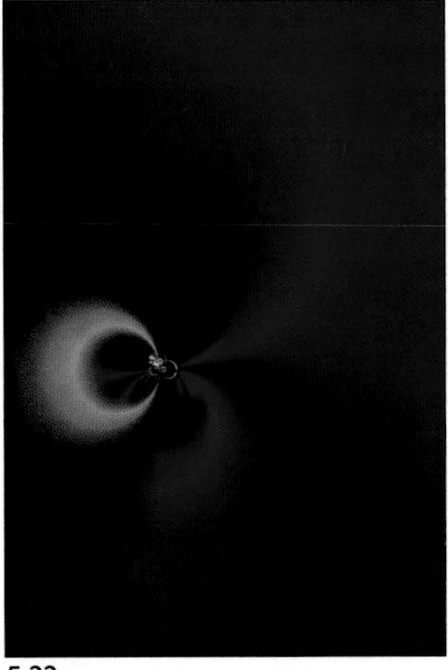

5.22

5.23

The image after applying the Vortex Tiling filter in Normal mode (5.22), and the final image after using the Difference Glue option (5.23)

Tie-Dye Diffusion

Some interesting tie-dye effects can be achieved by combining the KPT Pixel f/x filter with the KPT Gaussian f/x filter.

1. Select KPT Pixel f/x from the KPT 3.0 submenu.
2. Select Normal from the Glue Mode Gauge pop-up menu, choose Diffuse More from the Filter Mode Gauge, and adjust the

Intensity Sphere until the image is diffuse, but still recognizable. Modify the directional sphere if desired, and click on the OK sphere.

3. Choose KPT Gaussian f/x from the KPT 3.0 submenu.

4. Select Normal from the Glue pop-up menu, and Diamond from the Filter Mode Gauge. Set the opacity at 100 percent, and move the Intensity Sphere until the desired degree of the effect is achieved (85 percent in this case). The result is shown in Figure 5.24.

5.24

5.24 The tie-dye diffusion technique combines specular effects with directional blurs

Duotone, Tritone, and Quadtone Effects

Duotones, tritones, and quadtones are processes in which grayscale images are printed with one, two, or three additional colors, respectively, to enhance detail and sharpness in a portion of the tonal range. The process involves adding a printing plate for each color in addition to the black plate. When created properly, the result is a very pleasing, rich, and detailed multicolored image.

While duotone images can be created in Photoshop, which creates an image with separate channels that simulate the printing plates, it is possible to create a similar effect in KPT Gradient Designer. The effect can be achieved in either RGB or CMYK mode and is created using the filter's Grayscale Mapburst mode.

Creating a Duotone Effect

1. Open KPT Gradient Designer and select Grayscale Mapburst from the Mode control swatch (Figure 5.25).

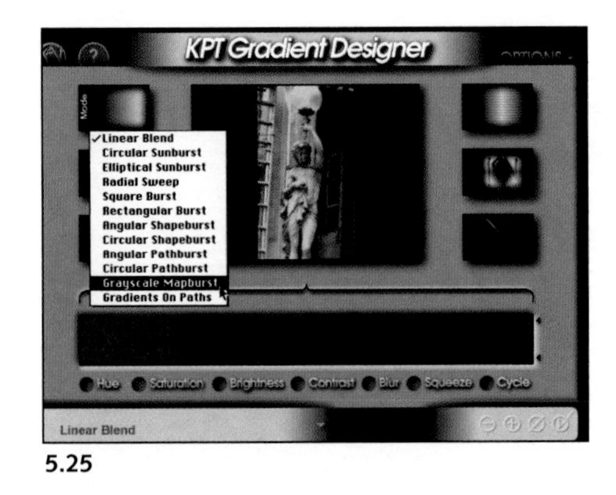

5.25

2. The color in the far right of the Gradient Bar fills the highlights of the image, and the color in the far left fills the shadow areas. Click and hold at the far right of the Gradient Bar and select a light color for the highlight portion of the gradient (Figure 5.26).

5.26

5.25 Select Grayscale Mapburst from the Mode control swatch

5.26 Select a highlight color in the color picker

3. Click and hold at the far left of the Gradient Bar and select a dark color for the shadow areas (Figure 5.27). The resulting duotone is shown in Figure 5.28.

5.27

5.28

5.27 Select a shadow color in the color picker

5.28 The resulting duotone

Creating a Tritone Effect

1. Follow the steps shown in "Creating a Duotone Effect."

2. Click on the center of the Gradient Bar and choose a third color, which will be assigned to the midtone areas of the image (Figure 5.29). (For best results, in each step select colors that simulate the highlight, midtone, and shadow portions of the tonal range.) The final image is shown in Figure 5.30.

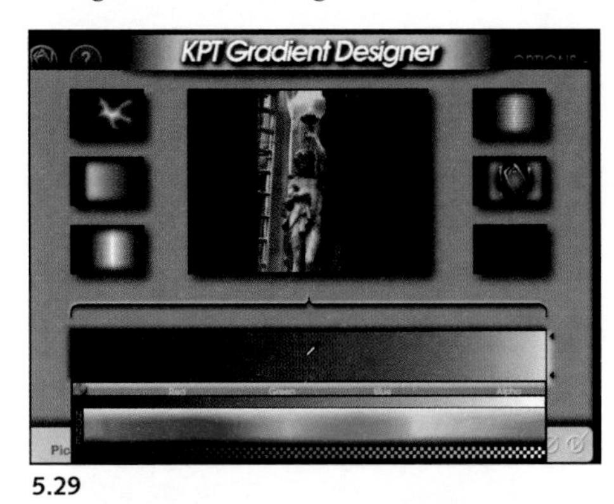

5.29

5.30

5.29 Selecting a third color for midtones

5.30 The resulting tritone

Creating a Quadtone Effect

1. Follow the steps shown in "Creating a Tritone Effect."
2. Click on the Gradient Bar at about the one-quarter point from the left end and drag toward the center of the bar to sample the original center color. This moves the midtone color to the three-quarter-tone portion of the bar.
3. Click on the far left end of the Gradient Bracket and drag it to the halfway point in the Gradient Bar. Click at the center of the Gradient Bar and sample a lighter color for the quarter tones (Figure 5.31). It is necessary to move the bracket in this case; otherwise, the selection of the quarter tones to the right will wipe out your previous color selections. The resulting quadtone is shown in Figure 5.32.

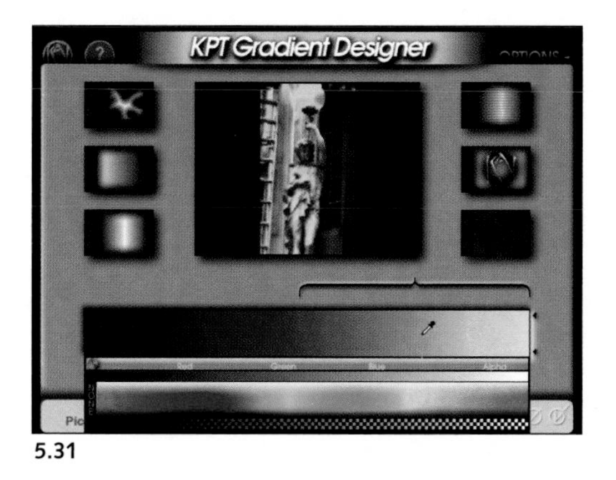

5.31

Once the colors are selected for the tonal areas, it is possible to tweak the effect further using the following methods:

- Using the image in the Preview window as a guide, click and drag on the Squeeze and Cycle buttons to push the color into other tonal areas of the image.
- Click and drag on the Contrast button to enhance the detail in certain areas of the image.
- Click and drag on the Hue button to cycle through various color sets.
- Press Command-F to flip the gradient colors, which transposes the shadow, highlight, and midtone colors.

5.31 Selecting the color for the quarter tones

5.32

Embossing an Image in KPT Spheroid Designer

This technique embosses a copy of an image onto spheres created in KPT Spheroid Designer.

1. Open the image to be embossed and select Save a Copy As from the File menu. Save the image as a PICT file (Figure 5.33).

5.33

5.32 The resulting quadtone

5.33 The original PICT file that will be mapped to the sphere

2. Close the original image file and open a new Photoshop file that is the size you want the sphere to be.

3. Open KPT Spheroid Designer from the KPT 3.0 submenu (Filter/KPT 3.0/KPT Spheroid Designer).

4. Click and hold on the Bump Map Menu, and select the Bump Map Manager from the pop-up menu (Figure 5.34).

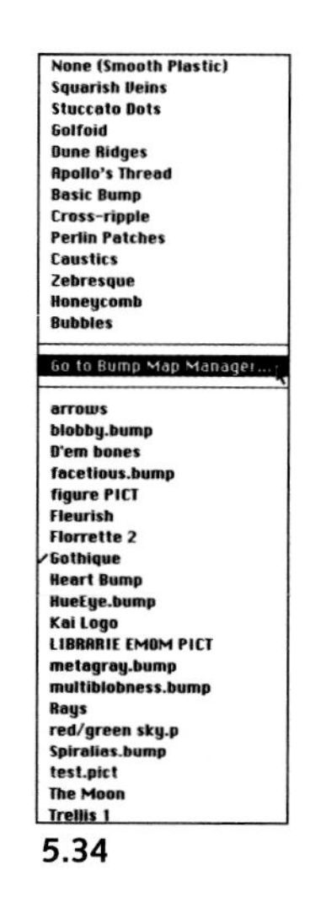

5.34

5. Click on the Import button, and select the PICT file you saved earlier (Figure 5.35).

5.35

5.34 Select the Bump Map Manager from the Bump Map Menu

5.35 Import the PICT file as a bump map

6. Click and hold on the Bump Map Menu again, and select the PICT file that you just imported (Figure 5.36).

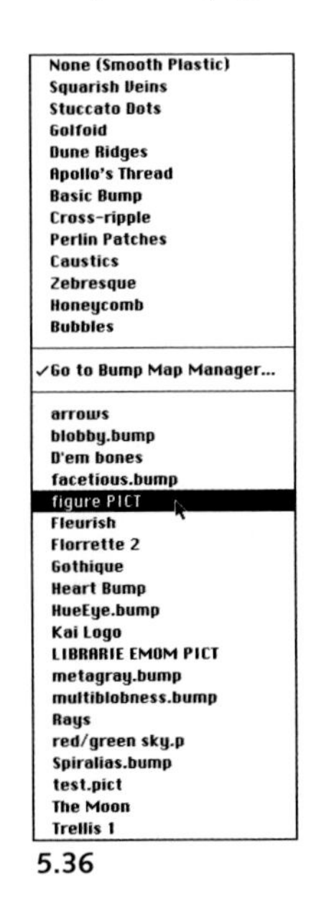

5.36

7. Click and drag in the Texture Swatch to position the desired portion of the image on the sphere.

8. Click OK to create the sphere. The result is shown in Figure 5.37.

5.37

5.36 Select the PICT bump map you just imported from the Bump Map Menu

5.37 The sphere created using the PICT-image bump map

Fractals Explained

The word *fractal* was coined by mathematician Benoit Mandelbrot in 1975 to describe the irregular, infinite shapes found both in nature and in his mathematical calculations. It comes from the Latin word fractus, which is derived from the verb frangere, meaning "to break." Fractals can be segmented into two groups: linear and nonlinear. Linear fractals are also called classical fractals, and their primary characteristic is that the smaller components, called seeds, resemble the overall shape exactly. The graphic designs of M. C. Escher demonstrate some of the principles of linear fractal calculations. Nonlinear fractals have smaller components that resemble the larger shape, but do not mirror it exactly. Therefore, they cannot be generated in a linear fashion, and instead map a given area that folds in on itself in endless repetition. These nonlinear fractals are the types explored in Kai's Power Tools; specifically, in the Mandelbrot and Julia sets.

5.38

Most artists who have worked with computer graphics for any length of time can easily recognize a fractal image (Figure 5.38). But ask them to describe the theory behind fractals and how they are generated, and you will often get blank stares. That is because what lies behind the fractal image is nothing but cold, calculated mathematics—and complex math at that. Given most artists' aversion to mathematics, we are faced with a paradox: We are drawn to the graphic images created by fractals, yet are repelled by the mechanics of how they are created.

This is what makes Kai's achievement in the KPT Fractal Explorer so significant. He has allowed us to experience all of the beauty that these images offer, without having to deal with any of the calculations. For example: The Mandelbrot set equals all points where the iterated function

5.38 A fractal image

$Zn=1 <- Zn2 + c$ (where the initial value $Z0 = 0$)

does not produce values that grow to infinity. This is the formula that creates the beautiful images in the Mandelbrot set. Kai has found a way for us to click and drag to intuitively explore the intrinsic beauty found in these images—without doing the math.

For those of you who want to know more, there are many excellent books available on fractal geometry, such as Exploring Fractals on the Macintosh by Bernt Wahl (Addison—Wesley, 1995). Fractals are created through the use of an imaginary number that is expressed as

$i = \sqrt{-1}$.

The result of this equation, when calculated once, equals a point on a graph called the complex plane. When calculated repeatedly, the results are plotted on the complex plane, and together define an area, thus creating the images you generate in KPT Fractal Explorer.

The colors generated by a fractal equation are also specifically delineated. The inside of the fractal is usually shown as a flat plane, and it is often colored black. The inside is flat because it represents points that will calculate themselves into infinity (generated by the square root of –1), and therefore they cannot be quantified. It is the outside of the fractal image that usually results in a variety of swirling colors. The outside colors are created by points that have moved outside of the infinite area after a number of calculations. They are said to have "escaped the set," and their color is a time-based rendering of the number of calculations it took for them to do so.

In KPT Fractal Explorer, you have the option of looking at the Julia set or the Mandelbrot set, or a combination of the two. Benoit Mandelbrot first plotted the Mandelbrot set with a computer in 1980, and the set refers to the area plotted by his equation. Mandelbrot was not the first to explore this subject, however. His work built on that of French mathematician Gaston Julia, who pioneered this area in the early part of the 20th century. Julia published a paper in 1918 that described a fractal set whose curve angles are distorted because their value remains constant. This set was one of the earliest fractal iterations, and it has been studied intensely ever since because of the variety and complexity within it. The amazing thing about the Julia set is that it was all calculated by hand, without any computerized assistance, and was communicated entirely as formula, save for a few hand drawings.

KPT allows you to explore the Mandelbrot and Julia sets either separately or in tandem (using a combination of the two formulas). Rather than pulling out your slide rule or programmer's manual, though, all you need is a mouse and a color monitor to experience the intense fractal visuals that Gaston Julia could only imagine.

Understanding and Using the Glue Options

The Glue swatch, which is present in almost all of the KPT interfaces, offers several ways to apply effects to your image. Glue options are also referred to as apply modes, channel operations (ChOps, for short—a term Kai coined), and calculations. The basic idea behind Glue is that the image data is combined with the filter effect to create a unique result. The various ways of combining—actually, comparing—the image with the effect achieves the different results. The available Glue options are Normal (sometimes referred to as Normal Apply), Procedural +, Procedural –, Difference, Lighten Only, Darken Only, Add, Subtract, Multiply, and Screen.

In pre-3.0 versions of KPT, as well as in version 3.0 of Photoshop itself, it was (and, for Photoshop, still is) important to understand what these options were and how they worked. It took a little work to apply these effects, which were somewhat intimidating for the uninitiated to master. But with KPT 3.0, Kai has made the ChOps (Glue) accessible to everyone with just the click of a button. Clicking and holding on the Glue control swatch provides a pop-up menu listing the options, or just clicking on it cycles through the options without making a menu selection.

In an experimental sense, you don't need to understand what happens when you select a Glue option, and it's always better to trust one's eyes than to trust a formula. For those who simply want to experiment, the details that follow are primarily for your curiosity. Given that the Glue result is based on the image as well as the effect, it will seem that the result is what it is, and all that remains is to look and see if you can use it. That's the nature of experimentation.

But what if you could do some preprocessing to enhance a particular result? For example, if you know that Lighten Only compares each pair of pixels in both the image and the effect and uses only the lighter of the two, what would happen if you lightened the image using Photoshop's Curves before opening KPT? Or what would happen if you created an effect in KPT by intentionally using tones that were lighter than those in the image? Knowing how these Glue options are applied allows you to be proactive in achieving certain results. The remainder of this section looks at how the Glue options work and discusses ways of going beyond the passive observation of results.

Comparative Test Strips

To illustrate how the Glue options work, I created a basic test strip containing three elements: a row of five tonal squares, a grayscale gradient above the squares, and a color gradient beneath the squares (Figure 5.39). Both the squares and the grayscale gradient represent the Photoshop image; the color gradient is a reference (I'll explain this more in a moment). The five squares have tints of 100 percent, 75 percent, 50 percent, 25 percent, and 0 percent black, and the smooth grayscale gradient ranges from 100 to 0 percent black. Both the grayscale tints and grayscale in the gradient represent the Photoshop image's tonal range (shadows to highlights). Note that all grays are made up of RGB values—equal amounts of red, green, and blue produce a neutral gray.

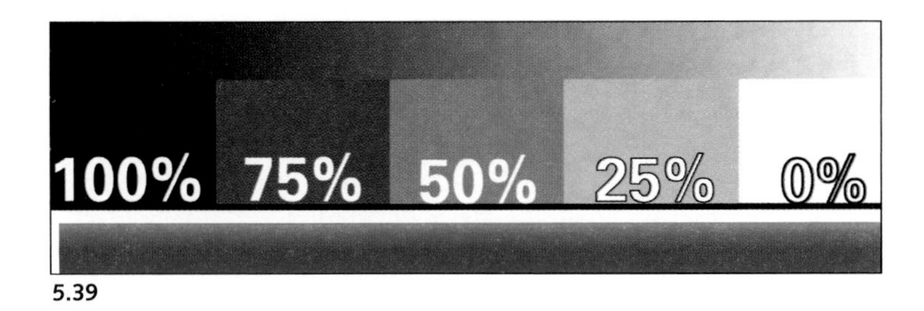

5.39

5.39 The basic test strip

For each Glue option, I used KPT Gradient Designer to create a red-to-blue vertical gradient that was identical to the reference gradient. The target for the KPT gradient was a bar-shaped selection that straddled the tinted squares and the grayscale gradient. After creating the same KPT gradient each time, I selected a different Glue option and clicked OK. In each test strip, the resulting KPT gradient shows how the KPT filter effect's impact on the Photoshop image changes, depending on the Glue option, and where in the tonal range those changes occur. (I used grayscale so these changes would be readily apparent.)

KPT filters manipulate a copy of the Photoshop image, generating a second set of image data for the KPT filter effect. KPT Texture Explorer, for example, generates its random textures from a copy of the Photoshop image. Once you click OK and the filter is applied, the KPT effect data overwrites the Photoshop image data. Glue options modify the KPT filter effect as it's applied by comparing the pixels in the KPT effect with the pixels in the Photoshop image, each in a different way.

This exercise does not show or explain how colors interact with each other—an entire volume could be written on the color theories behind the algorithms. But you can use the results as a guide for Glue options in any KPT filter, not just Gradient Designer. If you understand the tonal-value characteristics of the Glue options, you are off to a good start.

Normal

In the Normal option, the KPT effect is laid on top of the Photoshop image, obscuring it unless you build transparency into the effect (the KPT effect gradient is identical to the reference gradient; Figure 5.40).

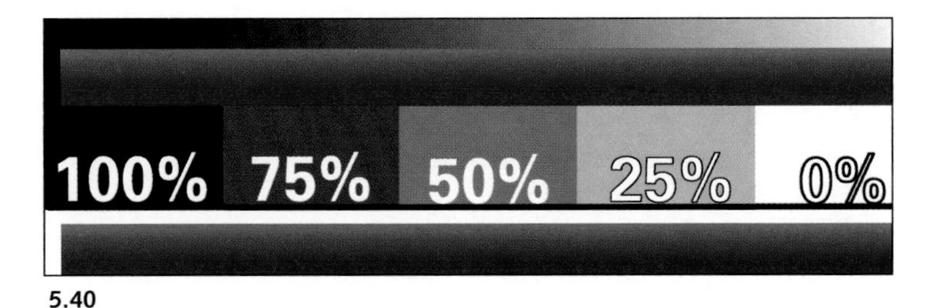

5.40

5.40 Normal test strip

Procedural +

The Procedural + option modifies the brightness of the KPT effect based on the pixel values in the Photoshop image. If the pixel in the Photoshop image is brighter than a 50 percent midtone, then the KPT effect is also brightened by the same amount. For example, if a pixel in the Photoshop image has a tonal value of 77 percent, the brightness of the KPT effect applied to it is increased by 27 percent (77 – 50 = 27). Following the same logic, any pixels with values below a 50 percent midtone would have a darker-than-average effect applied to it. As you can see in Figure 5.41, the natural extremes of white and black are left unchanged in the image, and the KPT effect is most obvious in the midtones. This allows KPT effects to be applied to Photoshop images so that the image remains intact (provided that the original Photoshop image has sufficient highlights and shadows, which are not altered by the Procedural + Glue option).

5.41

5.41 Procedural + test strip

Procedural –

The Procedural — option modifies brightness in the KPT effect, just as Procedural + does. The key difference is that Procedural — looks at the brightness of the KPT effect's pixels rather than the brightness of the Photoshop image's pixels (Figure 5.42). In comparing the test strips for Procedural – with Procedural +, you can see that the brighter areas of the Procedural – gradient remain constant across the test strip and are applied equally regardless of what is happening in the Photoshop image. In the areas of the KPT effect that are below average brightness, Procedural – is applied with less intensity to the Photoshop image, allowing more of the Photoshop image to show through. With the Procedural – option, the KPT effect tends to predominate over the Photoshop image, sometimes obscuring it altogether.

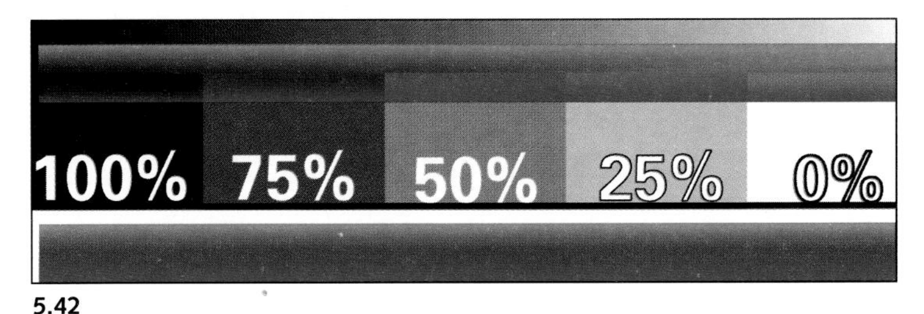

5.42

5.42 Procedural – test strip

Difference

Difference applies the KPT effect colors normally in the shadows and midtones of the Photoshop image, while reversing the KPT effect's colors in the highlight areas (Figure 5.43). The Difference option compares the RGB values of both the KPT effect and the Photoshop image pixels. It subtracts the lowest value from the highest, so that a positive number is always maintained. This means that if the KPT effect is the highest value, the Photoshop image is subtracted from it; if the Photoshop image is the highest value, the KPT effect is subtracted. The results are very dramatic because the calculations are applied to each channel rather than cumulatively. Therefore, calculating (i.e., subtracting the lower of the values from the higher) the blue-magenta color in the middle of the KPT gradient—which has an RGB value of R: 113, G: 29, and B: 161—and the midtone tint square, whose values are R: 146, G: 146, and B: 146, yields a color of R: 33, G: 117, and B: 15, which of course is very high in green and the opposite of magenta. The red and blue go toward their opposites, which are cyan and yellow, respectively. Difference almost always results in bright color effects that are more dramatic in the highlights and midtones and more stable in the shadows.

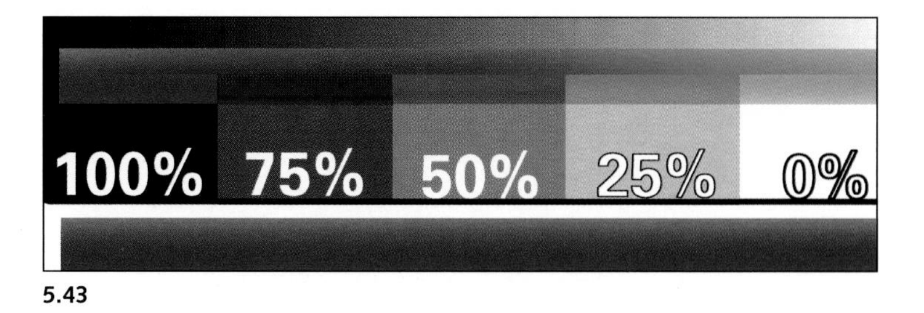

5.43

Lighten Only

Lighten Only applies the KPT effect primarily in the shadows and midtones, leaving the highlight areas of the Photoshop image relatively untouched (Figure 5.44). Lighten Only compares the RGB values of the KPT effect pixels and the Photoshop image pixels, and uses only the higher (lighter) of the two. For example, the 50 percent swatch in the test strip has equal red, green, and blue values of 146. In that area, all of the KPT effect values below 146 are eliminated and replaced with 146. Only the extreme blue and red areas, with values higher than 146, show through. Lighten Only reduces the effect in the highlights and applies it full blast in the shadows.

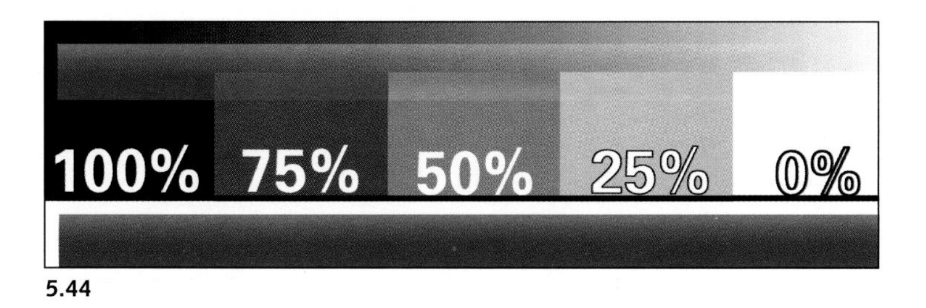

5.44

Darken Only

Darken Only applies the KPT effect primarily in the highlights and midtones, leaving the shadow areas of the Photoshop image relatively untouched (Figure 5.45). Many people mistakenly think that Darken Only is the opposite of Lighten Only. In fact, Darken Only looks at brightness values, while Lighten Only looks at RGB values. Darken Only darkens the KPT effect globally.

5.43 Difference test strip

5.44 The Lighten Only test strip

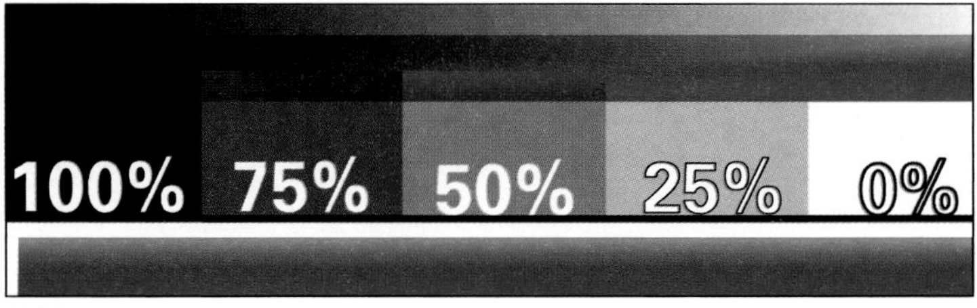

5.45

Add

As its name suggests, the Add option adds the RGB values of both the KPT effect and Photoshop image pixels, clipping the results at 255. This brightens the KPT effect as it is applied to the highlight areas of the Photoshop image, leaving the KPT effect at full strength in the shadows (Figure 5.46). Unlike the Lighten Only option, which chooses the lighter of two pixels, Add combines their values. This results in a much more luminous, glowing effect.

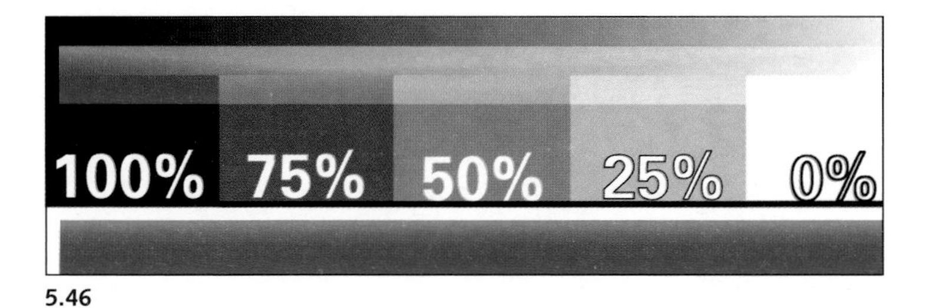

5.46

Subtract

In Subtract option, the color of the KPT effect is always reversed as it is applied to the Photoshop image (Figure 5.47). Applying a blue gradient with Subtract will add yellow to the image, while red gradients yield cyan and green gradients create magenta. In addition, the KPT effect is more subdued in the shadow areas of the Photoshop image and more intense in the highlight areas. The Subtract option is similar to the Difference option in that it subtracts the RGB values of the KPT effect pixel from those of

5.45 The Darken Only test strip

5.46 The Add test strip

the Photoshop image pixel. Unlike the Difference option, however, Subtract does not automatically subtract the lower from the higher value to maintain a positive pixel value. Instead, it always subtracts the KPT effect value from the Photoshop image value, which makes the KPT effect less obvious in the shadows.

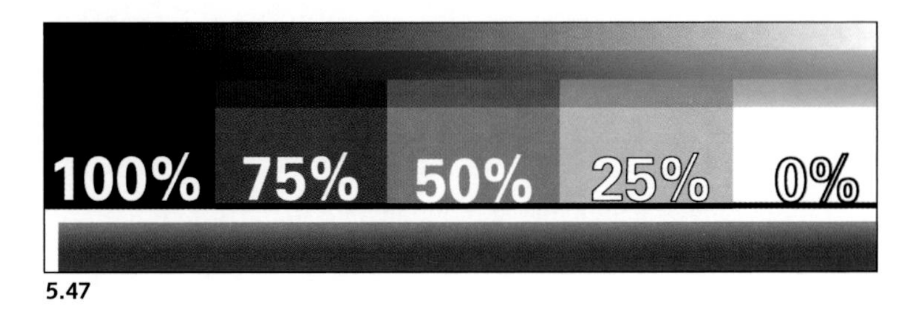

5.47

Multiply

The Multiply option acts like the opposite of the Add option, because it progressively darkens the KPT effect as it is applied (Figure 5.48). The results are achieved by comparing the brightness and decreasing the overall value. Rather than get tied up in the math on this one, just imagine both the effect and the image as slide transparencies. By laying one on top of the other and holding them to the light, they will block out more light where they overlap, getting progressively darker.

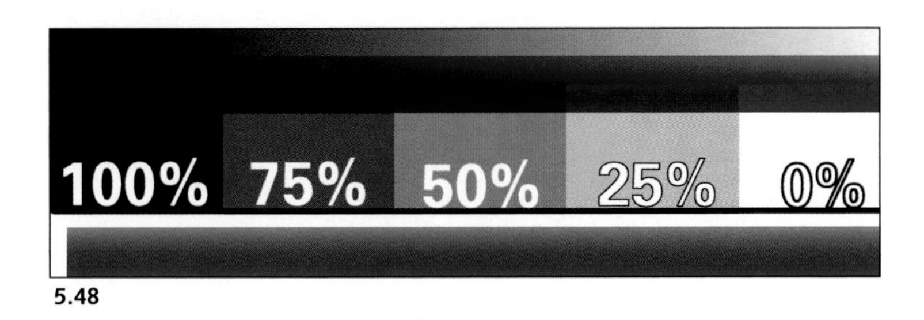

5.48

Screen

Screen applies only the lighter RGB values of the KPT effect to the Photoshop image (Figure 5.49). Unlike the Add option, which combines the pixel values to a maximum of 255, Screen simply

5.47 The Subtract test strip

5.48 The Multiply test strip

chooses the higher of the two. The two options are very similar, although more of the image shows through with the Screen option because its lighter pixels are left unchanged. In the Add option, the effect is more luminous, given that the values are combined to achieve a higher (brighter) value.

5.49

With the exception of Difference and Subtract, the Glue options do one of two things: They either lighten or they darken the effect as it is applied. These modifications can be based on the RGB values or to the luminosity, which dictates the overall brightness of the image. The modifications are either cumulative or selective; that is, they either add the effect and the image pixel values together, or they select the lightest or darkest values. These changes do not introduce any hues outside those present in either the effect or the image.

Subtract and Difference subtract the KPT effect from the Photoshop image pixel values (or vice versa), which results in dramatic color changes. Subtract follows a predictable course, since it tends to push the effect toward a darker tonal range. Difference is unpredictable, since it varies the way it calculates values in order to keep all values positive.

Knowledge Is Power

As mentioned earlier, the KPT Glue options have become so simple to use that it is not necessary for the casual user to understand the logic behind them. The variations can be seen by clicking on the Glue control swatch, and the results evaluated quickly and easily.

5.49 The Screen test strip

We have seen, however, that these options apply the KPT effects to various parts of the tonal range, affecting either brightness or RGB values, often being sensitive to either the highlights, midtones, or shadows. Knowing where the option is going to apply the KPT effect can help you determine which image to use or which KPT effect to apply. The exercises and examples in this section show just a few things that can be done when you consider the Glue options ahead of time.

Procedural +

Procedural + is effective for altering the midtones of an image. The easiest way to check for midtones is to go to the Channels palette in Photoshop and look at the grayscale renditions of the image in the Red, Green, and Blue channels. Areas that are free from pure blacks or whites will be most affected by the Procedural + option. Use the sponge tool in combination with the dodge and burn tools to reduce saturation and push specific pixel values toward the midrange. Procedural + is also very effective in coloring black-and-white images because of the way it leaves the shadows and highlights alone.

This exercise shows the benefits of using the Procedural + mode to alter the midtones of an image. The water in this image of a red beach toy looked a little lifeless to me (Figure 5.50). I wanted to add more contrast and perhaps more color saturation in the water, without affecting the red beach toy. In looking at this image in the Channels palette, I discovered that the red beach toy was considered either a highlight or a shadow by each of the Red, Green, and Blue channels, and that the remainder of the image was rich in midtone information. Thus, a KPT effect with the Procedural + option will be applied primarily to the water area and will ignore the bright red beach toy.

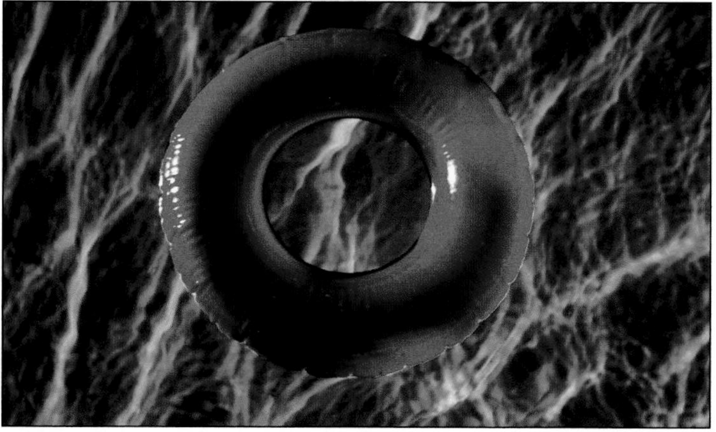

5.50

1. With the original image open, launch KPT Gradient Designer and select Procedural + from the Glue control swatch.

2. Create a gradient that achieves the desired effect (here, I added color saturation in the waves and bumped up the contrast). The Preview window shows the result (Figure 5.51).

5.51

5.50 Original image

5.51 The Preview Window updates all channels

3. Click OK to apply the effect. Procedural + allows the water area to be enhanced without affecting the bright red color (Figure 5.52). Without the Procedural + Glue option, the red would very likely have flattened out or oversaturated as the background was modified. (More examples using Procedural + are shown in Figures 5.53 and 5.54.)

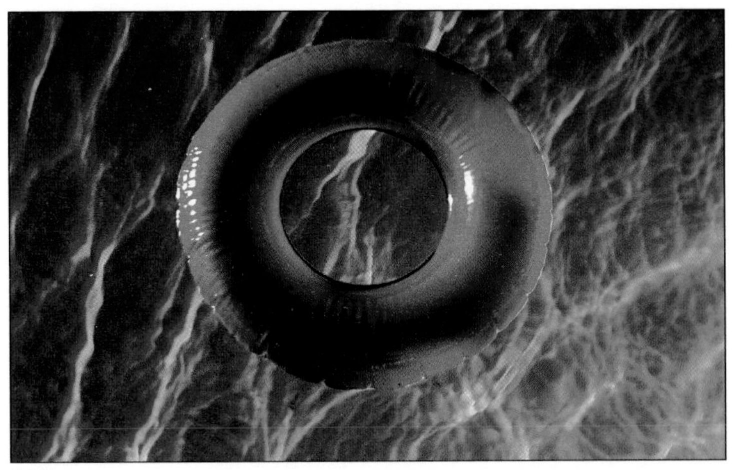

5.52

5.53

5.52 The image after applying the Procedural + option in KPT Gradient Designer

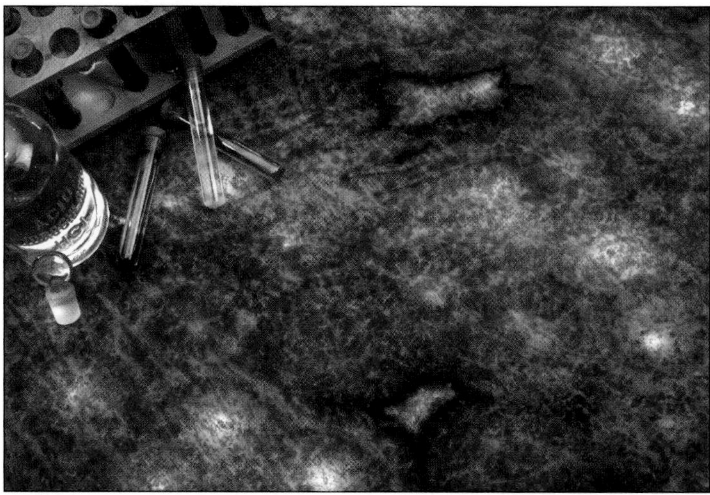

5.54

Difference

Difference is perhaps the most experimental of all the Glue options, creating striking and vibrant colors with strong hues. Difference tends to apply the KPT effect normally in the dark areas, and to reverse the color in the light areas. In Figures 5.55 through 5.57, notice how the KPT Gradient Designer effect is pushed into the black railing in the upper-left corner, as well as the dark corner in the lower right. It is in the lighter colors that Difference gets unpredictable, creating dramatic and sometimes beautiful results.

5.55

5.56

5.57

5.54 These before (5.53) and after (5.54) images show a KPT Texture Explorer effect pushed into the midtones using the application principles of Procedural +

5.55 The original image (5.55); the KPT Gradient created for it (5.56); and the image after the Difference Glue option is applied with the effect (5.57)

Combining Effects

Some very complex effects can be achieved by using the Glue options in combination with each other to make changes to different areas in the image. In some cases, it may be best to apply effects to only one of the RGB or CMYK channels, while at other times, isolating areas via selections seems to work best. This exercise uses both strategies to illustrate the wide range of results that can be achieved by applying Glue options in combination. It uses the same beach toy image shown in the Procedural + section (Figure 5.58).

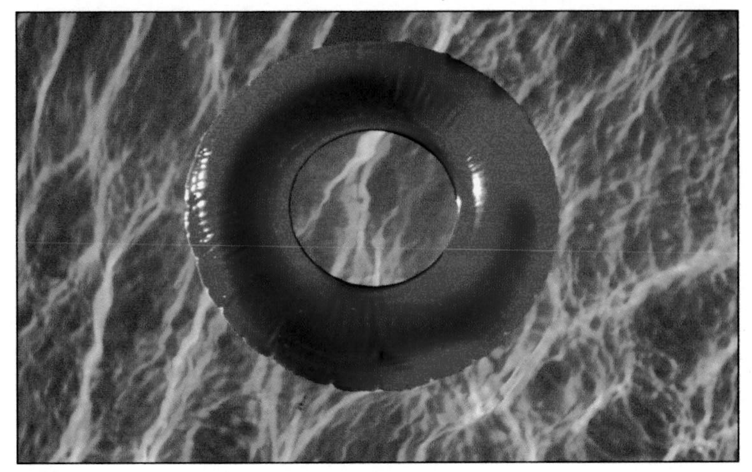

5.58

1. Select the red beach toy and make a copy of it.
2. Open the Channels palette in Photoshop and select only the Red channel; the image will change to grayscale (Figure 5.59). In this case, the Red channel has a lot of dark information in the water, with virtually no information in the beach toy (technically, the highlight area in this channel).

5.58 The original image

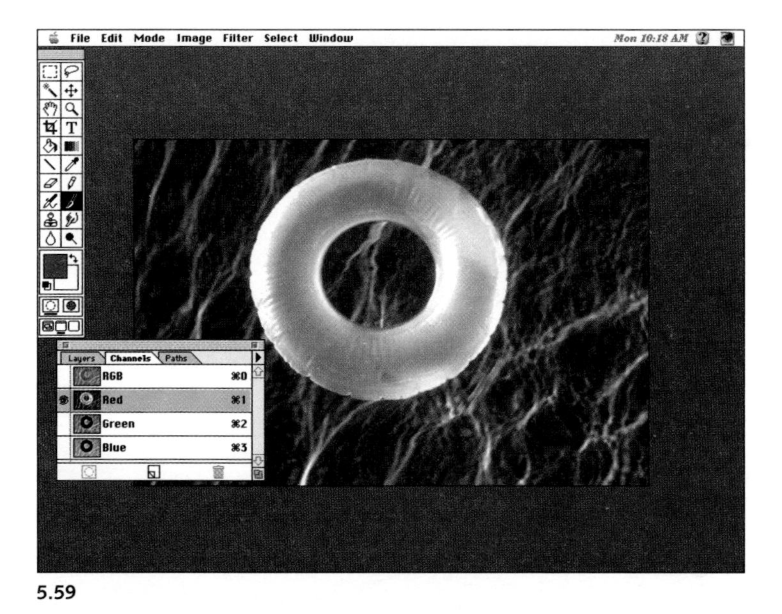

5.59

3. Select KPT Planar Tiling from the Filter menu, and click and drag in the Preview window to reduce the size of the tiles (the Scale) to 100, with a rotation value of zero (Figure 5.60).

5.60

4. Select Subtract from the Glue control swatch, and click OK. This reverses the tiled beach toys out of the water area and darkens the larger beach toy. Subtract acts like Difference in that it reverses the color of the KPT effect as it is applied to the Photoshop image. Since we are in grayscale mode, this results in making what was dark light, and vice versa.

5. Select the RGB composite channel in the Channels palette to view the results thus far (Figure 5.61). Given that the lighter

5.59 Select only the Red channel, which appears in grayscale

5.60 The KPT Planar Tile interface settings

areas of a channel show its respective color with more intensity, it comes as no surprise that the lighter areas of the Red channel (the tiled beach toys) show through as the brightest red. The large beach toy from the original image is no longer bright red, given that it was reversed to black by the Subtract option. When all three channels are viewed together, the Green and Blue channels partially obscure the tiled effect, creating greater depth in the image. This depth would not have been the same if the tiled effect had been applied to the image as a whole, rather than just to the Red channel.

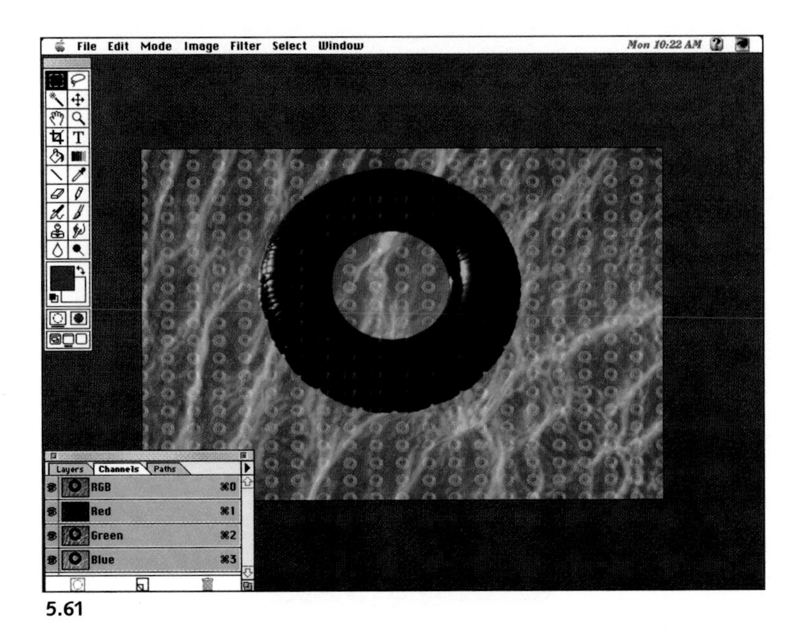

5.61

6. Having applied the KPT Planar Tiling effect, paste the previously copied selection of the beach toy into the image, and drag it into its original position. While it is still selected, drag the opacity slider to 50 percent (Figure 5.62). Save the selection (Select/Save Selection), leaving the channel name as #4.

5.61 The RGB results of KPT Planar Tile

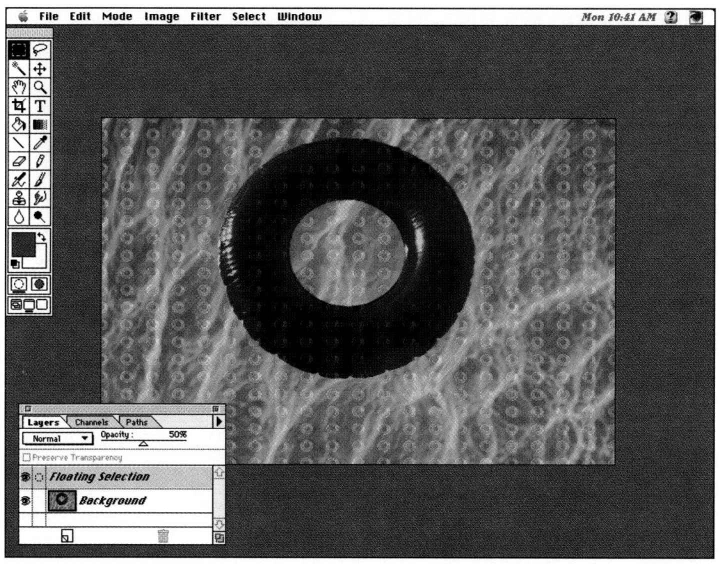

5.62

7. Choose Select None from the Select menu, and then choose Load Selection, specifying the #4 channel. The reason for saving the selection and reloading it is so that the entire area selected is impacted by the KPT effect. Otherwise, the effect is applied to only the floating selection, not to the entire area.

8. Activate KPT Vortex Tiling and create a vortex that introduces a pattern of beach toys into the selected area. Click and drag in the Preview window to place the center of the vortex in the middle of the circle. Drag on the Vortex Radius button to select an intensity value of 51. Choose Darken Only as the Glue option and click OK (Figure 5.63). The results are shown in Figure 5.64.

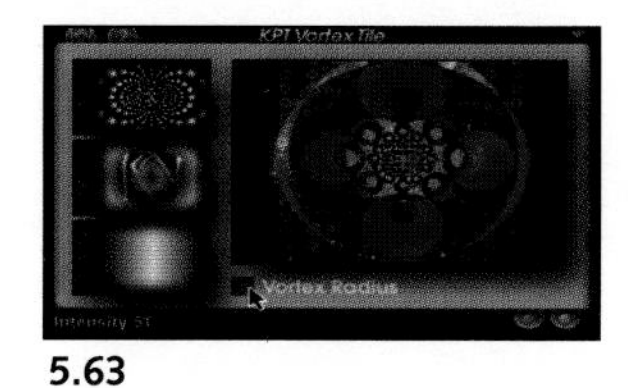

5.63

5.62 Paste the beach toy back into position and reduce its opacity to 50 percent in the Layers palette

5.63 The KPT Vortex Tiling interface settings

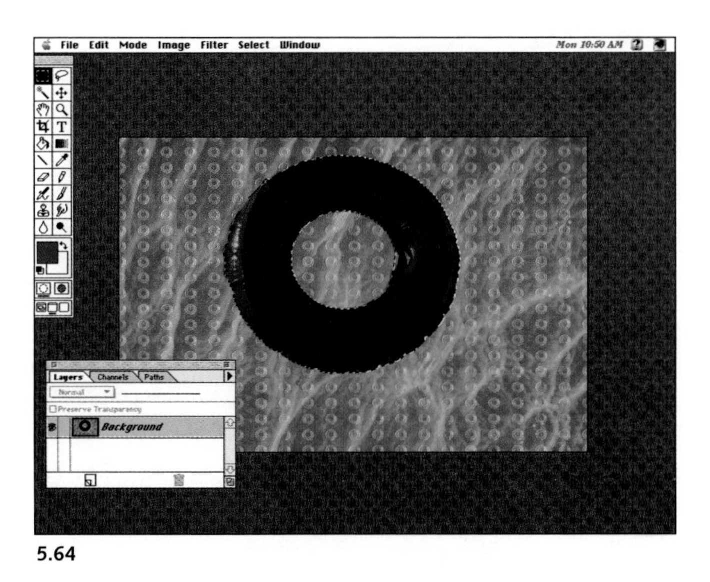

5.64

9. After the vortex effect is applied, select Paste Into from the Edit menu to paste another copy of the beach toy selection over the Vortex Tiling effect. Lower the opacity slider in the Layers palette to 51 percent, and deselect (Figure 5.65).

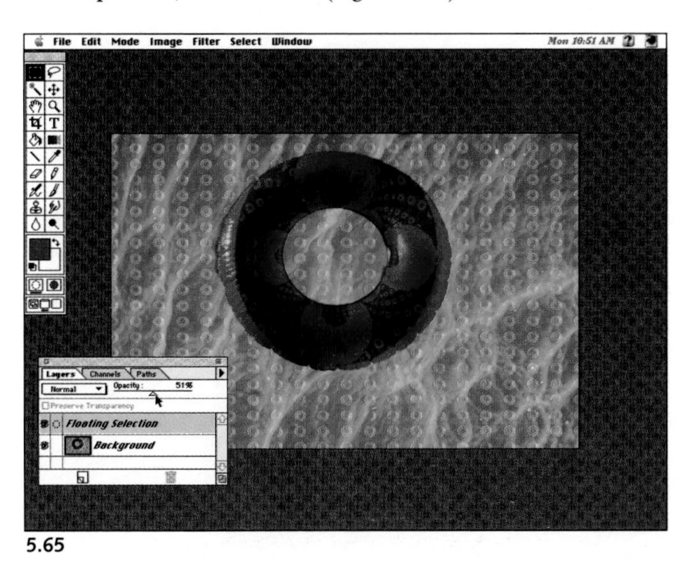

5.65

5.64 The results of KPT Vortex Tiling

5.65 Paste the beach toy again, lowering the opacity slider in the Layers palette to 51 percent

10. Complete the effect by selecting the rubber stamp tool, using the From Saved option in the Rubber Stamp dialog box. Paint in the

highlights at 100 percent opacity, and reduce the opacity to soften the transition edges from the Vortex effect to the original beach toy (Figure 5.66). The results are shown in Figure 5.67.

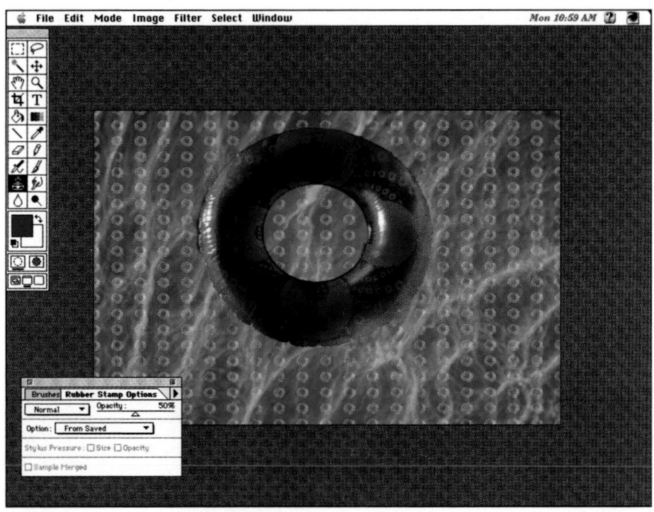

5.66

5.67

Kai's Power Tools keeps getting better and better. Interform and Spheroid Designer are great fun, especially with their animation potential. Animation effects are beyond the scope of this book, but they are worth taking the time to learn on your own. The KPT interfaces get easier to use as the buttons and procedures continue to fade into the background, allowing the creative process to remain at the forefront.

5.66 Using the Rubber Stamp tool with the From Save option, replace the highlights in the beach toy and soften the transition edges

5.67 The results show a high degree of detail seamlessly integrated into the image

Chapter 6

Exploring KPT Convolver

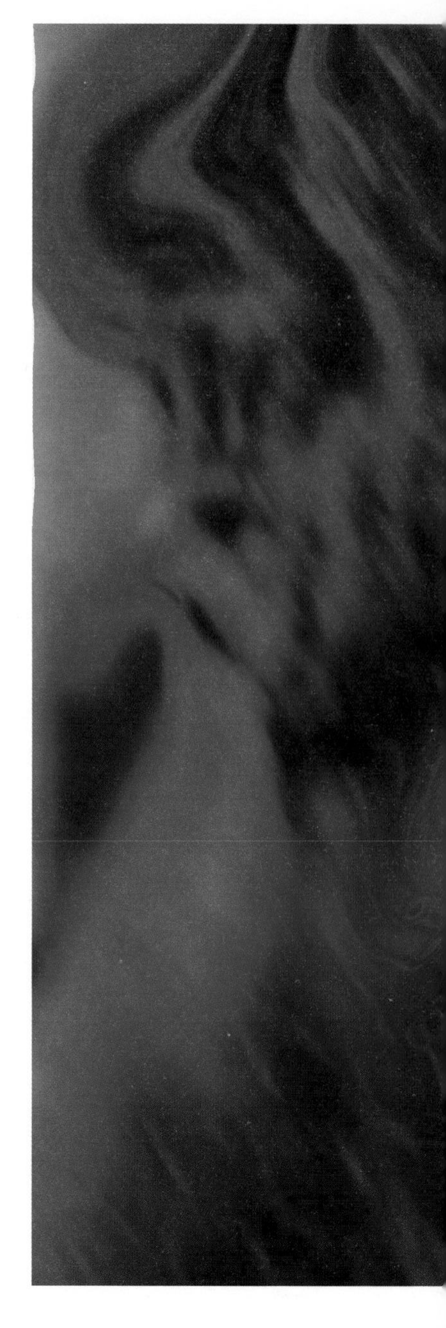

We have all heard that you can't have your cake and eat it too, that good things come to those who wait, and that the shortest distance between two points is a straight line. KPT Convolver takes a different view. It offers so much variety and control that, through intuitive exploration, you can have your cake and eat it now.

With Convolver, not only are you able to apply effects such as color, hue, saturation, and sharpen/blur from a single interface, you can vary the amount of each effect to an exacting degree. Apply a dash of sharpening, a pinch of color shift, and two cups of saturation to arrive at precisely the effect you're looking for. The program allows immediate and simultaneous access to all of its controls, is extremely fast, and is indulgent when you stray onto tangents rather than proceeding on a linear course.

The next section shows the KPT Convolver interface, with the main areas, icons, and tools labeled and described. You can use it as a reference and a guide for the information in this chapter.

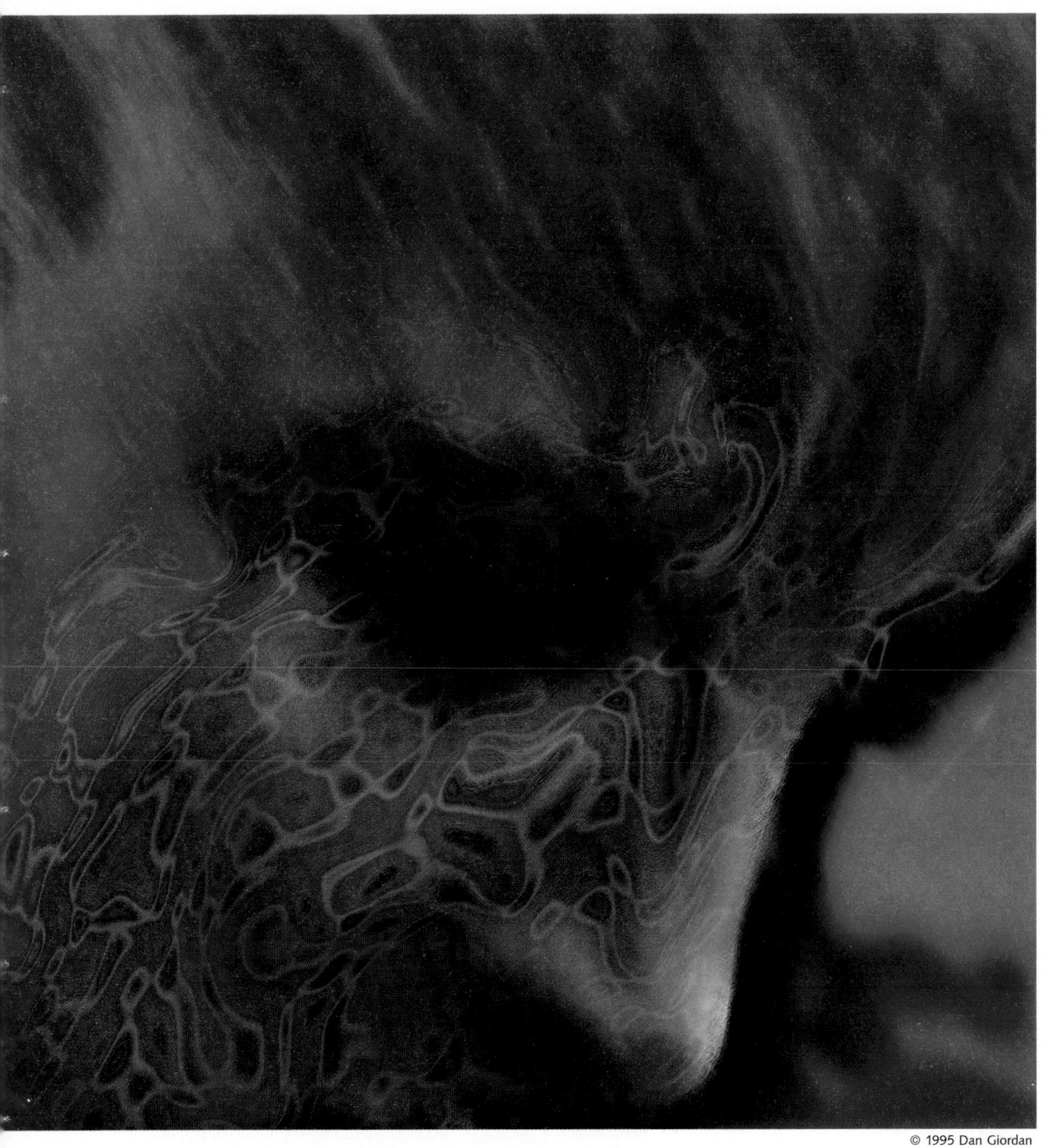

The KPT Convolver Interface

The tools and buttons in KPT Convolver can be found in three main screens: Explore mode, Design mode, and Tweak mode. The Explore, Design, and Tweak buttons allow access to their respective interfaces. The darkest button indicates the mode that is currently active. Certain controls and buttons are not available until you get your stars (see page 179 later in this chapter).

Explore Mode

The Explore mode is a great jumping-off point for all of the other modes and features in Convolver (Figure 6.2). Because there are so many possible directions, Explore helps you by making suggestions.

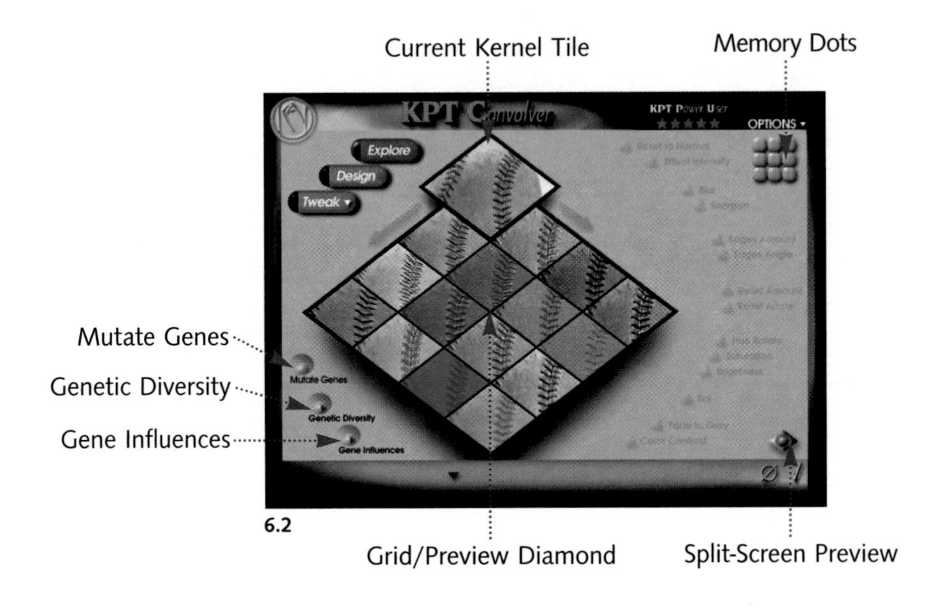

6.2

6.2 Explore Mode

The **Mutate Genes** marble generates a new set of image variations based on the variables selected in the Gene Influences pop-up menu.

The **Genetic Diversity** marble's pop-up menu determines the degree of diversity in the image variations that are created.

The **Gene Influences** marble's pop-up menu gives you control over which variables are modified. You can select overall texture or color control, and you have control over a color's hue, saturation, brightness, contrast, or tint. Texture controls allow modification of blur/sharpen, embossing, and edge detection.

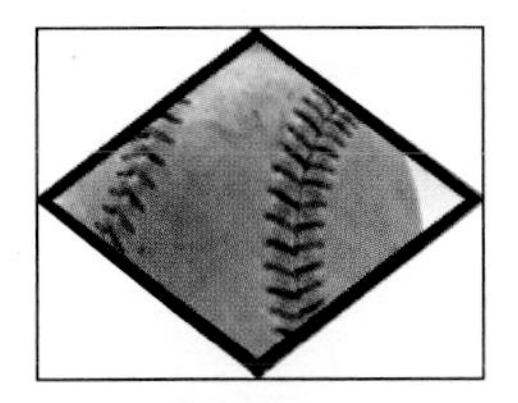

The **Current Kernel Tile** shows the results of the current kernel set, as applied to the image.

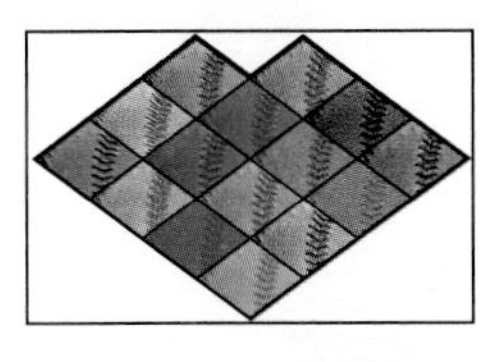

The **Grid/Preview Diamond** generates random kernel suggestions or, when in split-screen preview, compares the original image with the current effect.

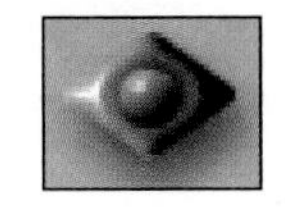

The **split-screen** preview button is added to the control set once you are awarded your second star; after activating the split-screen button in the lower right corner, you can then click on the Current Kernel Tile to divide the preview window, with half showing your original image and half showing the image with the effects you've applied to it. Split-screen is available in all three modes of Convolver.

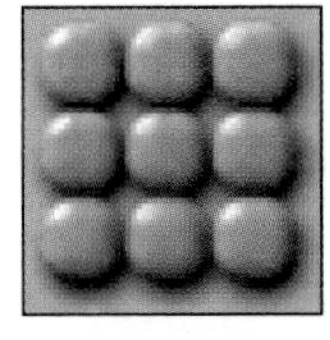

The **memory dots** are added as you are awarded your fourth star. Memory dots allow you to save specific settings as presets that can be stored as individual files or saved with the image file. They are active in all three modes; an effect can be added to them by clicking on a dot when the desired effect is shown in the Current Kernel Tile. To clear an effect from a dot, use Option-click.

Design Mode

The Design mode gives you additional creative control by allowing you to vary the degrees of polar opposites of an effect shown in the axis grid (Figure 6.3).

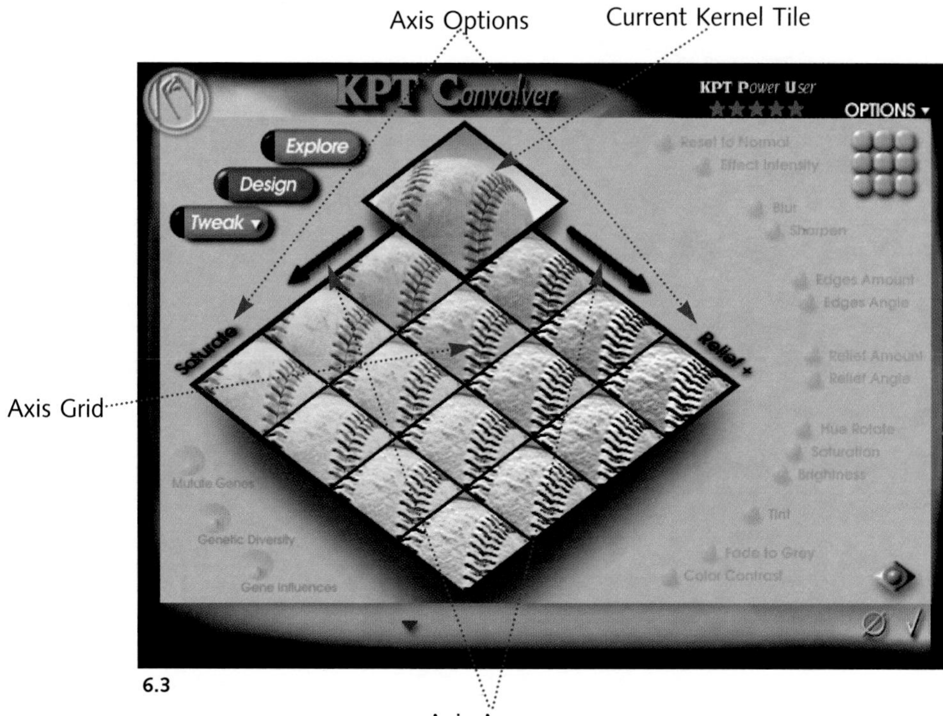

6.3

6.3 Design Mode

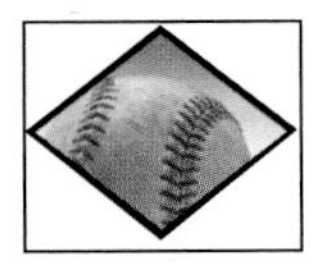

The **Current Kernel Tile** shows the results of the current kernel set, as applied to the image.

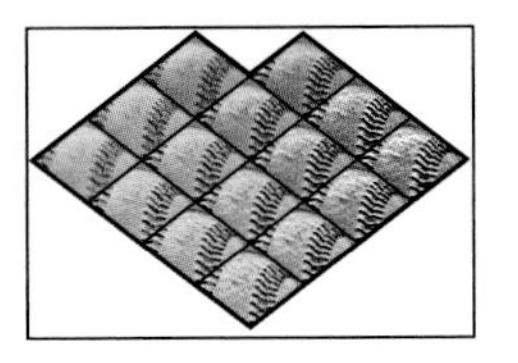

The Design mode's **axis grid** displays linear degrees of variation between the effects options selected in the pop-up menus at the far left corner and far right corners. Clicking on any square in the grid makes that effect the current selection; other variations flow from that value.

The **axis options** allow you to select an effect from the pop-up menus that appear when you click and hold on the words at the corners of the axis.

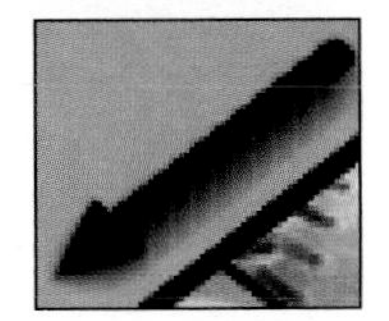

The **axis arrows** determine the degree of variation among the squares in the axis grid; variation is increased as the arrows are lengthened by clicking and dragging the arrowheads.

Tweak Mode

The marbles in Tweak mode are adjusted using a click-and-drag motion (Figure 6.4). As with a slider, dragging to the left decreases the effect's intensity; dragging to the right increases it. The only exception is the Tint marble, which has a circular control. Double-clicking on any marble returns it to its original state, applying no effect.

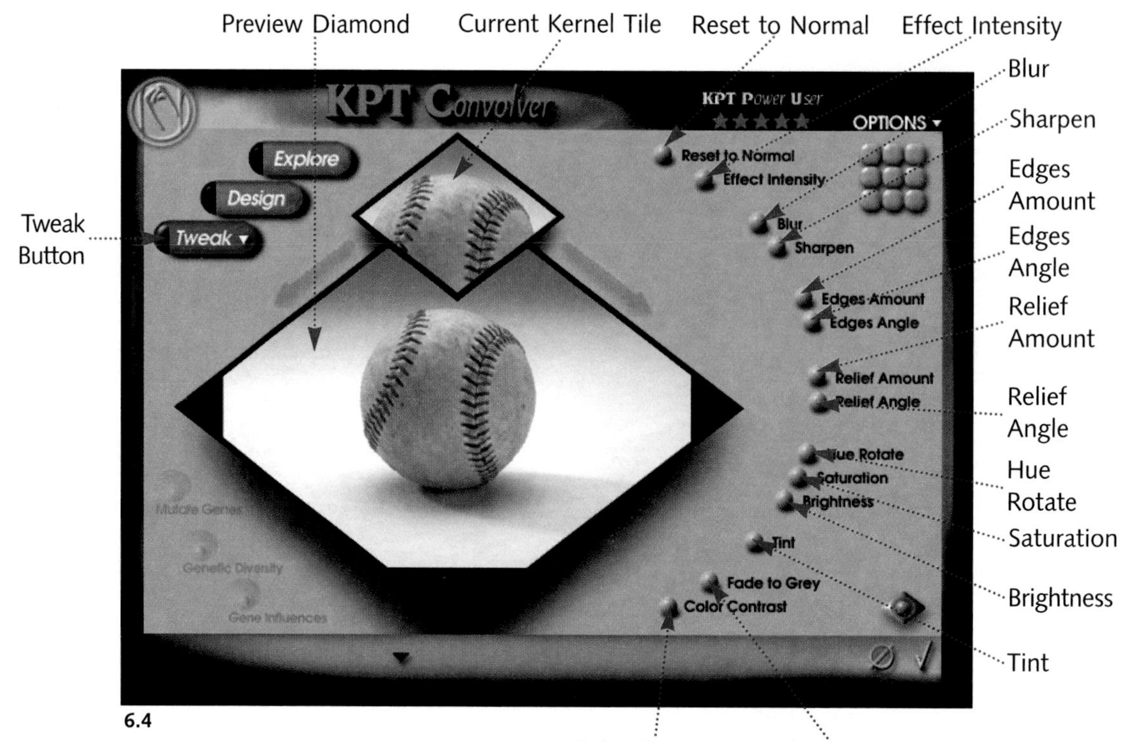

6.4 Tweak Mode

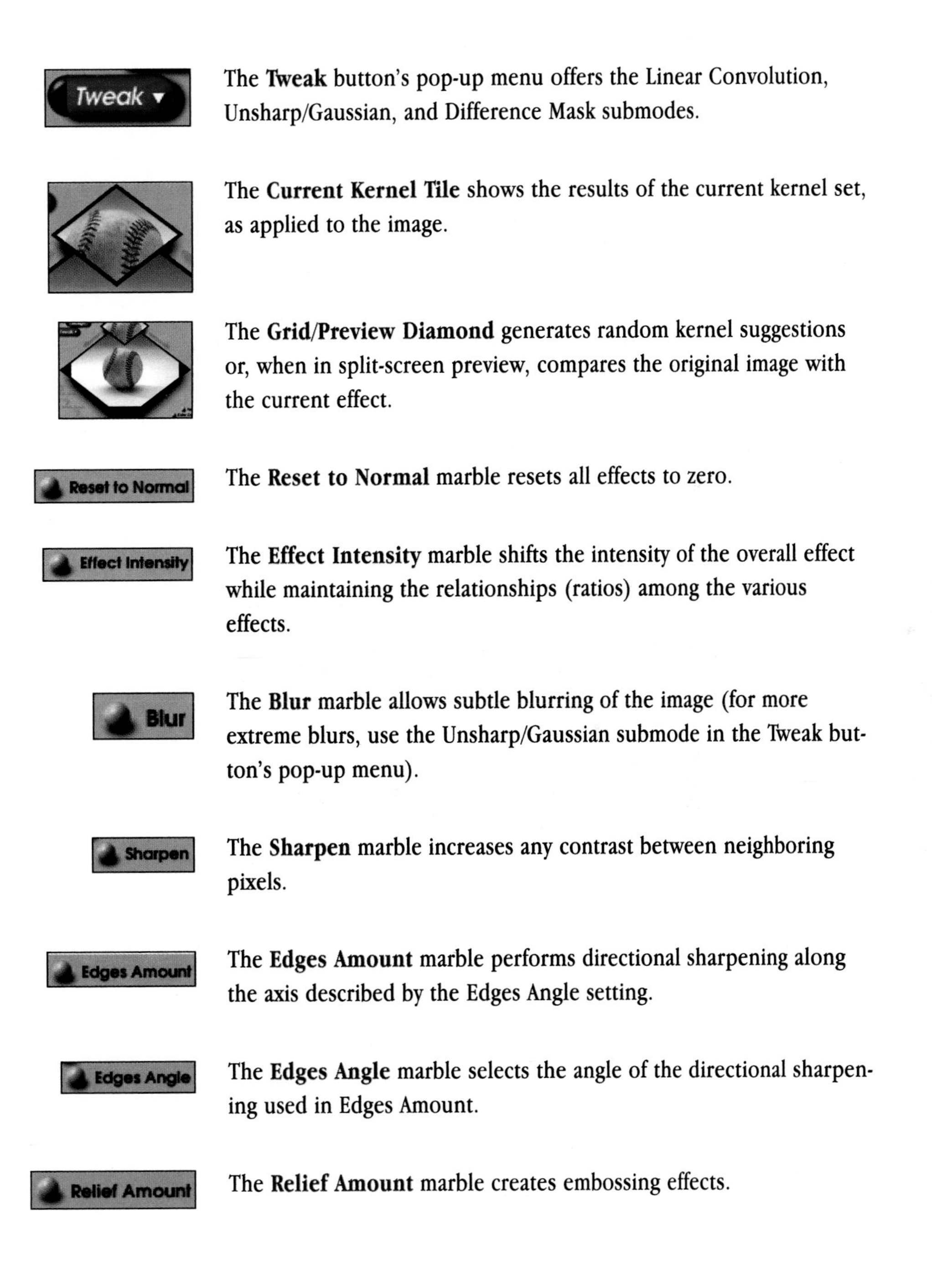

The **Tweak** button's pop-up menu offers the Linear Convolution, Unsharp/Gaussian, and Difference Mask submodes.

The **Current Kernel Tile** shows the results of the current kernel set, as applied to the image.

The **Grid/Preview Diamond** generates random kernel suggestions or, when in split-screen preview, compares the original image with the current effect.

The **Reset to Normal** marble resets all effects to zero.

The **Effect Intensity** marble shifts the intensity of the overall effect while maintaining the relationships (ratios) among the various effects.

The **Blur** marble allows subtle blurring of the image (for more extreme blurs, use the Unsharp/Gaussian submode in the Tweak button's pop-up menu).

The **Sharpen** marble increases any contrast between neighboring pixels.

The **Edges Amount** marble performs directional sharpening along the axis described by the Edges Angle setting.

The **Edges Angle** marble selects the angle of the directional sharpening used in Edges Amount.

The **Relief Amount** marble creates embossing effects.

Relief Angle

The **Relief Angle** marble determines the angle for the embossing effect set with Relief Amount.

Hue Rotate

The **Hue Rotate** marble globally changes the color of each image pixel through a "virtual color wheel."

Saturation

The **Saturation** marble increases or decreases color intensity.

Brightness

The **Brightness** marble adds or subtracts white to or from each pixel value.

Tint

The **Tint** marble allows you to select a color that tints the entire image; drag closer to the marble to decrease the saturation and further away for a more intense color change.

Fade to Grey

The **Fade to Grey** marble moves all color in the image toward neutral gray; you restore and intensify the color as you drag to the left.

Color Contrast

The **Color Contrast** marble increases the contrast of colors within the image; dragging further left desaturates the color toward gray and then moves into an inverted color space.

KPT Convolver Basics

KPT Convolver is an image correction application that operates as an Adobe Photoshop plug-in. Although sharpening and color controls are available in Photoshop itself, they have to be applied one at a time: Open the filter, tweak the Sharpen knob a little, now a little more, click OK, wait a minute for it to process, evaluate the results, and then repeat the process for a different effect. Applying filters linearly like this offers little chance of backing up more than one step should you change your mind. It also makes it tough to compare different combinations of effects, while Convolver allows you to apply multiple effects all at once, and you can view the results in real time—another Kai innovation.

The program provides access to its effects from three modes, each providing an increasing degree of control. You begin in Explore mode, which generates effects at random (Figure 6.5). When you see a direction forming, switch to Design mode, where you are able to manipulate the various effects and fine-tune what you started in Explore. Finally, Tweak mode offers complete control over all imaging options, allowing you to apply the final touches. Remember, it is not the effects that change as you progress through the modes, it is your degree of control.

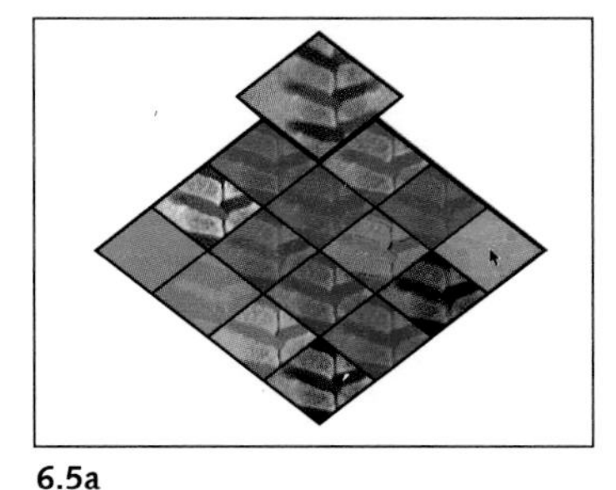

6.5a

6.5b

Clicking on a tile in Explore mode (Figure 6.5a) generates new effects at random (Figure 6.5b)

Convolver's functionality is based on the *convolution kernel,* a mathematical grid of nine numbers arranged like a tic-tac-toe board. Each kernel is in essence a preset algorithm; the specific kernel activated depends on the user's selections. The program allows you to apply a great variety of image effects, known as *convolution effects,* to an active image area or to the image as a whole. It also provides sophisticated control over color, sharpen/blur, edge and relief, and other effects. (It gives you so much control, in fact, that you may not want to leave the Convolver interface to go back to Photoshop!)

A convolution kernel is a set of numbers arranged in a $3 \times 3 \times 3$ matrix. The numbers chosen by the program for any particular matrix are carefully designed to modify the values of the image's pixels to create the desired effect. The cells in the matrix are superimposed over one pixel, with the center cell in the matrix aligning with the value of the image pixel being modified (Figure 6.6). The value of each pixel surrounding the center pixel is taken into account as the modification takes place. This provides a degree of equalization across the entire image, modifying the value of a pixel based on its context.

Convolver gives you simultaneous access to all of the convolution kernels in the application. Because of this, Convolver has been said to have a 27-dimensional space through which you can navigate. The linear push/pull of brightness and contrast in Photoshop and other image editing applications is replaced by a nonlinear, free-flowing space. All 10 polar opposites in Convolver—Blur/Sharpen, Edge Amount, Edge Angle, Relief Amount, Relief Angle, Hue Rotation, Saturation/Desaturation, Lighten/Darken, Contrast/Fade, and Tint—cross each other, with other factors pushing the total directional structure to 27.

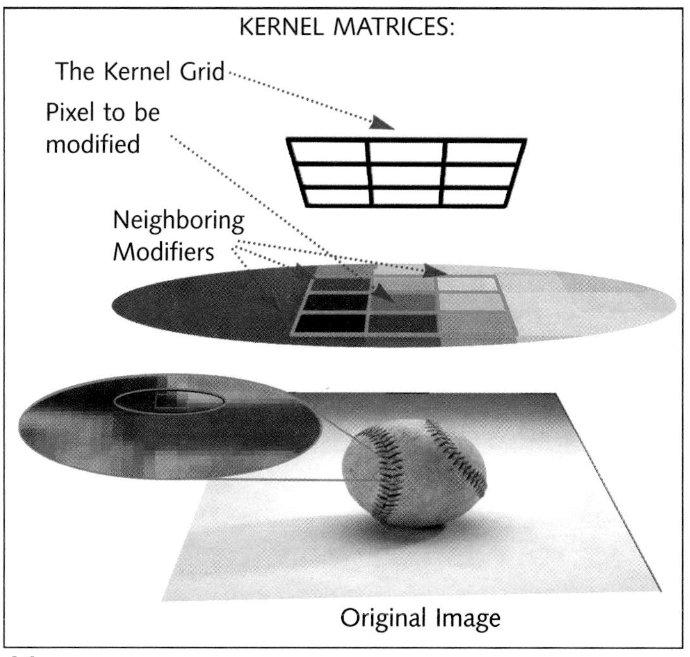

6.6

In the Convolver manual, Kai talks about all of the detail that lies hidden within an image. This all sounds very mystical, implying other worlds that mysteriously emerge from nowhere when a marble is tweaked. This is a good way to describe the phenomenon, because that is exactly what appears to happen. In reality, though, the convolution kernels are playing on the contrasting values of adjoining pixels. Those relationships are enhanced or reduced, giving the illusion of blurring, sharpening, or texture effects. A wide range of pixel values allows Convolver to bring out details you didn't think you'd be able to see. At some point, however, the illusion falls away as you reach the limits of how much the kernel can stretch and pull the values in the image. This is the point where individual pixels become obvious and it looks too grainy, or somehow unnatural.

6.6 The center cell of the kernel matrix aligns with the pixel to be modified

Underscoring all of this is the way we see images. Our eyes tend to move toward constructing and integrating image data, rather than breaking it down and tearing it apart. In a way, the convolution kernels in Convolver do the constructing and integrating as they play on the contrasting pixels within an image, helping us to see effects and details that were previously invisible.

Kernels are especially valuable when the desired effect requires the algorithm to alter the relationships among sets of pixels, rather than changing their values globally. Take a blur effect, for example. Decreasing the overall contrast in the image (a global change) will reduce the highlight/shadow distinctions in the image without blurring it. Decreasing the contrast between pixel sets, as a kernel matrix does, maintains overall contrast while softening the edges, thus creating a blur effect. The effect is noticeable (especially in high-contrast areas) when the contrast between pixels is reduced—the edges soften and the image becomes homogenized. To achieve this effect, each pixel's value must be modified based on the value of the pixel next to it. This is exactly the way convolution kernels work.

The Evolution of KPT Convolver

KPT Convolver was the first Macintosh product developed completely in-house at MetaTools since the release of Kai's Power Tools. Although it was not released until December 1994, KPT Convolver got its start two years earlier when Ben Weiss skipped his college studies to attend a seminar on image processing in San Jose, California.

"I was attending Harvey Mudd College at the time, and it was the week before finals week when Martin [Schmitt] and I went up," said Ben, who is now the imaging scientist at MetaTools. "We had just released KPT at that time and I was thinking about creating a kernel explorer that would work similar to the Texture Explorer. It would generate random sets of kernel numbers, creating various effects." After taking a backseat to other company projects, such as KPT Bryce and Live Picture, Ben's kernel explorer eventually became the Explore mode in Convolver.

Kai told me that the Convolver name was one of his little jokes that stuck, with the code name surviving the development and beta phases and the product coming to market with the name intact. It's a play on the word convolution, which *Webster's* defines as "a complication or intricacy of form, design, or structure." *Convolution* means something much more specific in the imaging world. In the KPT Convolver manual, Ben Weiss ties the word *convolution* to image enhancement and the extraction of detail.

The interface, which began in black and white with lots of buttons, took shape as everyone began to understand the program's capabilities. Ben said, "There is a very large space of things you can do in there, and the biggest challenge was creating an interface that would help navigate that."

Kai has said that a good interface is one that masks complexity, presenting options to the user as simply and concisely as possible; in that regard, Convolver truly succeeds. The pitfall of elegant simplicity, however, is that people sometimes fail to grasp the power hidden behind the design. In a recent interview, Kai said, "There's a technical side to the story as to what happens when you look at a pixel and you take its neighbors into account and so forth. That's all fairly straightforward, but that's not what [Convolver] was about to try to do. A lot of people have missed the advantages and subtleties as to what that thing is and what it does. Some of them have really gotten it."

KPT Convolver and Kai's Power Tools

Because both are plug-ins and both perform texture effects and image correction, people sometimes confuse the capabilities of Kai's Power Tools and KPT Convolver.

In general, you will find that you can easily spot a KPT image. While that is not true of all artists or of all of the features of KPT, it does hold true for much of the feature set. Page Curl and Glass Lens, for example, are one-shot effects that leave their stamp on every image that uses them (Figure 6.7). This tends to codify and homogenize the image to some extent, removing some of the individuality that the artist might put into it.

6.7

KPT can also create beautiful images from nothing at all. Begin with a white screen; add some noise, blur, or sharpen; apply a gradient; and you're on your way. KPT generates preset effects, and it allows you to apply paint in the form of gradients and, to a lesser extent, noise and texture.

In contrast, there is no signature look to a Convolver image that makes it easy to spot. Convolver begins with the image itself and doesn't go very far without one. The next time you create a new document in Photoshop, while the screen is still white, select Convolver and begin exploring. You will see colors change as you go, but there are no texture shifts and the colors are not very exciting. It's hard to go very far without some sort of pixel contrast available for Convolver to exploit.

Think of Convolver as a mathematical equation that multiplies a given number. If the number is zero (that is, no color), then the result will be zero as well. If the number has a value, the

6.7 The KPT Page Curl effect

equation will make its value increase exponentially. In general, the higher the original number's value, the greater the equation's result. The reality is that Convolver needs an image to work from—some contrast in value, color, or texture. And the more quality and variation there is in the image, the more options you have to develop and explore.

Getting the Most out of KPT Convolver

The following section presents some strategies for approaching KPT Convolver. Although there is no one "best" way to use Convolver, these are basic approaches that everyone can make use of. Beyond these, there are any number of ways to explore, since Convolver adapts to your own personal approach and way of working.

Earning Your Stars

Convolver evolves as you use it, and in a very unique way. As you work with it, the program awards you "stars" that give you new tools and increased functionality—so it actually rewards you for exploring (Figure 6.8). There are five stars in all, associated with four new features (the first star is just to let you know that there are stars). You'll be working along and suddenly a screen will pop up from nowhere, congratulating you and telling you about the new feature that has been added to the application.

6.8

6.8 KPT Convolver stars

The Convolver stars add so much functionality to the application that it is worth focusing on them first. As you explore certain features, a message pops up and congratulates you, explaining the new feature that has been added to the program, and telling you how to use it. As a bonus, in the course of gathering your stars, you'll get an excellent tour of Convolver's capabilities.

There are five stars in all, and they offer the following capabilities:

Star 1

Adds nothing, but alerts you to the fact that the stars exist. Use each of the modes once, and it will appear.

Star 2

Enables the split-screen preview, which allows you to compare the original image side by side with the current cumulative effect (Figure 6.9). This feature is available in any of the three modes, and it is activated by clicking on the button that shows up in the lower right corner. Frequent use of the full-screen preview (say, five times) in the Explore mode earns you this star. (Simply click on the Current Kernel Tile to select the full-screen preview.)

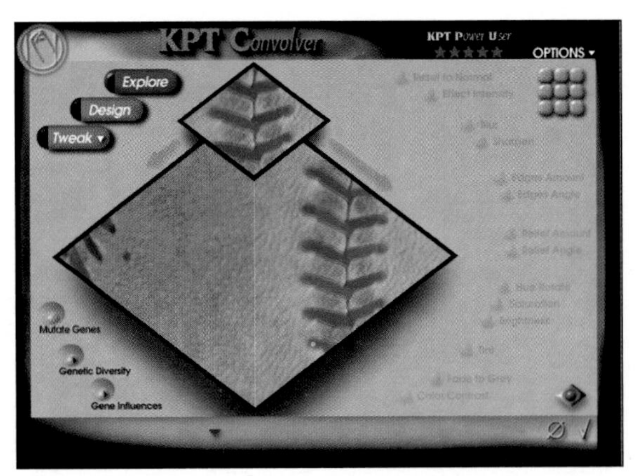

6.9

6.9 Split-screen preview

Star 3

This star brings with it an algorithmic tint wheel for the Tint marble in Tweak mode (Figure 6.10). This wheel makes it easier to select specific colors intuitively and quickly. Click on the Tint marble 20 times or so, and this star appears.

Star 4

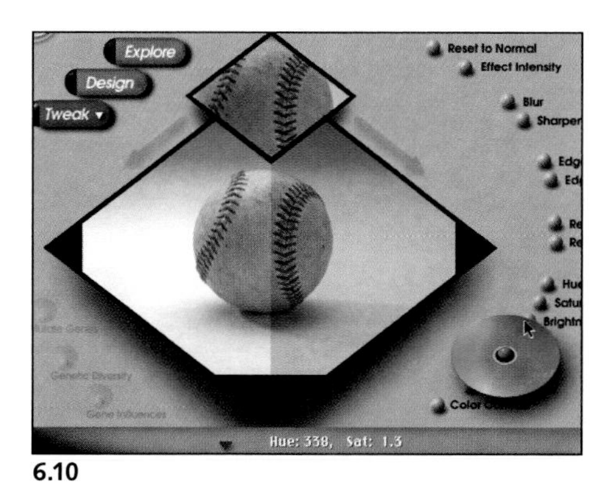

6.10

The fourth star adds something called memory dots to the interface. (See page 182 for more information.) Cycle through the Explore, Design, and Tweak modes until this star appears. This could take three or four revolutions, but the memory dots are worth the effort (see page 166 for the location of memory dots in the Convolver interface).

Star 5

The fifth and crowning star in the Convolver set adds an Animate Random command to the pop-up menu items in the Explore mode's Gene Influences button (Figure 6.11). Click this button and Convolver will begin to animate the various colors and textures, cycling through all of the options. Clicking the mouse stops the action and activates the last effect. This star is added through scrubbing (see page 182). About 15 attempts at scrubbing should reveal the fifth star.

6.10 Tint marble's tint wheel

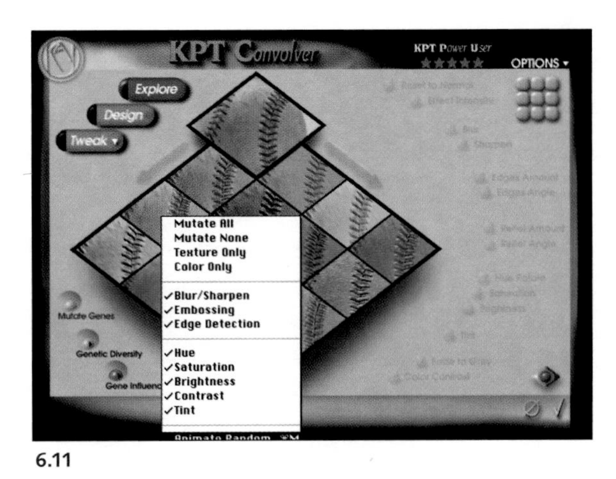

6.11

6.11 The Animate Random command

Memory Dots, Animation, and Scrubbing

Memory dots are like bookmarks that save specific effects so you can come back to them later. When you're exploring and you come across a color or effect that you like, click on a memory dot to save it and move on. You can save up to nine settings and retrieve each by clicking on the same memory dot you used to save it. To remove a saved effect, Option-click on a dot, which clears its contents. (And we can acknowledge Kai's cleverness in building the dot pad in the shape of the 3 × 3 × 3 convolution kernel.) Convolver also allows you to save sets of memory dots as files, which means that you can go indefinitely without running out of room. Fill the first nine, save them as a file, erase the current dot grid, and start over.

When you got your fifth star, you were given the ability to animate. While in Explore mode, select Animate Random from the Gene Influences menu to start the animation, and click the mouse once to stop it. Details about animation speeds and controls are listed in the splash screen you saw when you got your star. You can review this information at any time by Option-clicking on the fifth star. The standard animate sequence cycles through the variations among the current kernel tile and other kernels that are randomly generated. Once you have accumulated a set of memory dots, you have the power to animate those as well; select Animate Dots from the Options menu to start this process.

Scrubbing is a feature in the Explore and Design modes that allows you to combine the current effect with an effect in one of the grid squares, creating a hybrid of sorts. You can think of scrubbing as a controlled, manual version of animation. Clicking on any grid square and dragging away from it will combine (interpolate) the effect in the grid square and the effect in the Current Kernel Tile. Scrubbing is a directional control, so you can dictate which effect dominates and which one influences.

A Quick Tour

This exercise will get you familiar with the kinetic and interactive qualities of KPT Convolver, as well as introduce you to some of its capabilities.

1. In Photoshop, open this baseball image from Kai's Power Photos (you'll find the low-resolution version on the CD-ROM that comes with this book). Take a snapshot of the entire image (Figure 6.12).

Edit
Can't Undo ⌘Z
Cut ⌘X
Copy ⌘C
Paste ⌘V
Paste Into
Paste Layer...
Clear
Fill...
Stroke...
Crop
Create Publisher...
Publisher Options...
Define Pattern
Take Snapshot

6.12

6.12 The Photoshop Take Snapshot command

2. Using a combination of the Lasso and the Magic Wand tools, select the baseball and press Command-H to hide the edges (Figure 6.13).

6.13

3. Launch Convolver (Filter/KPT Convolver). Begin by clicking on the Explore button, and then click on the button in the lower-right corner of the screen, which enables the split-screen preview (available after earning your second star; see page 179). With split-screen enabled, you can compare the current state of the Explore effect with the original image by clicking on the top diamond (Figure 6.14).

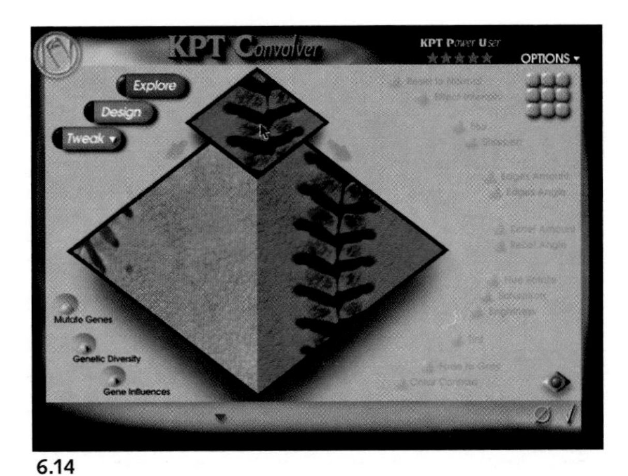

6.14

6.13 The Master Palette

6.14 Use the split-screen preview

4. Click on the Mutate Genes marble; scramble the effects until you see one you like, and then click on a memory dot. Repeat the process two or three times. The dot turns dark gray to show that an effect is assigned to it. Here, two effects were assigned to memory dots while in Explore mode (Figure 6.15).

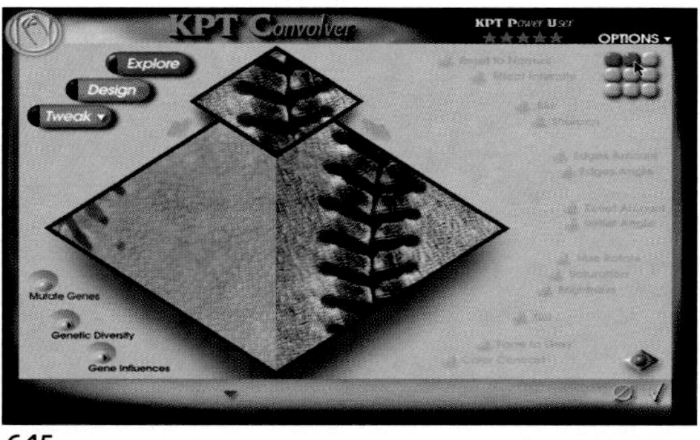

6.15

5. Before leaving Explore mode, select Texture Only from the Gene Influences pop-up menu (Figure 6.16), and then click on the Mutate Genes marble a few times. The color values, which were interesting, will remain constant while you modify only the texture of the image.

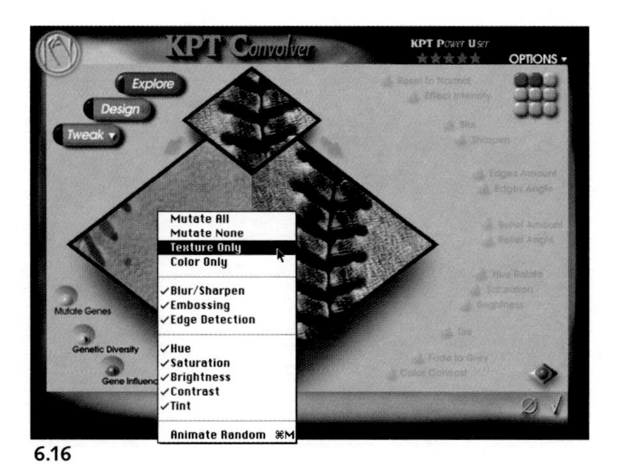

6.16

6.16 The Texture Only selection in the Gene Influences menu

6. Now click on the Design mode button for more control over texture. For the axis values, select Edges Angle and Edge Detection (Figure 6.17). Select the degree of texture modification you like. (Edge Detection adds texture by increasing the contrast between neighboring pixels, or a blur effect by reducing contrast.)

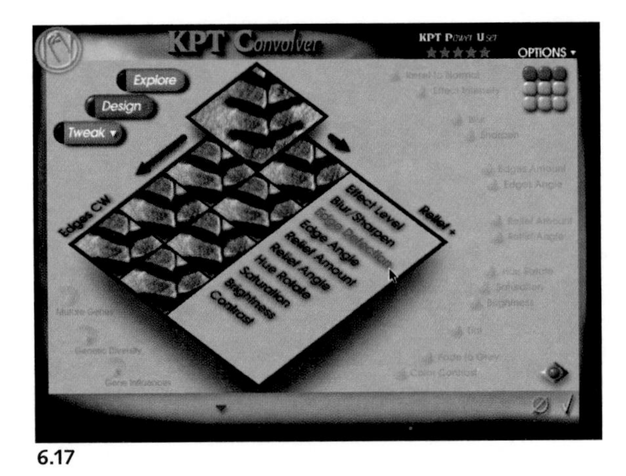

6.17

7. Click on the Tweak mode button. Increase the brightness of the image by tweaking the Brightness marble (Figure 6.18), and apply the effect to the baseball by clicking on the check mark in the lower-right corner.

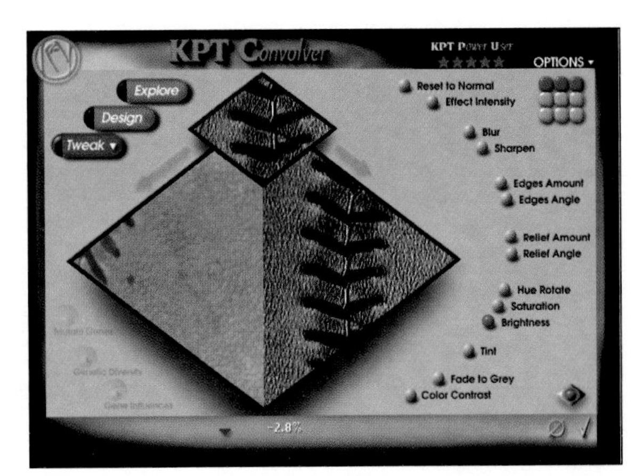

6.18

6.17 Select Edge Detection as one axis value

6.18 Adjust the brightness in Tweak mode

8. Back in Photoshop, invert the selection (choose Select/Inverse) so that the background rather than the baseball is active (Figure 6.19).

9. Relaunch Convolver. In any mode, you can reposition the sample that shows through the Preview Diamond so you can see the effects on the ground plane. To do so, choose Reselect Sample from the Options menu, which brings the entire image into view (Figure 6.20). Click and drag on the diamond and move it to the point where the ball meets the ground plane. Release the mouse button; the Preview Diamond now shows the ground plane.

10. In Explore mode, select Color Only from the Gene Influences menu, and then click on the Mutate Genes marble until you see a green cast in the ground plane (Figure 6.21).

6.19 Invert the selection in Photoshop

6.20

6.21

11. Switched to Tweak mode, and use the Edges Angle and Edges Amount marbles to modify the image until the ridges in the texture run horizontally (Figure 6.22). Keep in mind that the changes you see in the window apply only to the selected area, in this case the ground plane but not the baseball. Apply the effect to the selection by clicking on the check mark in the lower-right corner.

6.20 Choose the Reselect Sample Icon

6.21 The ground plane with a green cast

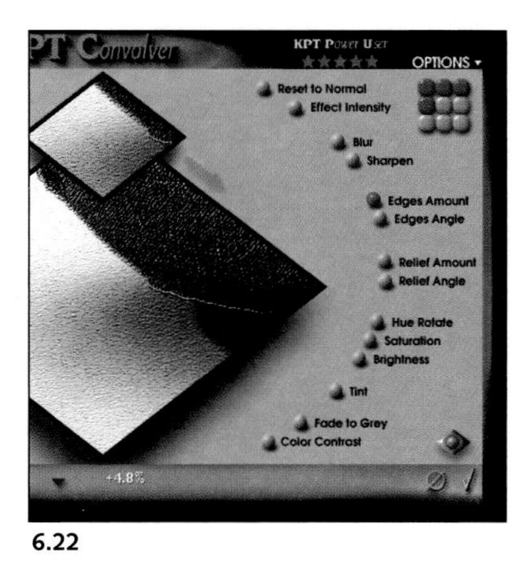

6.22

12. Give the baseball a worn appearance. In Photoshop, use the Magic Wand tool with a tolerance of between 75 and 100 to select random patches of the ball's texture (Figure 6.23). Use the Lasso tool to fine-tune the selected area. Press Command-H to hide the edges.

6.23

13. Select Fill from the Edit menu. In the resulting dialog box, choose Snapshot from the Use pop-up menu, and select Normal mode and 100% opacity. Click OK. This process fills the selected areas with the snapshot of the original image that you took in step 1 (Figure 6.24).

6.22 Create texture using Edges Amount

6.23 Make random selections using the Magic Wand tool

6.24

14. What if you change your mind and decide you like most of the original background better? To restore the portions you want, select the Rubber Stamp tool; in the Rubber Stamp Options palette, choose the From Snapshot option, Normal mode, and 100% Opacity. Set the brush size to 100 pixels, and brush the original background back into the image (Figure 6.25). The final image is shown in Figure 6.26.

6.25

6.24 The baseball takes on a worn appearance

6.25 Restoring portions of the original background

6.26

6.26 The final image

In this exercise, each effect evolved from a loosely generated effect in the Explore mode, which was tightened up in the Design and Tweak modes. The memory dots and unlimited undos gave you complete freedom to explore without worrying about losing what you had already developed. The next section discusses the extensive undo capabilities in Convolver.

Undos by the Hundreds

In a bit of self-revelation, I must confess that I used Convolver for a month before I realized that extensive undo capabilities are built into it. I asked Phil Clevenger, director of new technologies at MetaTools, when they were going to build it in, and he walked over to a machine and began shamelessly flipping through the 256 levels of undo, looking at me as if I had just asked Adobe to add brushes to Photoshop.

Perhaps you are familiar with this feature already and are wondering why I am mentioning it here. I find that many artists know that it's there but do not utilize it as much as they could. The creative process thrives on large amounts of visual information, and the successful designer or artist often runs through as many variations and iterations of the design as possible—if you don't experiment, you may be missing something. So make use of Convolver's undo feature; don't settle for the first good image, or the 10th, or even the 100th—you have 256 levels to go. Convolver allows you to push forward with confidence, knowing that there is a way back to that effect that was perfect only in retrospect.

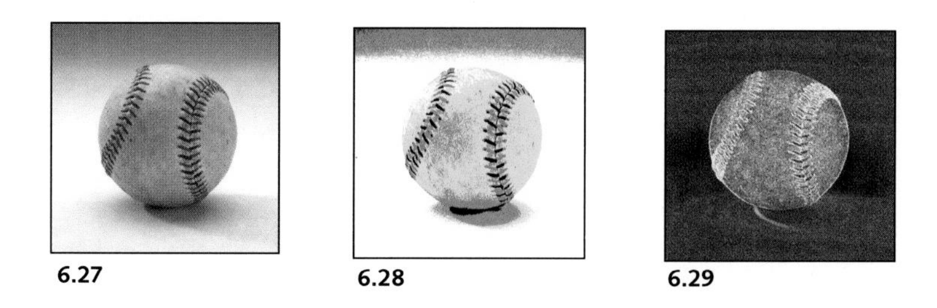

6.27 6.28 6.29

A great use for all those undos is to combine them with the Difference Mask option in the Tweak mode button's pop-up menu. The Difference Mask compares the original image with the current effect. If you have done nothing to the original image, you will see a black screen. If you have applied one effect, you will see the difference between that and the original image, which can be pretty dazzling (Figures 6.27 through 6.29).

But let's say you've been exploring, and you have gone through 50 or 60 different effects. Difference Mask will compare the most recent effect with the original image, but pressing Command-Z will undo one level at a time and compare the previous effect with the original. You can back up all the way to the start if you like, looking at all of the variations along the way.

Explaining Convolver is a lot like explaining an artist's brush. You pick up paint on the bristles and apply it to the canvas. To appreciate Convolver, you must approach it the same way. Convolver responds to ideas and intentions with a degree of subtlety and control seldom seen before—in the hands of an artist it truly comes to life.

6.27 Original image

6.28 Image with standard Convolver effects

6.29 Image with Convolver Difference Mask applied

Chapter 7

Exploring KPT Bryce

KPT Bryce is a 3D design program that generates realistic and fantasy landscapes. It has an open, intuitive interface that combines ease of use with exceptional power and depth. Although you can generate complete scenes of amazing complexity within the first 15 minutes of installing Bryce, you will still be mastering its controls weeks and months later.

The name Bryce refers to Bryce Canyon, Utah—a place of stunning landscapes—and Kai originally named the program Bryce: New World Explorer. As Bryce moved through the alpha and beta stages of development, New World Explorer was dropped, but Bryce stuck.

The next section shows the KPT Bryce interface, with the main areas, icons, and tools labeled and described. You can use it as a reference and a guide for the information in this chapter.

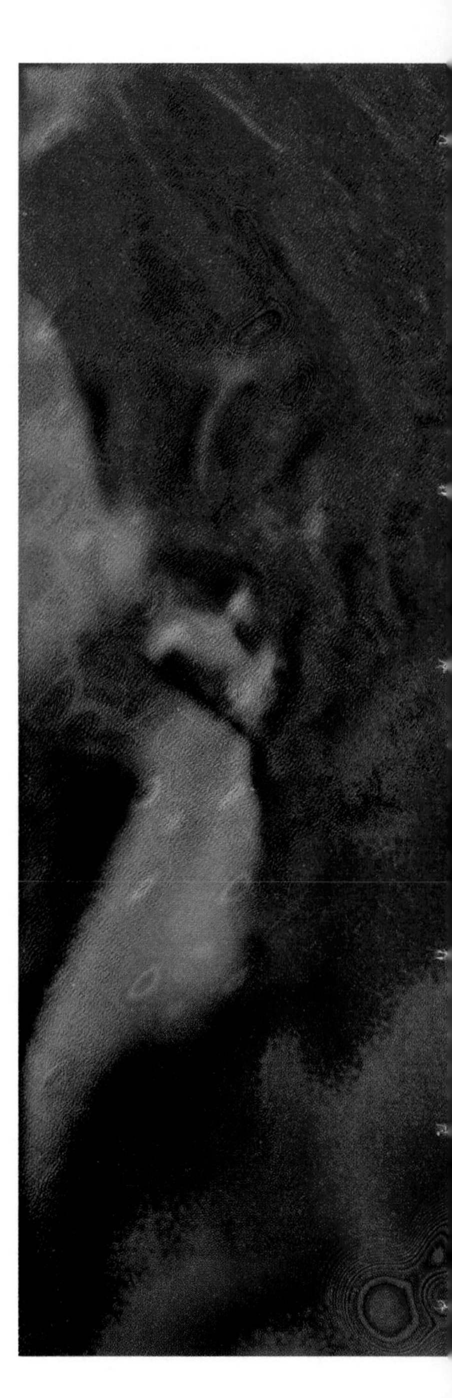

The KPT Bryce Interface

The KPT Bryce interface has five palettes: a constant Master Palette, through which you can access the other four; and the Create, Edit, Sky and Fog, and Render palettes, which roughly correspond to the steps you take in creating a landscape.

Master Palette

The Master Palette allows navigation, camera-angle modification, and other methods of controlling a landscape (Figure 7.2). Nearly all of the tools are accessed by clicking on their icons.

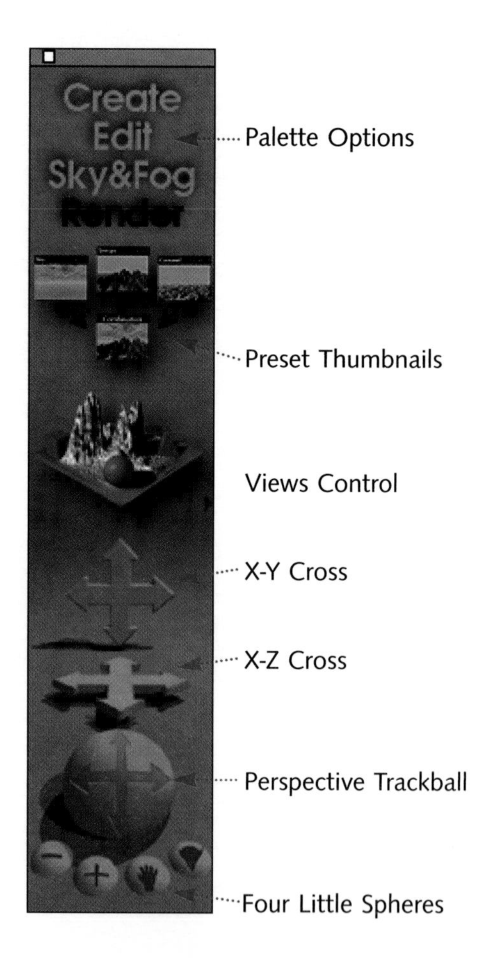

7.2 The Master Palette

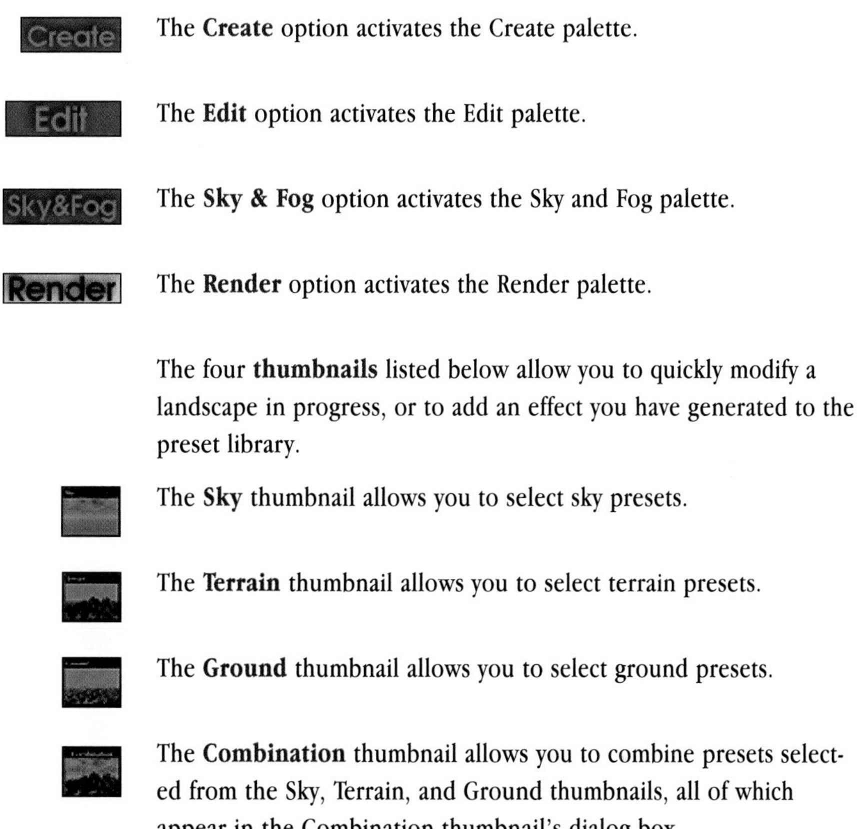

The **Create** option activates the Create palette.

The **Edit** option activates the Edit palette.

The **Sky & Fog** option activates the Sky and Fog palette.

The **Render** option activates the Render palette.

The four **thumbnails** listed below allow you to quickly modify a landscape in progress, or to add an effect you have generated to the preset library.

The **Sky** thumbnail allows you to select sky presets.

The **Terrain** thumbnail allows you to select terrain presets.

The **Ground** thumbnail allows you to select ground presets.

The **Combination** thumbnail allows you to combine presets selected from the Sky, Terrain, and Ground thumbnails, all of which appear in the Combination thumbnail's dialog box.

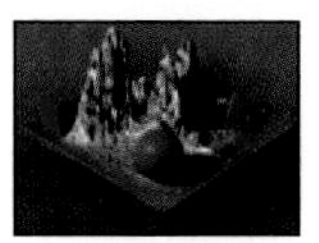

The **Views** control's pop-up menu allows you to select one of the four default views—Main, Top, Front, and Side—or you can add one of your own, or select from several camera controls.

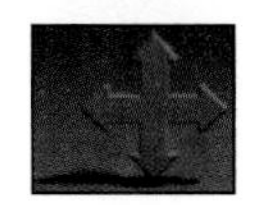

The **X-Y Cross** moves the camera horizontally (along the x axis) or vertically (along the y axis).

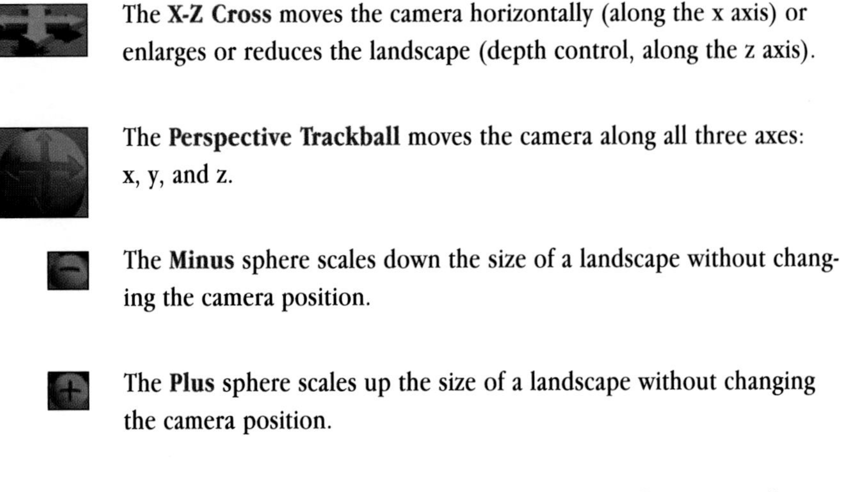

The **X-Z Cross** moves the camera horizontally (along the x axis) or enlarges or reduces the landscape (depth control, along the z axis).

The **Perspective Trackball** moves the camera along all three axes: x, y, and z.

The **Minus** sphere scales down the size of a landscape without changing the camera position.

The **Plus** sphere scales up the size of a landscape without changing the camera position.

The **Hand Tool** sphere moves the scene horizontally or vertically without changing the camera position.

The **Focal Control** sphere controls the focal setting of the camera lens, allowing for wide-angle viewpoints, without changing the camera position.

Create Palette

The Create palette is the starting point for most Bryce designs, since it is here that you generate the basic forms for the landscape (Figure 7.3).

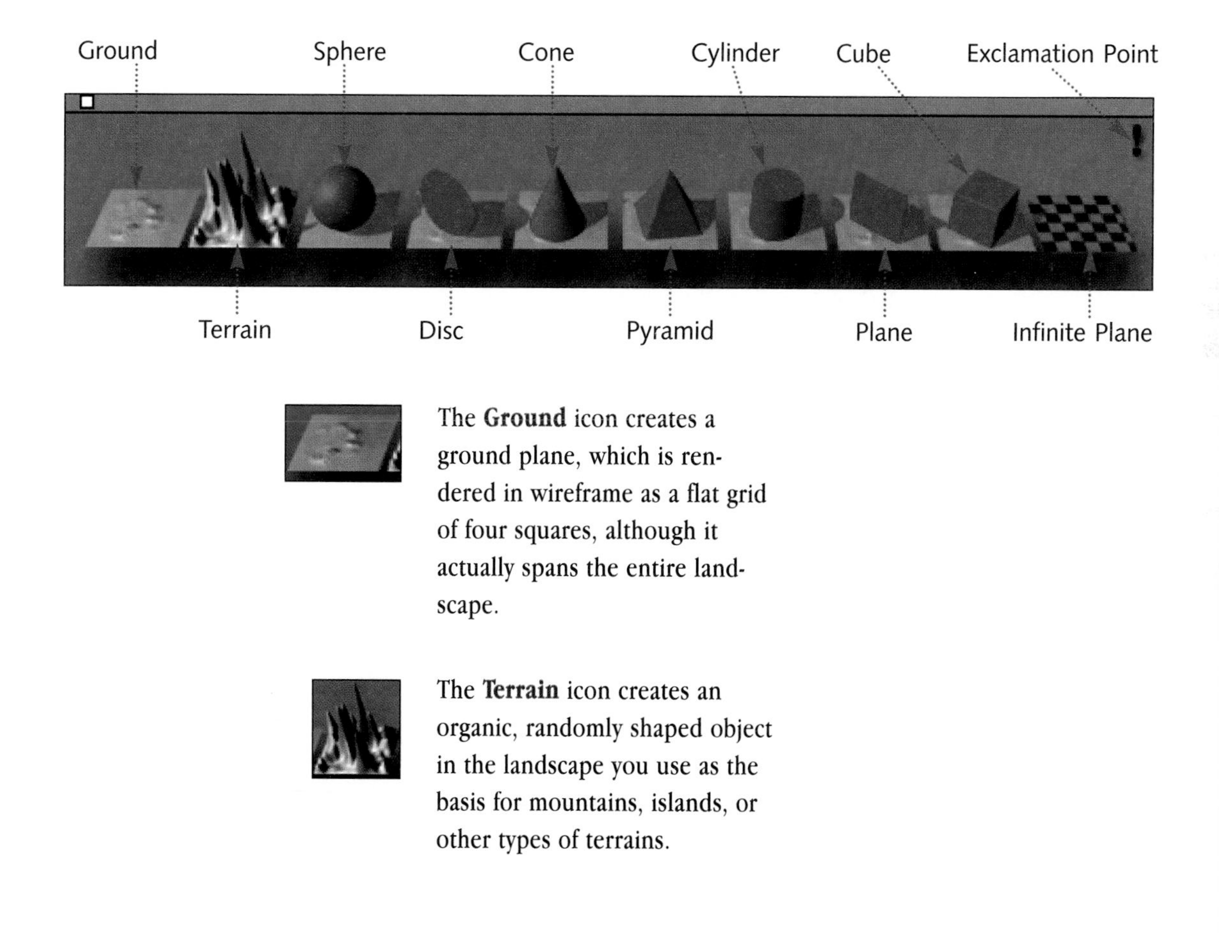

The **Ground** icon creates a ground plane, which is rendered in wireframe as a flat grid of four squares, although it actually spans the entire landscape.

The **Terrain** icon creates an organic, randomly shaped object in the landscape you use as the basis for mountains, islands, or other types of terrains.

7.3 The Create Palette

Primitives icons create seven basic shapes:

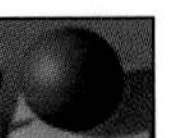

Spheres

Discs

Cones

Pyramids

Cylinders

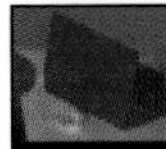

Planes

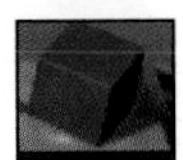

Cubes

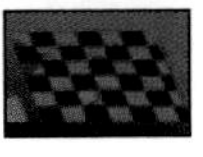

The **Infinite Plane** icon creates an infinite plane, which is similar to a ground plane but has more flexibility. It is a useful surface for mapping clouds, oceans, or PICT images.

The **exclamation point** gives you the option of viewing links among objects.

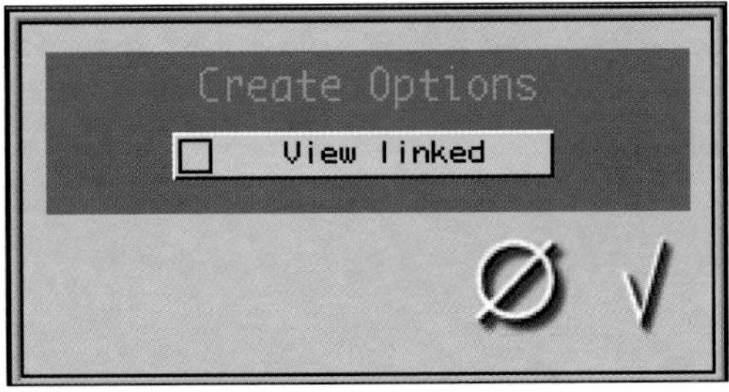

7.4

7.4 The Create Options dialog box

Edit Palette

The Edit palette allows you to change the attributes of any selected form (Figure 7.5). In addition to proportional and size changes, it also includes the Terrain Editor and Materials Editor (Figures 7.6 and 7.7). The Materials Editor controls the texture surface of an object, and the Terrain Editor controls the shapes of hills and mountains.

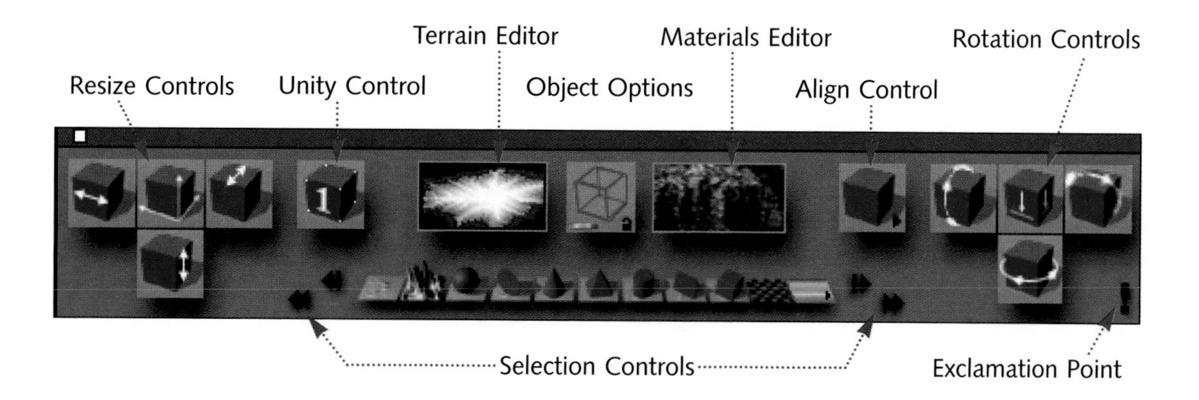

7.5 The Edit Palette

Before Bryce objects can be edited, they must first be selected using the following **Select** controls:

The **bottom-left arrow** selects the first object created.

The **top-left arrow** toggles through each object, from the last to the first created.

The **top-right arrow** toggles through all objects, selecting from the first to the last created.

The **bottom-right arrow** selects the last object created.

The **Ground Plane** icon selects all ground planes.

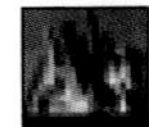

The **Terrain** icon selects all mountains, islands, and other terrains.

The **Primitives** icons select:

All spheres.

All discs.

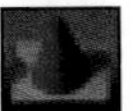

All cones.

All pyramids.

All cylinders.

All planes.

All cubes.

All infinite planes.

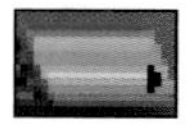

The **colored plane**'s pop-up menu allows you to select objects by wireframe color.

The **Resize** controls constrain resizing:

Along the **x axis** (horizontally).

Along the **y axis** (vertically).

Along the **z axis** (depth).

In **equal proportions** in all directions.

There are two **Alignment** controls:

The **Unity** icon returns selected objects to their original size, undoing any rotation that you applied, and snaps them to the closest position on Bryce's 3D grid.

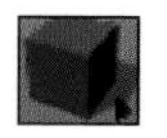

The **Align** icon's pop-up menu enables you to flip or align selected objects along the x, y, or z axis; scatter the selected objects randomly; or snap the objects to the nearest position on Bryce's 3D grid.

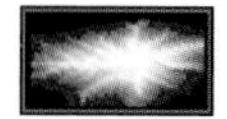

The **Terrain Editor** icon activates the Terrain Editor dialog box (Figure 7.6), where you can customize the contours of terrain objects.

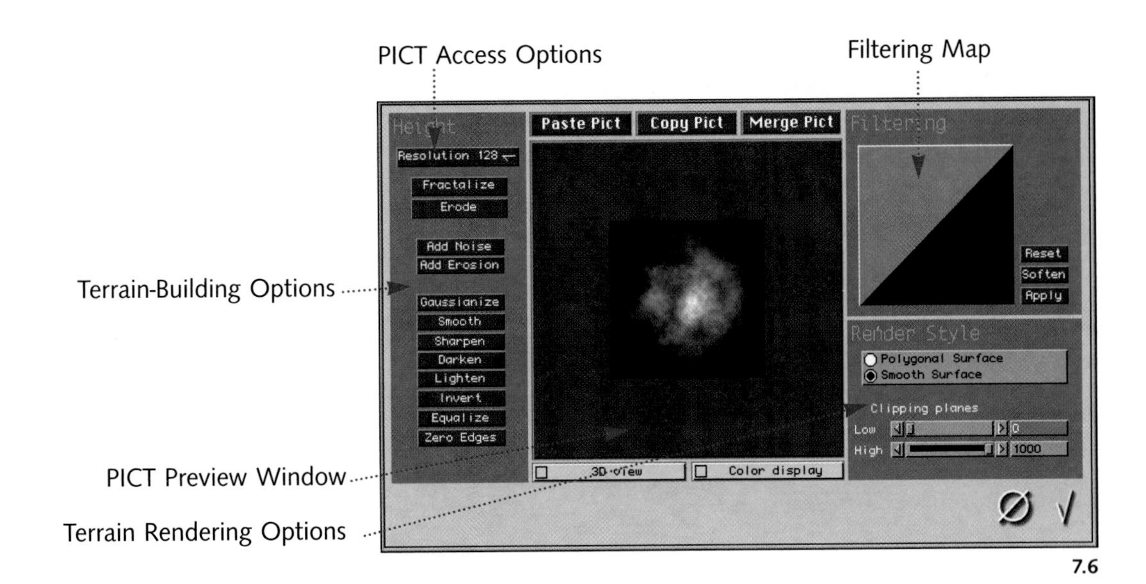

7.6

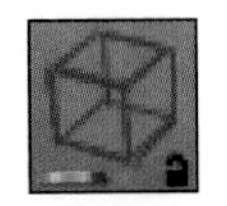

The **Object Options** icon allows you to assign colors to or lock objects, and to display objects as a box.

The **Materials Editor** icon activates the Materials Editor dialog box (Figure 7.7), where you can control the look and feel of Bryce objects.

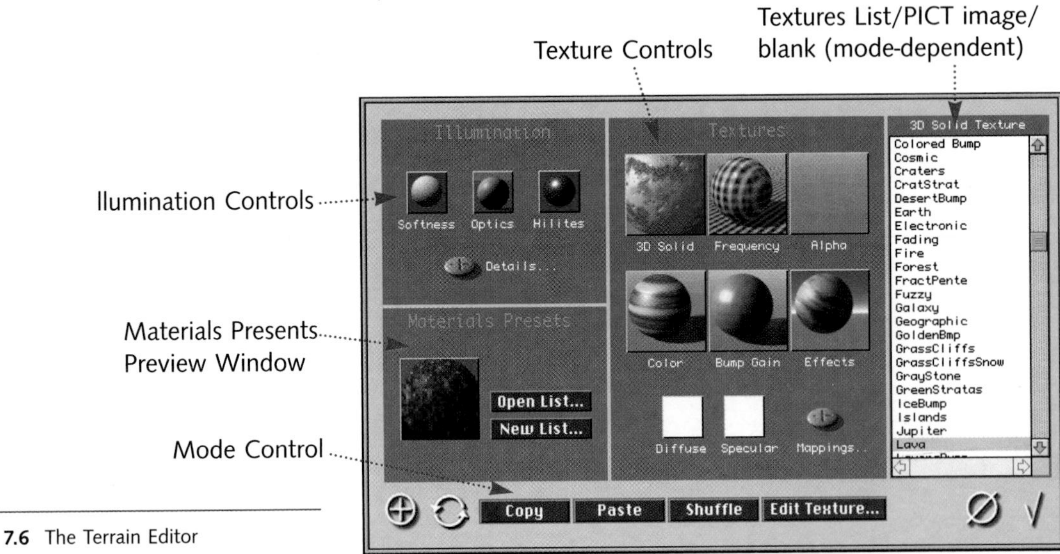

7.7

7.6 The Terrain Editor

7.7 The Materials Editor

The **Rotation** controls rotate an object:

Around its **x axis**.

Around its **y axis**.

Around its **z axis**.

The **ground-align** tool aligns the bottom surface of an object with the default ground level.

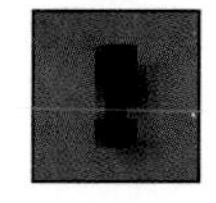

The **exclamation point** allows you to toggle Center Scaling, which scales an object around the center point rather than the bottom of the object (Figure 7.8).

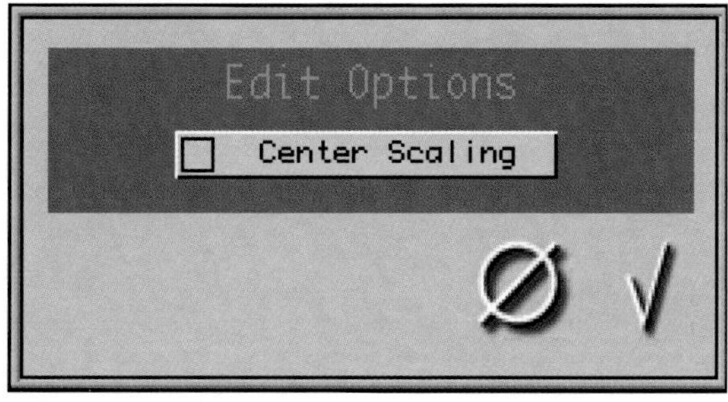

7.8

7.8 The Edit Options dialog box

Sky and Fog Palette

The Sky and Fog palette allows you to add clouds, fog, haze, and other atmospheric effects (Figure 7.9).

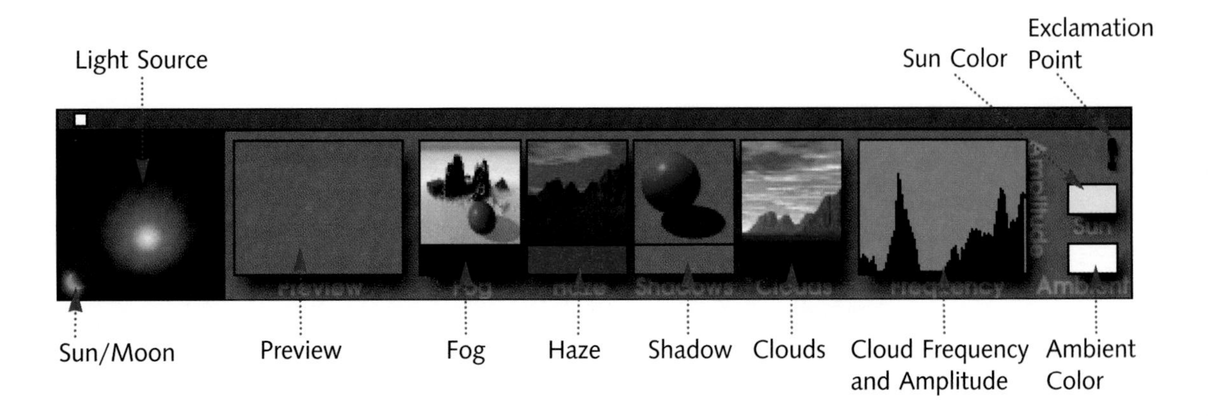

7.9 The Sky and Fog Palette

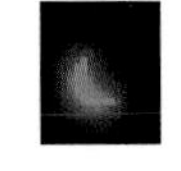

The **Sun/Moon** icon toggles between sunlight and moonlight.

The **Light Source** sphere controls the direction of light in a landscape. With the landscape positioned at the center of the sphere, moving the Light Source there creates a "high noon" lighting effect. Otherwise, the Light Source is mapped to a compass—placing it at the very top of the sphere creates a light on the northern horizon in the landscape; when it's at the far left it creates a light on the western horizon; and so on.

The **Preview window** provides a quick update of all Sky and Fog parameters as they are modified.

The **thumbnail controls** allow you to modify your sky, both graphically and numerically; pop-up color pickers in the lower rectangles of all but the Shadow thumbnail allow you to select a color for those effects.

The **Fog** thumbnail controls the fog effect in a landscape; horizontal dragging controls the density (the first of two numbers shown as you edit), while vertical dragging controls the amplitude (the second number shown).

The **Haze** thumbnail controls the degree of haze at the horizon of an infinite plane in the landscape.

The **Shadow** thumbnail controls the intensity of the shadows cast by objects.

The **Clouds** thumbnail controls the amount of cloud coverage in a landscape.

The **Cloud Frequency and Amplitude** window controls the number and appearance of clouds. Dragging up creates high spikes on the graph, which give you clearly delineated cloud forms; low spikes soften the clouds' edges. Dragging to the right creates more spikes, and thus more cloud formations.

The **Sun Color's** pop-up color picker allows you to select the color of sunlight.

The **Ambient Color's** pop-up color picker allows you to select the color of shadows.

The **exclamation point** activates a dialog box that gives you more precise control over most Sky and Fog effects (Figure 7.10).

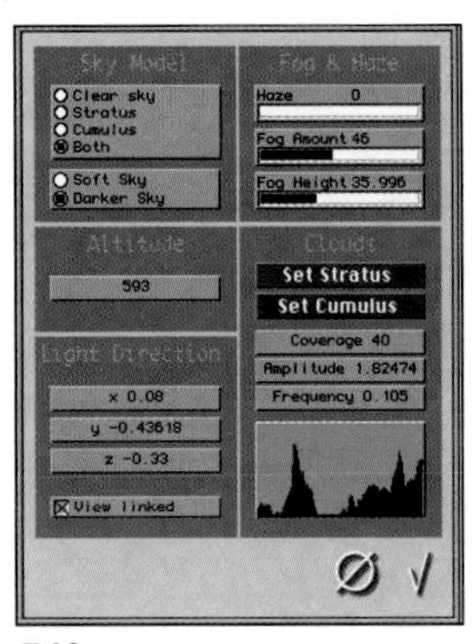

7.10

7.10 The Sky and Fog options dialog box

Render Palette

The Render palette controls how an object is rendered as a PICT file. Attributes such as file size, atmospheric effects, and perspective effects can all be controlled from this palette.

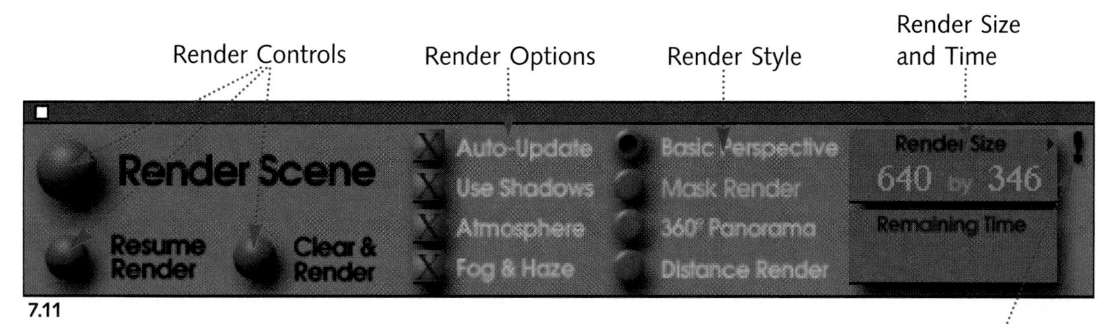

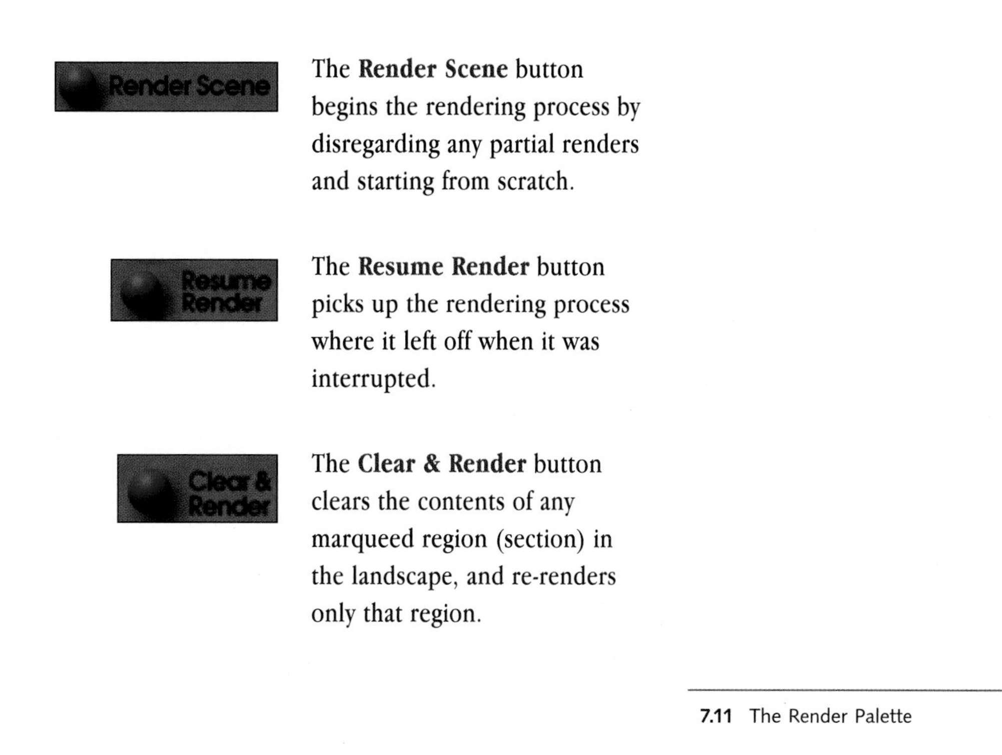

The **Render Scene** button begins the rendering process by disregarding any partial renders and starting from scratch.

The **Resume Render** button picks up the rendering process where it left off when it was interrupted.

The **Clear & Render** button clears the contents of any marqueed region (section) in the landscape, and re-renders only that region.

7.11 The Render Palette

Auto-Update

The **Auto-Update** button updates any changes you make in the Sky and Fog palette by automatically re-rendering the marqueed region (section); it re-renders the entire scene if no region is marqueed.

Use Shadows

The **Use Shadows** button determines whether shadows in the landscape are rendered; eliminating shadows speeds up rendering.

Atmosphere

The **Atmosphere** button determines whether the sky is rendered with the landscape; eliminating skies speeds up rendering.

Fog & Haze

The **Fog & Haze** button determines whether the fog and haze effects are rendered with the landscape; eliminating these effects speeds up rendering.

Only one **Render Style** button may be chosen for each render.

Basic Perspective

The **Basic Perspective** button renders the scene exactly as depicted in the window.

Mask Render

The **Mask Render** button renders any selected objects in black, anti-aliased against a white background, for use as a mask or alpha channel.

360° Panorama

The **360° Panorama** button renders the landscape in a strip that appears as though the camera were rotating 360 degrees within the scene.

Distance Render

The **Distance Render** button renders images in grayscale, with the closest objects black, more distant objects in lighter and lighter shades of gray, and the object farthest away in white.

The **Render Size** area displays what the resolution of the rendered landscape will be; its pop-up menu allows you to select the format (wireframe window) size for the scene.

The **Render Time** button displays the estimated rendering time for the image, not including anti-aliasing time.

The **exclamation point** activates a dialog box that allows you to toggle anti-aliasing on and off, and to set the resolution (Figure 7.12).

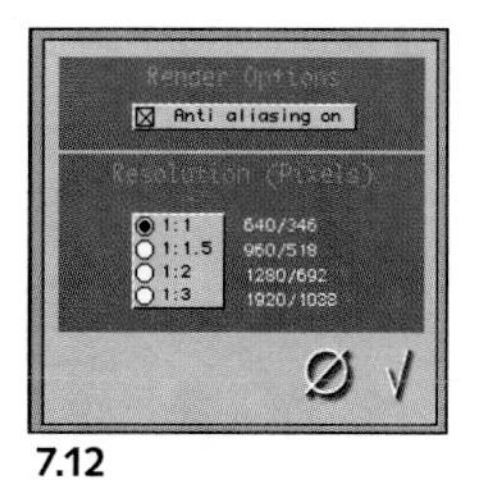

7.12

KPT Bryce Basics

When you first launch KPT Bryce, you are presented with a group of three windows containing preset elements of landscapes—skies, terrains, and ground planes (Figure 7.13). There is also a fourth window that displays a composite of the elements selected in the other three. By clicking on each element window, you can scroll through a handful of presets and view the resulting composite in the Combination window. (You can also access this dialog box at any time by clicking on the Combination thumbnail in the Master Palette.) In this way, you can create a landscape only seconds or minutes after launching Bryce for the first time. Although this method is simplistic, its results are impressive.

7.12 The Render Options dialog box

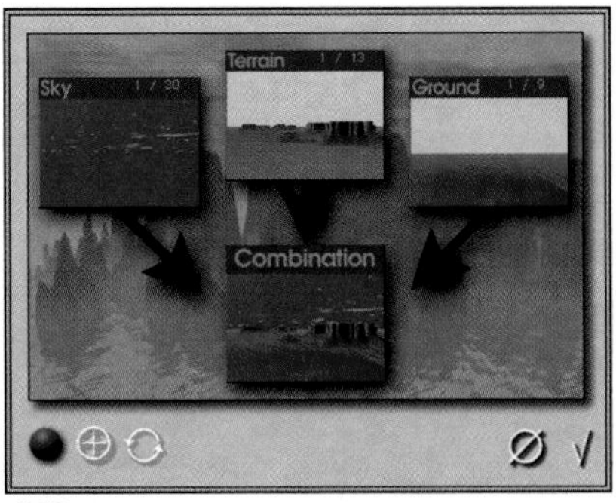

7.13

7.13 The startup presets dialog box

The Evolution of KPT Bryce

The original concept and development for KPT Bryce was done by Eric Wenger, an artist and software developer with a real passion for landscape imaging. In the five years he had spent developing it, Eric built an exceptional amount of power and control into Bryce, and he envisioned it selling for around $5,000 per copy to just a few hundred professionals. In an interview, Kai told the story of how it became a $99 program for everyone.

"As I was visiting [Paris] to see Live Picture, Andreas [Pfeiffer] tried to mention that there is another kind of a crazy guy I'm supposed to see. You know, this happens all the time—people say, "You gotta see this, you gotta see this." So I went there expecting very little, frankly, and Eric showed me a slide show of images and I thought it was great. It's exactly what you see at Siggraph [graphics conference] all the time. It only then dawned on me to what degree he had dove into the mathematics of the thing. See, when I saw it he had 14 palettes laying around. He would type in the xyz angle for the light ray; he would type in the location of the objects—it was amazing.

"Eric still had in his mind that the thing should cost $5,000; it should work for a few dozen people that needed landscapes. He thought it was a very high-end thing, and he didn't think there would be more than a few hundred people who would ever buy it. . . . The only way I convinced him, actually, is that we played for the right to determine the price over a game of Go. I royally killed him, and earned my right to set the price. I told him, 'You're not going to like it, it's going to be 99 bucks.' And that's what we did."

As Kai and Eric developed and polished the application, its power and depth remained, although it was enhanced by an intelligent, approachable interface. When it was released it was another bestseller, and especially notable in that it created a whole new audience for 3D imaging.

Creating Landscapes

Although some may never go further than this, it's not difficult to begin working with Bryce's more powerful features. Bryce allows you to create landscapes by generating wireframe models of various scenic components. These components include skies, mountains, and oceans, as well as basic forms such as spheres, cylinders, cubes, cones, and pyramids. The program gives you full control over the size and proportion of each shape. Forms are generated and placed within a three-dimensional space, where you can click and drag them into position. Views from different angles aid in the placement of objects within the 3D space.

With the basic shapes in place, colors, textures, and properties such as reflectivity or transparency are assigned to each shape. These controls allow you to generate materials such as chrome, glass, and even clouds. These materials properties are mapped onto the objects you create, and you can control the exact amount of reflectivity, transparency, and so on.

Bryce uses a method called ray tracing to render a smooth, antialiased landscape from the wireframe model you create (see page 216 for more details on ray tracing). Ray tracing allows Bryce to offer some very sophisticated atmospheric controls, such as fog effects, cloud cover, the colors of the primary and ambient light, and the direction and intensity of light. After assigning materials to the wireframe objects in your scene, you would then assign these atmospheric properties, which are applied globally to the entire 3D space (Figure 7.14).

All through the process, you have the ability to render parts of the scene, or the entire scene, in order to preview your work. This is usually not necessary while you are generating shapes and editing their proportions, since their appearances will change dramatically once materials are applied to them. From the materials point on, however, rendering becomes an important component in evaluating your work in progress (see step 14 on page 234).

7.14

Finally, you render your image after defining the proportions of the image, its size in pixels, and the camera perspective. Although the design process in Bryce is quite fast, and its controls are intuitive, the rendering phase can grind things to a halt. Kai says that he and Eric designed Bryce to be uncompromising with regard to the details rendered in the image, and that level of quality comes with a time requirement. He also likes to say that Bryce was designed to make use of the computer's "idle hours." Kai often equates sleep time and lunch time with render time, suggesting that we set up images to render and then walk away from the computer, leaving Bryce to work its magic. It is also possible to render scenes in batches to further maximize off-hour processing.

You will also find that things go faster and smoother if you group specific tasks, such as assigning materials to wireframes, or colors to different object shapes for easy selection. For example, when you first open Bryce and place an object, its surface has a basic, gray-plastic texture (this is the No Textures option in the Materials Editor; see page 221 in this chapter). Objects render very quickly in this mode, so place all of the objects in your landscape before you apply more complex surface characteristics through the Materials Editor. Once the objects are placed, you can adjust their placements and render them quickly to ensure alignment and basic composition.

7.14 The same image shown in wireframe (right), with textures added (middle), and with atmospheric effects added (left)

Navigating 3D Space

If you're coming to Bryce from the 2D world, you must first get used to working in three dimensions. The 3D space is structured along the x, y, and z axes, and all of the movements and positioning you do in Bryce are carried out in relation to these axes (Figure 7.15). The x axis runs horizontally; the y axis runs vertically; and the z axis moves away from you (the z axis may be considered the third dimension, representing the object's depth).

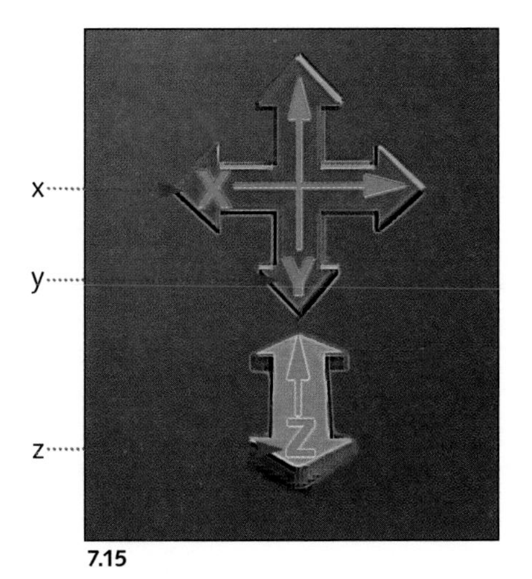

7.15

7.15 The x, y, and z axes

As you begin adding objects to your landscape in the Main view, you will see that they are all placed at approximately the same spot. You can move objects up and down or side to side, but it is hard to tell what's happening when you move them forward or backward in space. But if you switch to Top view, you can see and maneuver the z axis, which controls depth. You might even begin in Top view so you can get good feedback right from the start.

Good navigation allows you to set camera angles and exercise complete control over composition. You can create emotion and drama in the landscape by adjusting scale, point of view, and similar properties. Mastering these controls is essential in moving beyond the dabbling stage and taking advantage of the true power of KPT Bryce.

Getting the Most out of KPT Bryce

Once you've mastered the basic Bryce tools, you can go deeper into the program to create objects and effects that are not obvious. There are ways you can generate trees, for example, or import pictures to use as backdrops. The strategies in this section will get you started.

The Elements of Ray Tracing

Ray tracing is the rendering process that brings 3D wireframe models to life. It is not essential for the Bryce user to know what ray tracing is or how it works; for most it is enough to know that those great fog and water effects are brought to you by this sophisticated rendering method. For those who must have all the details, read on.

The process is used by many 3D modeling applications because it is able to render objects in a lifelike manner. One problem with ray tracing, though, is that it tends to render objects with very little surface texture—it creates surfaces so smooth that they appear unrealistic. Bryce solves this problem by combining ray tracing with sophisticated bump-mapping controls, which allows an object's complex textures to be described and integrated along with its lighting attributes. Ray tracing's strength is in its capability to describe how a surface reacts when illuminated. It is able to differentiate between a shiny surface such as chrome, a transparent surface such as glass or water, and a matte surface such as felt or cloth. It works by creating an imaginary light path that is traced from the "viewer's eye" to the objects in a scene, and then bounces off of them as it makes its way back to the light source. If the light path should encounter a shiny or transparent surface, ray tracing creates additional beams that trace how light would reflect off of or pass through the object.

When light passes through an object—say, a glass of water or a crystal ball—ray tracing is able to describe the distortion that takes place via the transmitted ray. Reflected rays would predominate with a surface such as chrome or polished steel. If an object has a matte surface, with no reflective or transparent qualities, then the light beam is traced directly back to the light source. Therefore, when a light path strikes an object, ray tracing will create an additional reflective or transmitive beam, if necessary, to describe a shiny or transparent surface (Figure 7.16).

Although ray tracing creates reflective and transparent beams only when required by the object's surface texture, there is another kind of beam that it creates in almost all instances: the shadow ray. A shadow ray is created each time a light beam bounces off a surface. The intensity of the shadow ray is controlled by the intensity of the reflected light beam. This allows more transparent objects to cast lighter shadows, while a dense object (which would reflect the light beam more sharply, with less transparency) casts a crisp, deep shadow. The shadow ray travels through the scene until it either hits the light source or strikes an opaque object, where it describes the shadow.

The entire ray-tracing process happens for each and every pixel in the image. The light source, shadow, reflective, and transparent beams all combine to calculate the value of that one pixel, which is described using RGB values. This is why the path is traced from the eye to the light source rather than from the light source to the eye. Some light beams, such as those that strike the backs of objects, never reach the viewer's eye and therefore do not directly impact the way the scene looks. By tracing from the eye to the light source, ray tracing describes only the pixels needed to create the final rendered image.

Ray tracing is the base technology, and you access that technology through the Bryce interface. The Illumination section in Bryce's Materials Editor (see page 201 in this chapter), for example, allows you to control how matte, reflective, and transmittive surface attributes combine and interact with each other in countless variations. You can combine these components in various degrees by using the Softness, Optics, and Hilites spheres. Softness controls the matte qualities of an object; Optics controls its transmittive qualities; and Hilites controls its reflective qualities.

So think about this the next time you're impatient with Bryce for taking 20 minutes or an hour to render your image: There are a lot of mathematical light beams bouncing around in your computer, all making your seascape a little more realistic and your surface a little more shiny.

7.16 Ben Weiss

7.16 The detail in this Ben Weiss image highlights the variety of materials that can be rendered using ray tracing

Mastering Camera Controls

The Bryce camera controls the Main view of the scene. In the Side, Front, or Top views, you can adjust the camera either by moving the little blue box, which represents the camera itself, or by moving the blue projection line, which represents the camera angle, that extends from the blue camera box. You can drag the projection line around the scene to dictate the Main view.

(See page 196 in this chapter for a picture of the palette's interface, which you'll refer to often in this section.)

The camera angle can add a drama to your scene, so you should consider it carefully. The objects in the landscape may dictate the angle you choose, for instance, if you want to play off of the variations in their physical attributes. Once you've created the scene as a place, set up the camera to show the viewer what this place is all about. Experiment with the wide-angle lenses or in working with dramatic camera angles, such as ground-level and bird's-eye views (Figures 7.17 through 7.21).

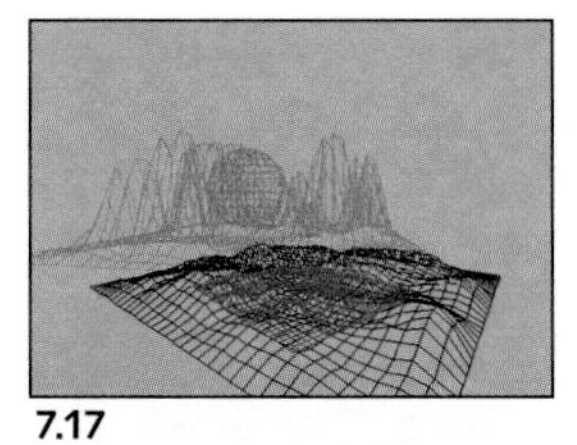
7.17

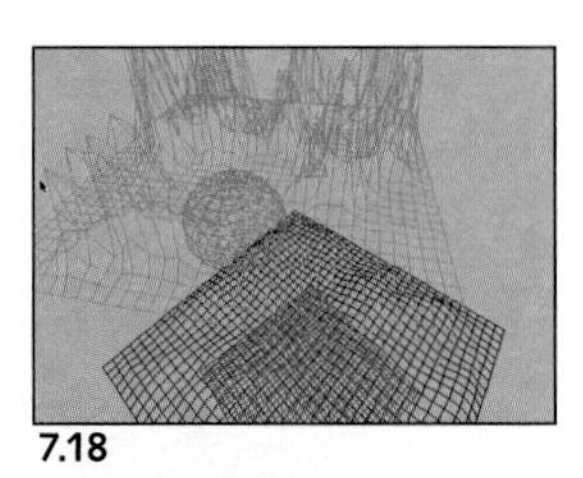
7.18

7.19

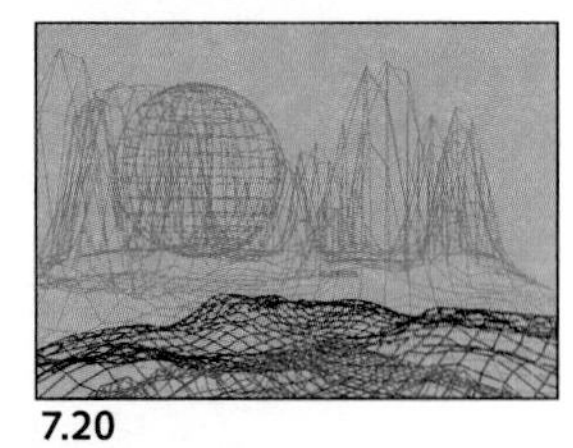
7.20

7.21

7.17 Camera set to Main View

7.18 Camera set for bird's-eye view

7.19 Camera set at ground level

7.20 Camera set at Main View, with a focal length of 34 degrees

7.21 Camera set at Main View, with a focal length of 127 degrees

For a wide-angle view, click on the Focal Control sphere (see page 196) and drag to see the change in the focal length. Note that the camera itself is not moving; rather, the scene is expanding and compressing, just as it would appear if you used a fish-eye or telephoto lens with a camera. For greater precision, double-click on the Perspective Trackball to enter numeric values for the camera angle and focal length.

The same focal length will do different things, depending on how close it is to an object. A longer focal length will result in greater distortion of objects that are closer to the camera; a shorter focal length will depict a narrow slice of your scene and will allow you to get closer to objects with less distortion.

While you're experimenting with different focal lengths, try dragging the camera through the scene and resetting the projection line. For example, creating a birds-eye view is quite simple: Using the Side view, drag the blue camera box above the entire scene, and point the projection line down to the landscape below.

A good place to start for any of these camera placements is the preset camera angles in the Views menu in the Master Palette. Click and hold on the small triangle next to the Views icon, and choose Ground Camera, Top, or Side to see your scene from these points of view. Selecting Add View As in the Views menu allows you to add your own camera angle to the preset list of views.

A well-thought-out and composed Bryce landscape, such as those created by Kai and Eric Wenger that are included on the KPT Bryce CD-ROM, should make you curious: What's around that corner? What's on the other side of that rock? What's behind me? These artists evoke that response because they've mastered Bryce's camera controls—and so should you. Experiment by moving the camera in all directions, looking for the perfect angle, the perfect shot.

Creating Trees in KPT Bryce

It might surprise you to hear that Bryce does not create trees. After all, you are making a landscape, and who ever heard of a landscape without trees? Although this seems like an obvious omission to an otherwise fine program, a little thought about what it would require will put it into perspective. To create a tree, Bryce would have to make a randomly generated trunk, with hundreds of branches and thousands of leaves attached. And that's for just one tree; most landscapes contain several trees at least; sometimes dozens or hundreds. Generating that kind of complexity in a wireframe model with full scalability and modification, and then rendering it in detail would compromise Bryce's design speed, and its rendering times would increase dramatically, given all of the additional surface calculations.

Nevertheless, perhaps you have seen Bryce images with trees in them. You were not entirely deceived, for there are ways for clever and aspiring digital imagers to place trees in a Bryce landscape, including the three described here.

In the first method, you create a PICT image of a tree in Photoshop, create an alpha channel as a mask, and import the image into Bryce. Once imported, you project the image onto a flat plane, along with the mask, and place it within the Bryce landscape (see page 228). In this way, the image picks up some of the lighting effects and integrates well with the scene. The limitations are that it is a flat plane, and the viewing angle cannot be altered without distorting the tree.

The second method is to create trees, piece by piece, from the simple shapes available within Bryce. But man, oh man, what a task. The result would be either that the tree looks clunky, or that you have acquired the patience of Solomon. This method produces the most artificial result for all but the 0.00001 percent of Bryce users who are true imaging masters.

The third method is to go outside of Bryce to a third-party application that is designed for creating trees in wireframe. The complexity of this undertaking is underscored by the fact that several complex, high-end applications have been created just for making trees. One such program, from Onyx Software, is called TREE Professional. It creates the entire tree to your specifications, allowing you to dictate the tree's type, size, shape, and angle. Programs such as TREE Professional provide the fastest, most professional results—if your budget can afford them.

Working with 3D Solids

The 3D Solids controls in the Materials Editor can be one of the most confusing aspects of KPT Bryce. There is a lot of power housed in the Materials Editor dialog box, and along with that comes a certain degree of complexity. It is important to understand the options available when you assign a texture to an object, and when those options should be exercised.

(See page 201 in this chapter for a picture of the Materials Editor interface, which you'll refer to often in this section.)

The word material in Bryce refers to the way a texture interacts with light within the landscape. The components governing that interaction are the color and texture of the object, its reflective nature, its level of highlight, its degree of transparency, and how it bends or refracts light if it is transparent. The lighting effects, textures, and surface mappings that are controlled in the Materials Editor dialog box all go into the creation of a material. It's important not to confuse any one component with the entire process.

In the lower-left corner of the Materials Editor dialog box is a box labeled Materials Presets. These are preset combinations of lighting, reflectivity, and textures. Click and drag on the icon to visually scroll through them.

At the center of the dialog box is the Textures area, where you assign the physical properties to the material you are creating. The first of the six icons (the upper far-left icon) governs the origins of the texture—its type and source. The options here are No Texture, 2D PICT, and 3D Solid. Although you can select No Texture to create glass and water effects, or choose 2D PICT to map a PICT image onto the surface of your object (see page 228), you'll probably spend most of your time working with 3D Solid textures. These textures are noise-based algorithms and are central to Bryce's ability to make clouds, marble, and other complex textures.

When you select 3D Solid, a Texture List appears in the box to the right with the names of 3D Solid textures that underlie any 3D Solid material you are using. Experienced Kai's Power Tools users will see this list and immediately assume that these are presets like those in KPT, so it's important to note that these are not materials presets. Think of them as raw materials, a starting point. You can add transparency, reflectivity, and many other properties to these raw materials, transforming them into hundreds of variations.

When working with 3D Solids, the Color icon (the lower-left icon) in the Textures area is also important. This icon assigns the color information from a 3D solid texture or 2D PICT to the highlights, midtones, and/or shadows of the selected object. The color is made visible in the object via three light channels—Diffuse, Ambient, and Specular—either alone or in combination.

The Diffuse light channel applies to matte surfaces, which reflect light evenly. Color that exhibits Diffuse characteristics is usually focused in the midtones of an object. Ambient light can be thought of as light that exists without an apparent direct source. When emphasized in the Materials Editor, Ambient light can make an object appear self-illuminating, like the sun. In most cases, however, the Ambient light channel affects the color in the shadow areas of an object. The Specular light channel has to do with the reflective qualities of an image; Specular lighting focuses on the highlights of an object.

The Color icon dictates which of these three light channels reveal the color in a the 3D material or PICT image. The channels may be designated either individually or in pairs. It is not possible to combine all three components in the same object using the Color icon alone. The two white boxes at the bottom of the Textures area, labeled Diffuse and Specular, address this limitation. These options allow you to force a color into one the light channels, effectively controlling all three components.

For example, if you selected a color scheme that revealed color in the Specular and Ambient regions of an object, clicking and holding on the Diffuse box and selecting a color from its pop-up color picker allows you to force a color into this area as well (Figure 7.22). These boxes are only used if the color scheme chosen does not include these properties. If the scheme does contain these properties, then the color selected by the color picker will be overridden.

7.22

Working with Illumination

The visual characteristics of any object we see are due as much to the way light interacts with the object as it does with the physical properties of the object itself. In other words, an object assumes the characteristics of the light that shines on it. A white ball viewed under incandescent light looks somewhat yellow; if it's viewed under fluorescent light, it looks a little green; and when viewed outdoors, it looks slightly blue. And if the white ball is placed on a blue surface, the shadows of the ball and other areas near the blue surface will take on a blue cast. This is called reflected light, and some materials reflect light more than others.

7.22 The Diffuse box and its color picker

In the Illumination area of the Materials Editor, you can control light properties in two ways. The most direct way is to click and drag on the area's Softness, Optics, and Hilites spheres. Softness controls the combination of Specular and Diffuse settings in the selected object; Optics modifies transparency and reflectivity; and Hilites provides additional control over specular highlights.

(See page 201 for a picture of the Materials Editor interface, which you'll refer to often in this section.)

The second method is through the controls available in the Details dialog box (click on the Details button in the Illumination section; see Figure 7.23). These are Ambient, Diffuse, Specular, Reflectivity, Transmitivity, and Refract Index. As mentioned in the previous section, Ambient, Diffuse, and Specular refer to a scene's shadows, midtones, and highlights, respectively. The Reflectivity slider controls how shiny an object is; the Transmitivity slider controls the object's transparency; and the Refract Index slider controls the amount of distortion that results when light passes through a transparent object (for example, the distortions are distinctly different for light passing through water, crystal, and a windowpane).

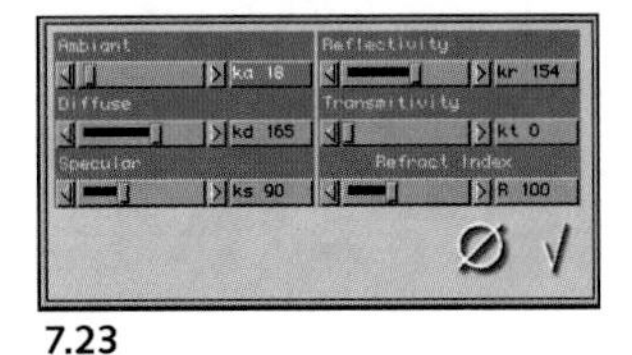

7.23

When you consider all of the materials characteristics together, you will see that their variations within Bryce are virtually unlimited. The key is to think about the materials components in the context of the landscape you are creating, and then add them to the properties of an object. Another thing to keep in mind is that there is no law that says you can't blur the lines between a 3D Solid characteristic and an Illumination component. For example, if you are working on a landscape with a slightly blue light

7.23 The Details dialog box

source and you are not satisfied with the way the mountain range is picking up the blue cast, you can go into the Materials Editor and edit the 3D Solid material, adding a bit of blue to help it blend with the landscape.

Using PICT Images in the Terrain Editor

The Terrain Editor allows you to modify the shapes of mountains and hills. Combining the basic scaling controls in the Edit palette with the Terrain Editor's shaping capabilities allows you to create most hill and mountain formations.

The first thing you'll notice in the Terrain Editor dialog box is the grayscale-to-height map in the middle. Although you cannot edit the map directly, you can see how it looks in 3D view and/or color by clicking on the corresponding checkboxes at the bottom of the dialog box.

(See page 201 in this chapter for a picture of the Terrain Editor interface, which you'll refer to often in this section.)

To create a terrain, Bryce generates a grayscale PICT file and fills it with fractal noise (this is the same kind of noise generated by the Photoshop Noise filters). The fractal component of the noise ensures that it is always unique, asymmetrical, and abstract; in essence, it is organic, as a mountain should be.

Bryce converts the grayscale noise file to a terrain using a grayscale-to-height algorithm (thus, the name of the map). This process converts tonality to altitude, with the white areas of the image representing the highest points in the scene, and the black areas of the image representing the lowest points. This concept is similar to the visual coding used by map makers, in which white indicates mountaintops and brown and green indicate low-lying areas. Instead of color, however, Bryce relies on shades of gray to shape its terrains.

To edit the grayscale-to-height map, you can use any of the controls in the Height section. These controls modify the tonal relationship within the grayscale noise file that is used to generate the terrain. Some commands, such as Lighten and Darken, directly affect the tonal range of the file. Since white represents the highest points in the terrain, lightening the image overall has the effect of raising the altitude of the entire terrain. Darkening has the opposite effect, lowering the overall height of the terrain. In this way, Bryce can create sharp peaks through greater contrast, or rolling hills through more subtle, graduated tones and a narrower tonal range (Figure 7.24). Hills become mountains and vice versa, and they can be stretched or smoothed into exactly the type of terrain you want.

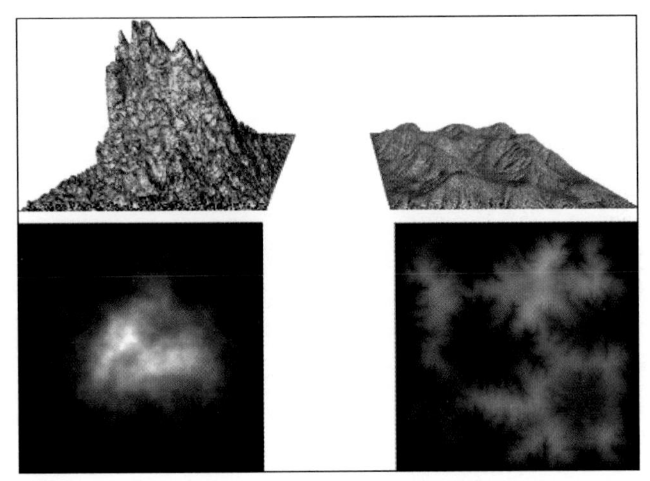

7.24

But what if you substituted that randomly generated grayscale noise file with some other grayscale file, such as that of a fractal image or a photograph? Mountains can be created from the contours of a person's face, and any shape can be mapped onto a terrain. The Terrain Editor provides some of the more impressive effects Bryce has to offer, so it is definitely worth taking the time to master.

7.24 Two terrains, one rough and one smooth, with their corresponding grayscale-to-height maps—Notice how the white areas in the map correspond with the highest points in the terrain

Bryce also allows you to import a PICT file, such as a photograph or design, into the Terrain Editor, where it can be used in the grayscale-to-height calculation of a terrain. When used without modification, this imported PICT image may be merged into an existing terrain so that its characteristics are softened, or it can be edited using the Height controls. The grayscale PICT file you import should be square and of a moderate resolution. If you want the image to be easily recognized in the terrain, you should increase the contrast to emphasize broad tonal differences rather than minute details, which can get lost in the shuffle. If you use Photoshop to generate your initial PICT file, use the Curves, Levels, and Contrast controls to prepare the PICT file for Bryce. A little time spent on the front end of this process will pay big dividends later.

In the Terrain Editor, there are three buttons above the greyscale-to-height map: Paste PICT, Copy PICT, and Merge PICT. When you click on the Merge PICT button, a new dialog box appears showing the current terrain, an empty window for importing another PICT image, and an empty Blend window, which will show how the two other images look when combined (Figure 7.25). Moving the slider beneath the windows controls which of the images dominates in the final image; move the slider all the way to the right if you want to show only the image you've imported. The radio buttons beneath the Blend window provide control over how the images are combined.

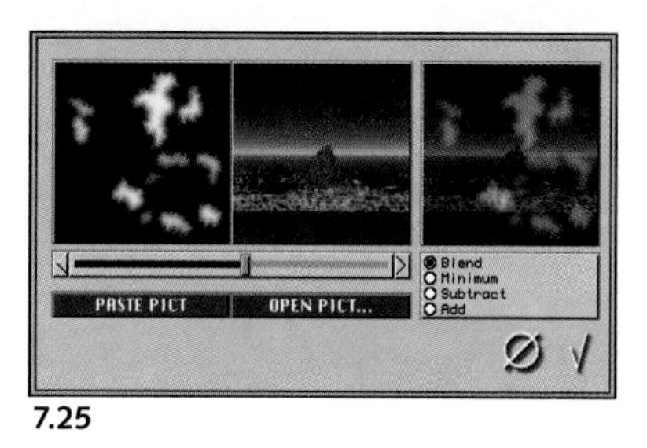

7.25

The factors that will work against you in trying to add recognizable features to your terrains are miniscule detail, perspective, and lack of resolution. Assuming that you have chosen a suitable image and simplified it into basic tonal areas, the image you'll see in the greyscale-to-height map should look pretty much like your original PICT. Click on the 3D View and Color Display buttons to see the terrain more clearly.

7.25 The Merge PICT dialog box

If the PICT image being mapped onto the terrain has loads of detail, set the resolution in the Height section all the way up to 512 or even 1024. Keep in mind, however, that if the image will be placed in the distance in your scene, it is probably a waste to set the resolution this high. Reserve the highest resolutions for the closest objects in your scene.

After fine-tuning your image and finding the right resolution, you'll need to consider perspective and camera angle. Think of the 40-foot images carved into the ground in the Andes Mountains in South America; these images of birds and other elaborate designs are impossible to recognize from ground level, yet they can be seen clearly from the air. In the same manner, the higher your camera is off the ground and the more it is pointing downward in a bird's-eye view, the more recognizable your terrain image will be (Figure 7.26).

7.26 The importance of height in being able to recognize an image in a terrain

Experiment with fractals generated in Kai's Power Tools, or with your own randomly generated noise patterns. Don't get too caught up in the pattern of the fractal itself, however. Remember that it is the tonal values in the image, and their relationship to each other, that have the biggest impact on the Bryce terrain.

Mapping PICTs onto Planes

There are times when you just need to add a photograph to your Bryce landscape. This is not difficult to do, but, as with the greyscale-to-height maps, it does take a little practice. PICT images can be brought into Bryce and mapped onto any object, showing the full detail of the PICT image. The mapped file is flat, however, so the angles in the scene become more critical.

In selecting an object surface on which to map the PICT image, choose one that is as flat as possible, as in a box or plane. Other objects, such as spheres or cones, will distort the image (though often with interesting results). Be sure to use the Side, Top, and Front views to ensure that the angle of the object surface works well in relation to the camera.

After creating and positioning the object for mapping, select it and open the Materials Editor in the Edit Palette. Click on the top-left icon in the Textures area until the 2D PICT icon appears (Figure 7.27). You'll see the 2D Picture Preview window to the right in the dialog box. If a PICT image has already been assigned to the object, it will be shown here.

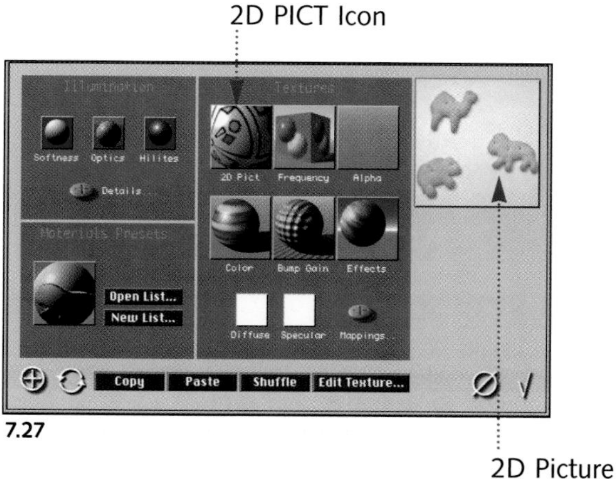

7.27

If nothing has been assigned yet, you'll see the Bryce PICT splash screen. Click on the splash screen to open the PICT Scrapbook dialog box (Figure 7.28), and open, copy, or paste your PICT image. Then do a quick render to see how the PICT image looks when mapped onto the object you selected.

7.27 The 2D PICT icon selected in the Materials Editor

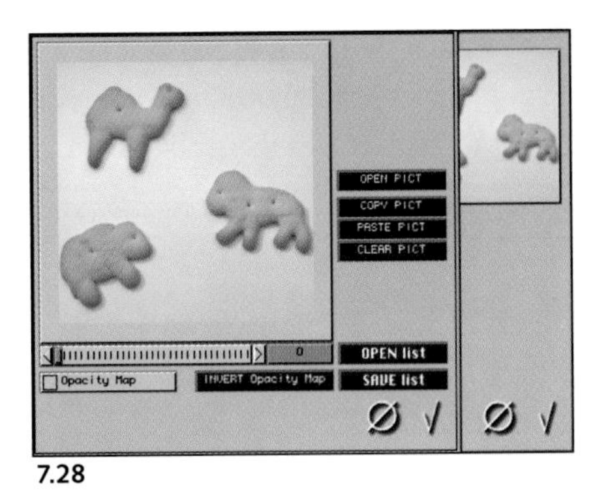

7.28

Creating Silhouetted PICT Files

At times, you may want to place a PICT file in a scene as a silhouette. Silhouettes can be created by using alpha channels in Photoshop that serves as a mask in Bryce. The black areas of the alpha channel will be ignored by Bryce as it maps the PICT, and the white areas will reveal your image. The following exercise takes you through this process.

1. Open a PICT file in Photoshop and make a selection of the object you want to silhouette in the Bryce scene (Figure 7.29).

7.29

7.28 The PICT Scrapbook dialog box

7.29 Select the object to be silhouetted

2. With the selection active, select New Channel from the Channels palette; in the resulting dialog box, choose Masked Areas in the Color Indicates area and click OK.

3. The image window will be all black, with the selection still active in the new channel (Figure 7.30). Set the background color to white and press Delete.

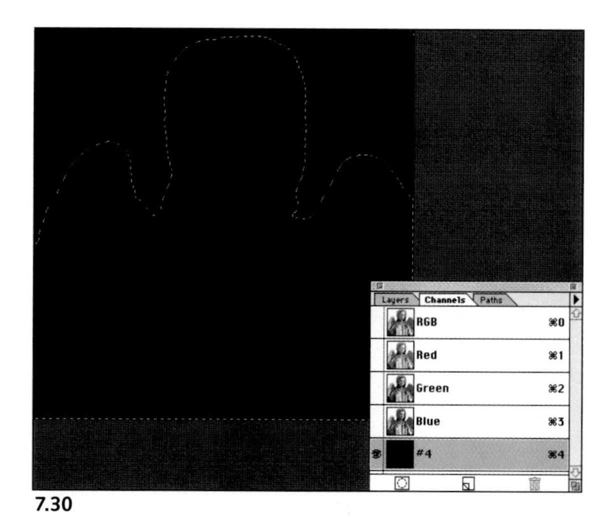

7.30

4. In the Channels palette, highlight the new channel and choose Select All.

5. Copy the selection, create a new PICT file, and paste the selection in it. The new file should be in Grayscale mode since only the grayscale channel was copied from the original file. Save the new file, which is the alpha channel; give it the same name as the original, but add the suffix *.mask,* and place it in the same folder as the original file (Figure 7.31).

7.31

7.30 In the new channel, the selection is still active

7.31 Save the new file with the suffix .mask, and place it in the same folder as the original file

6. Launch Bryce and create a square by selecting the plane icon in the Create palette.
7. Using the tools in the Edit palette, rotate the square until it directly faces the camera (Figure 7.32).

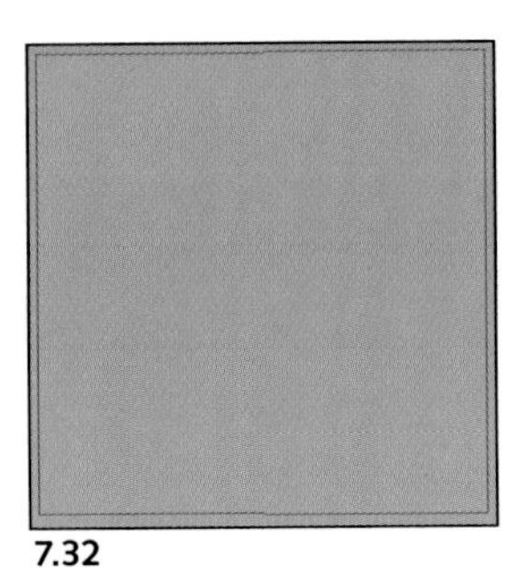

7.32

8. While still in the Edit palette, double-click on the square to open the Materials Editor.
9. In the Materials Editor, click on the upper-left icon until 2D PICT appears.
10. Click on the Bryce PICT splash screen to open the PICT Scrapbook.
11. Click on Open PICT, and select the original PICT image that you created (Figure 7.33). Check the Opacity Map checkbox at the bottom of the screen, which reveals the alpha channel, and click on the OK check mark (Figure 7.34).

7.33

7.32 Position the square so it faces the camera

7.33 Select the original PICT image

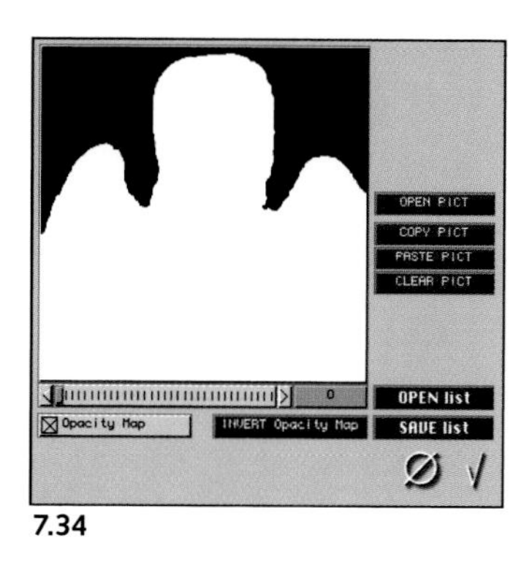

7.34

12. Back in the main interface for the Materials Editor, click on the Alpha icon (the upper-right icon) until the Transparent mode is active (the bands on the sphere have a matte surface, and you can see through to the back of the sphere. Figure 7.35). As always, check the Materials Presets preview to see how the object will look when rendered.

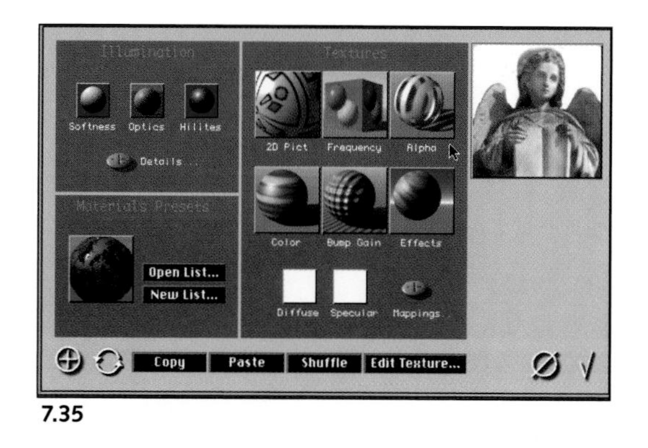

7.35

13. In the Details dialog box (click on the Details button in the Illumination section), move the Ambient and Diffuse sliders to the far right so the PICT mapping will look as close to the original as possible (Figure 7.36). If your image has a color cast, it is probably because the HiLites sphere in the Illumination box has a color cast assigned to it. To remove or change the cast, click and drag on the sphere until it shows the desired color of light. Click on the OK check marks to return to the Edit palette.

7.34 Clicking the Opacity Map checkbox reveals the alpha channel for the image

7.35 Set the Alpha icon to Transparent mode

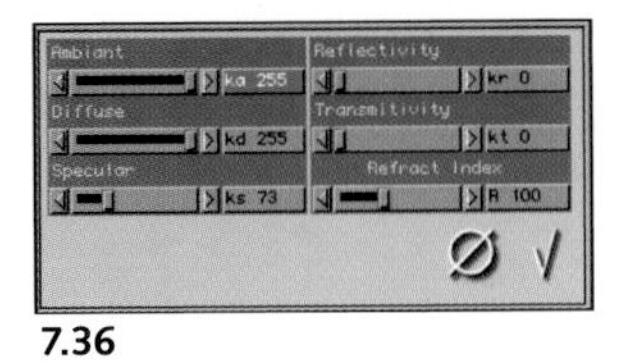

7.36

14. Select the Sky and Fog palette, and click on any control to start a full-screen render. Once it starts, click anywhere in the window to stop it. Drag a marquee over the square and click on any control again to render the marqueed region. This will allow you to view the results so far (Figure 7.37). If you're satisfied with your changes, continue building the rest of the scene, and then do a full-screen render to see the results (Figure 7.38).

7.37

7.36 Use the Details dialog box to fine-tune the appearance of the PICT mapping

7.37 The results of the silhouetting

7.38

For some stunning effects, you can also combine 2D PICT images with PICT-generated terrains, varying the opacity of each. To do this, first generate a terrain from a PICT image (see page 225). Then map a PICT image onto the terrain using the above exercise—but do not activate the Alpha icon. If the direction of the light is placed correctly, this procedure allows you to cast realistic shadows from the mapped PICT image onto the surface of the object.

As you continue to explore Bryce after mastering PICT terrains and mapping, start experimenting with Alpha effects. And if you have a taste for it, dig deep into the Materials Editor and see what 3D textures you can create with it. Whether you focus on new materials, combining PICT objects with Bryce objects, or even setting up elaborate worlds to explore with your camera, Bryce will continue to reveal its rich feature set as you work with it. Not bad for a program that lets you build your first scene in 10 minutes.

7.38 The PICT image integrated into a full Bryce scene

Annunciation

Working with KPT Gradient Designer

IVUE Correction in Live Picture

Masking in Live Picture

Working with Stencils in Live Picture

Compositing in Photoshop

Color Correction with Curves in Photoshop

The creation of this image began at the precise moment that I snapped the central photograph of my wife, Barbara. We were walking through the streets of Florence—exploring, really—looking for interesting places that were off the beaten track. I noticed one particular door that was ajar. It was facing the street and looked quite ordinary and nondescript. We had already walked past it when I called Barbara back and slowly opened it.

It opened onto a courtyard with beautiful trees and bushes, a terrific contrast to the sepia and ochre colors of Florence. Across the courtyard was another door that our curiosity refused to ignore. Behind that one was the most wonderful little chapel—dark, secluded, and very intimate. The art in this space was superb, topped off by an altar piece by Renaissance artist Filippo Lippi. Since it was late afternoon, daggers of light streamed through some unseen upper windows, as if from nowhere. Barbara was seated in just the right spot, bathed in a tiny beam of light (Figure 8.1).

I used two other source images for this piece, which I also photographed during our stay in Florence: one of an angel, from an anonymous 18th-century fresco on an outdoor wall (Figure 8.2), and the other of a section from the interior murals of the Church of Santa Croce in Florence, which were painted by Giotto, the great Renaissance mural artist (Figure 8.3). I combined these images to recreate our feeling of being in that particular chapel at that particular time. We never did find out the name of the chapel, but I call the resulting image *Annunciation.*

For more detailed information on how to create this image, see the Creative Exercises folder on the CD-ROM.

Praying for Rain

IVUE Correction in Live Picture

Silhouetting and compositing in Live Picture

Working with textures in KPT Texture Explorer

Using Layers to combine effects in Photoshop

This image, which I call *Praying for Rain*, relies heavily on the strengths of Live Picture's IVUE Correction tools, especially in the way they integrate composite images by homogenizing the color of light. A key factor in any composition, whether it is abstract or realistic, is that all of the components must have the same color of light to convince the viewer that they share the same space. That point is dramatically expressed in this image, but is just as important in a realistic photo composite.

For more detailed information on how to create this image, see the Creative Exercises folder on the CD-ROM.

Moonscape

Setting up a basic scene in KPT Bryce

Atmospheric effects in KPT Bryce

Working with clouds in KPT Bryce

Illuminating objects in KPT Bryce

When I started using Bryce, I wasn't interested in the levels of control that lurked beneath the surface; it was enough simply to create landscapes that appealed to me. After a while, though, it became less satisfying just to press a button and be presented with a mountain. It had to be a specific mountain, with a specific shape, texture, and color.

What I've found is that you need to let the requirements of the scene dictate your skill level in Bryce. Don't concern yourself with learning the deep Materials Editor until you have a requirement that the existing materials components cannot support. When such a requirement does arise, learning becomes easier because it has a context.

That's what happened with this *Moonscape* image: It motivated me to learn how to control skies within an image. I was always able to get skies to "fit in" with my images, but I wasn't sure how to make them stand out. With a scene like this, which has very few objects, the sky had to be terrific to create any interest at all.

For more detailed information on how to create this image, see the Creative Exercises folder on the CD-ROM.

The Eye of David

Sharpening in Live Picture

Compositing in Live Picture

Difference-based textures in KPT Convolver

Opacity variation in Live Picture

Area-based textures in KPT Texture Explorer

I created this composite for the sidebar in Chapter 5 that discusses the differences and similarities between Photoshop and Live Picture. When I started I had no idea that it would become so elaborate. The idea was to merge some of the common elements of each interface into a simple design.

Being on deadline, there wasn't time to scan images or request high-resolution artwork for the composite. Besides, I figured the final image would never run larger than 3 or 4 inches in either dimension, which reduced my dependence on high-quality scans. So I began taking screen shots, cropping and compiling them, and making many discoveries along the way.

One of the biggest discoveries was that for certain tasks, you can get away with extremely low-resolution originals using a few of Live Picture's Sharpen/Blur layers. Live Picture doesn't eliminate every need for a high-res scan, but for some things, it just might surprise you.

This image involved a lot of back and forth between Live Picture and Photoshop as I built the image in stages, adding filter effects and compositing along the way. I saved it at different intervals, and brought these into Live Picture and merged them together, varying the intensity of the effects to get a subtle, intricate result.

For more detailed information on how to create this image, see the Creative Exercises folder on the CD-ROM.

Gallery

Welcome to the Gallery.

These images, contributed by artists from around the country, reveal the wide range of creative possibilities using the four MetaTools programs featured in this book. Some are pure Bryce; some are pure Live Picture; some are amalgams of several programs. Together, they underscore the theme that the technology does not create vision; it simply facilitates it.

Sometimes, images created with a software program have a signature look, prompting viewers to say, "That's a [software name] image." That kind of generalization will be difficult to make with the images in this gallery. In the same way that a master chef combines ingredients and cooking techniques to achieve a unique and cohesive result, these artists combine image and technique using the full range of tools the programs provide.

In addition to myself, the contributors include Kai and eight guest artists: Susan Kitchens, Bill Ellsworth, Jackson Ting and Robert Bailey, Scott Tucker, Dan Ecoff and Ron Shirley, and Justin Thyme. From the beautiful Bryce abstractions by Bill Ellsworth to the swirling fractals of the Absolut Kai image, the Gallery presents a full complement of interpretive vision.

Shoreline
©1995 Susan A. Kitchens
KPT Bryce

April's End
©1995 Bill Ellsworth
KPT Bryce, KPT Convolver,
Adobe Photoshop 3.0

Absolut Kai
©1995 Kai Krause
Adobe Photoshop,
Kai's Power Tools

Frisco Dawn

KPT Bryce, Kai's Power Tools,
Adobe Photoshop,
Adobe Illustrator

Shiny Earth
©1995 Justin Thyme
KPT Bryce

Food for Thought
©1995 Daniel B. Ecoff and Ron Shirley
Adobe Photoshop 3.0,
Live Picture 2.0

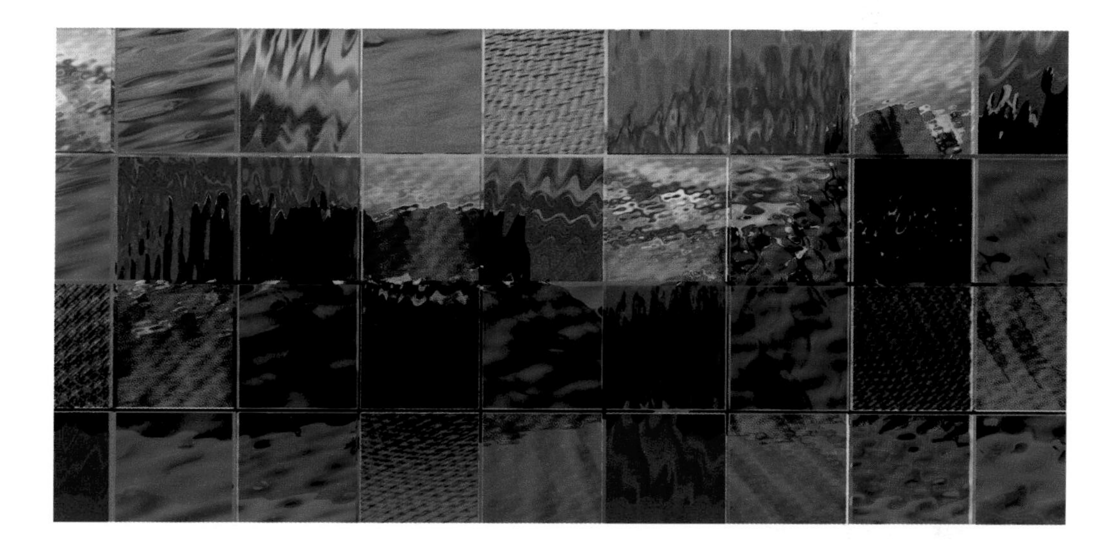

Glassblocks

KPT Bryce

Pastorale 3

KPT Bryce

Cambrian Pipeline
©1995 Jackson Ting
and Robert Bailey/ArtEffect
Design Studio
KPT Bryce, Kai's Power Tools,
Adobe Photoshop,
Adobe Illustrator

This One's for Ansel
©1995 Scott R. Tucker
KPT Bryce 1.1,
Adobe Photoshop 3.0.4

Steel Rosette
©1995 Bill Ellsworth
KPT Bryce

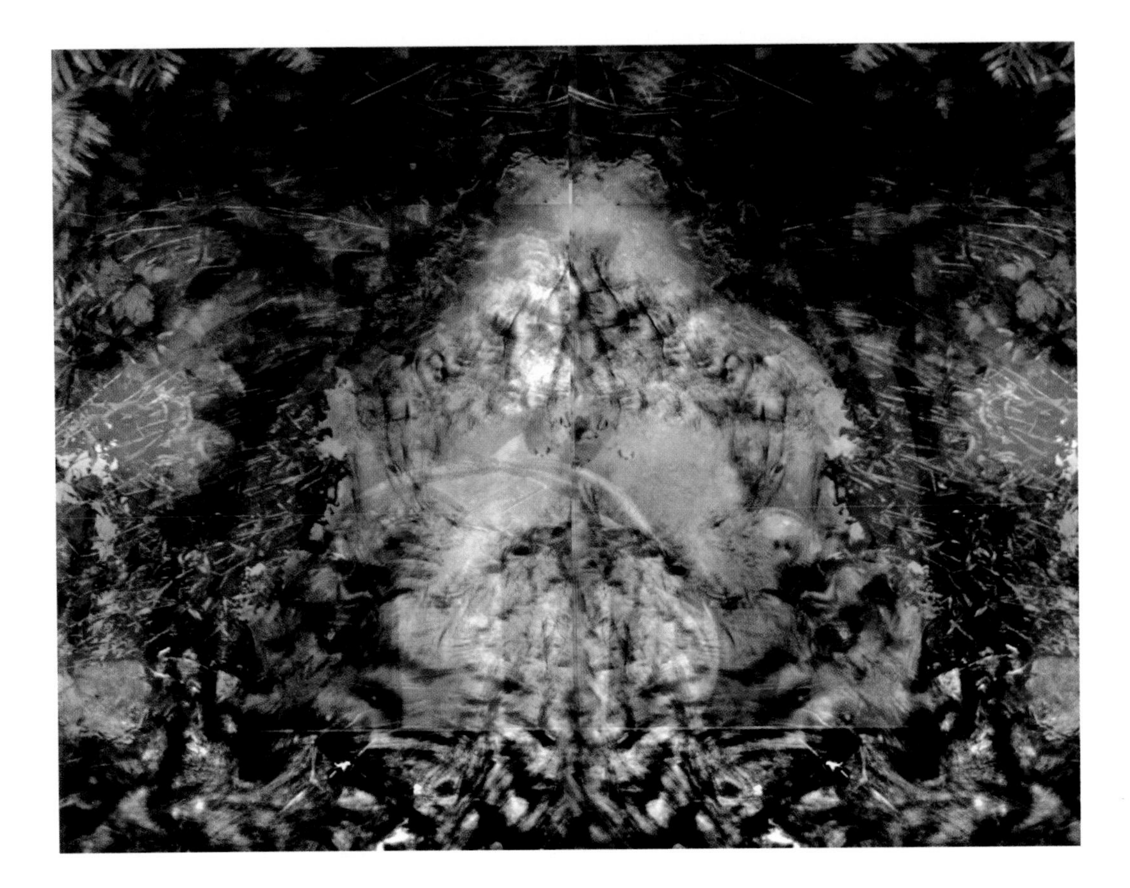

AngelGrass
©1995 Daniel Giordan
Live Picture, Adobe Photoshop

Tian Chi

KPT Bryce

The Passage of Time
©1995 Daniel Giordan
Live Picture, Adobe Photoshop

Poster for MACWORLD Tokyo
© Kai Krause
KPT Bryce, Adobe Photoshop,
Kai's Power Tools

Cover for *Playboy* magazine's
Annual Report
© Kai Krause
Adobe Photoshop,
Kai's Power Tools

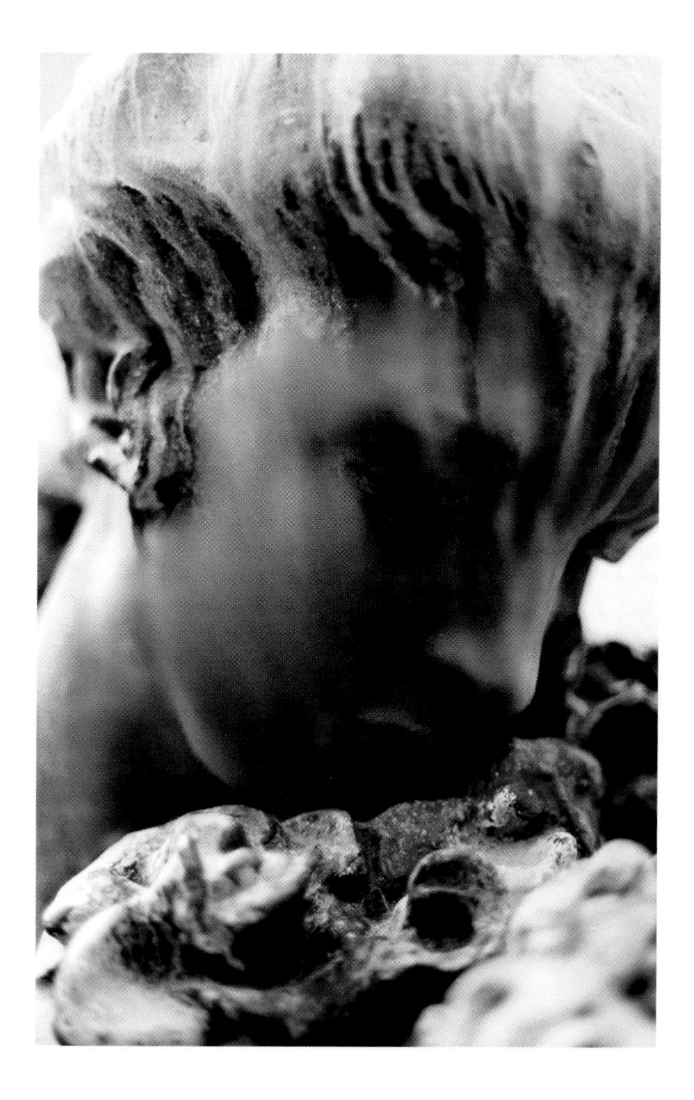

Transformation

Live Picture

The Abandonment of Hope
©1995 Daniel Giordan
Live Picture, Adobe Photoshop,
Kai's Power Tools

Appendix

Contributors

ArtEffect Design Studio

Phone: 818-996-8391; fax: 818-342-7397. E-mail: AFX Robert@aol.com or TingJ@aol.com.

ArtEffect Design Studio, founded by Jackson Ting and Robert Bailey in 1994, specializes in digital design, illustration, and photography. Jackson's natural-media background as an illustrator and designer meshes with Robert's photography and digital imaging background, making ArtEffect an innovative and multifaceted design studio.

Robert Blumberg

Live Picture Inc., 2425 Porter Street, Suite 16, Soquel, CA 95073; 408-464-4200.

Robert Blumberg is a cofounder and vice president of Live Picture Inc.

Clio Awards Ltd.

Michael A. Demetriades, Vice President/ International Director, 276 Fifth Avenue, Suite 401, New York, NY 10001; phone: 212-683-4300; fax 212-683-4796.

Honoring advertising excellence worldwide

Roger Dean

Daniel B. Ecoff Photographix

15002 Magnolia Boulevard, Suite 9, Sherman Oaks, CA 91403; 818-788-6892.

Digital design, digital imaging specialist, photography

Bill Ellsworth

24120 Old Hundred Road, Dickerson, MD 20842; 301-349-5380. E-mail: LOA9@aol.com.

Bill Ellsworth is an artist in both the analog and digital realms. Beginning in 1994, he has worked with Macintosh computers to create his unique brand of art using Adobe Photoshop, KPT Bryce, and Kai's Power Tools. His work has appeared in various publications and can be seen in the MetaTools forum on America Online.

Susan A. Kitchens

Phone: 818-303-7367. E-mail: auntialias@aol.com.

Susan A. Kitchens is a graphic designer and digital artist. Her work includes graphic design, calligraphic lettering, and digital imaging for print, Web, and multimedia. In addition, she is a writer, consultant, and trainer. She has contributed to Sherry London's *Photoshop 3.0 Special Effects How-To* (Waite Group Press) and Nick Clarke's *Kai's Power Tools: An Illustrated Guide* (Addison-Wesley). She also wrote *The KPT Bryce Book,* published by Addison-Wesley in 1995.

Kai Krause

c/o MetaTools Software, 6303 Carpinteria Avenue, Carpinteria, CA 93013; 805-566-6200. E-mail: Kai@aol.com.

MACWORLD Expos

MetaTools, Inc.

6303 Carpinteria Avenue, Carpinteria, CA 93013; 805-566-6200.

Mitch Hall Associates

1400 Providence Highway, Norwood, MA 02062; 617-551-9800.

Mitch Hall Associates is an event-management organization that has received worldwide acclaim for its management of MACWORLD Expo.

Playboy Inc.

Martin Schmitt

Ron Shirley Photo Imaging

8945 Exposition Boulevard, Los Angeles, CA 90034; 310-837-5659.

Advertising photography and digital imaging

TBWA

292 Madison Avenue, New York, NY 10017; 212-725-1150.

Advertising agency (Absolut Vodka)

Justin Thyme

1212 Grafix, 146 W. 57th Street #51A, New York, NY 10019.

Justin Thyme is a New York-based artist, as well as a poet, writer, dancer, and musician. He is the founder and owner of the graphic design firm 1212 Grafix. Justin is thrilled to have his work included in a book about Kai Krause.

Scott R. Tucker

1036-D Delta Drive, Lafayette, CO 80026-2869; 303-666-3395 (day) or 303-666-6588 (evening). E-mail: Tuckersaur@aol.com.

By day: data processing professional. By night: the digital undead. Last year I bought my Mac to digitally enhance my photographs. I went in thinking, 'Won't it be great to crank up the colors on this sunrise.' Little did I know I'd soon be using it to enhance the one I 'shot' in Bryce—by converting it to black and white! I've enjoyed art ever since I was a kid, but my profession leaves me little time for traditional illustration. The computer gives it all back. I am available for freelance work; drop me an e-mail.

Ben Weiss

E-mail: kptben@aol.com; America Online: KPT Ben

For the past three years, Ben Weiss has worked closely with Kai in developing Kai's Power Tools and related products. Besides work, his major pastime is surfing the blue Pacific. Ben lives on the beach in Carpinteria, California.

Index

A

B

I

J–K

L

M

N–O

P

Q–R

S

T

U–W